Sir JOHN URE PRIMROSE, Bart., LL.D.

Chairman of Directors from 1912 to 1923.

See page 253.

THE STORY OF THE RANGERS.

First published
in 1923 by
The Rangers Football Club, Limited
Ibrox Park, Glasgow

This facsimile edition published
in 2004 by
DESERT ISLAND BOOKS
7 Clarence Road, Southend on Sea, Essex SS1 1AN
www.desertislandbooks.com

British Library Cataloguing-in-Publication Data.
A catalogue record for this book is available from the British Library.

ISBN: 1-874287-95-3

Printed in Great Britain
by
4Edge Ltd

Publisher's note:
The first edition of this book was published
in Crown size (180 x 120 mm).
In this edition the text has been magnified by 7½ per cent.

The STORY of THE RANGERS

FIFTY YEARS OF FOOTBALL

1873—1923

By JOHN ALLAN

DESERT ISLAND BOOKS

FOREWORD.

THE Story of the Rangers is a plain tale of practical deeds. It is a tale of a humble origin, testing hardships, critical days when existence hung by a thread, indomitable spirit and some victories. It is told because 1923 is the club's Jubilee Year, and, also, because it is worth telling. Whether under the old amateur or modern professional regime, the Rangers have tried to play a creditable part in the development of a great national sport. As to their successes in the field of competitive play, these pages bear ample witness. Up to the close of season 1922-23, 401 International honours were conferred upon Rangers' players, a valuable contribution to the sporting prestige of Scotland. In the legislative sphere, Rangers men have laboured assiduously in building up the football edifice. Here, in brief, are the outstanding features of the club's history:—

Up to the end of season 1922-23, Rangers had played in

12 Scottish Cup Finals	-	Won	4
22 Glasgow Cup Finals	-	Won	15
23 Charity Cup Finals -	-	Won	11
57			30

These figures are inclusive of the 1901-2 Glasgow Cup Final when, after a drawn match, Celtic scratched. In 1901 Rangers won the Glasgow Exhibition Cup, virtually the equivalent of a Scottish Cup victory.

Members of the First Division of the League since the competition was instituted in 1890, the Rangers have won the Championship 12 times, inclusive of 1890-91, when they were joint-champions with Dumbarton. In 1904-5, they obtained the same number of points as Celtic and were defeated in a match played to decide the championship. The following table shows that only once have the Rangers occupied a position lower than fourth:—

Position					Seasons
Champions, -	-	-	-	-	**12**
Runners-up, -	-	-	-	-	**8**
Third, -	-	-	-	-	**9**
Fourth,	-	-	-	-	**3**
Fifth, -	-	-	-	-	**1**

From the 948 League matches played, 1,420 points have been obtained. In 1898-99, Rangers won every League match, a feat never equalled in any country. From a possible 84 points in 1920-21, the team amassed 76, the greatest aggregate ever compiled in any country.

As illustrating the colossal advance in popularity made by the game, and the influence exercised by the Rangers club in creating that popularity, the following points are interesting:—

The club's first pitch was on the open space of the Fleshers Haugh on Glasgow Green. Ibrox Park embraces 14·140 acres and is the largest ground in Scotland.

8,000 people witnessed the Scottish Cup Final of 1876-77 between Rangers and Vale of Leven. The attendance at the fourth-round Scottish Cup-tie between Rangers and Celtic, in 1919-20, at Ibrox Park, was 83,000.

In 1882-83, the club had to borrow £30 from the President to pay debts. In 1919-20, the total income exceeded £50,000.

In 1883-84, Rangers' total income from seven Scottish Cup-ties was £90. At the Scottish Cup-tie with Celtic in 1919-20, £3,020 was drawn at the gates exclusive of tax.

In the Club's first Glasgow Cup-tie, in 1887-88, with Third Lanark, the total drawings were £96 8s. In 1907-8, the three games in the Glasgow Cup Final with Celtic were watched by 192,000 people, who paid £4,972 17s. 8d.

The attendance at Rangers' first league match in 1890, when the Hearts visited Ibrox, was 3,400. In 1919-20, 75,000 people witnessed the League match with Celtic at Ibrox.

What will the next fifty years have to show?

CONTENTS.

1873.

The Beginning—A Historic Match—Brothers M'Neil— Forming the Club—Choice of a Name—The Colours— Splendid Pioneers—Brave Hearts.

IN the summer evenings of 1873 a number of lusty, laughing lads, mere boys some of them, flushed and happy from the exhilaration of a finishing dash with the oars, could be seen hauling their craft ashore on the upper reaches of the river Clyde at Glasgow Green. As keen then was their enthusiasm for the sport of rowing as it became, in later years, for the game of football; for these lads were the founders of the Rangers Football Club. Mostly natives of the Gareloch, young crusaders who had come to the great city to woo the twin goddesses, Fame and Fortune, the spirit of adventure was strong within them. So, watching the " giants " of the old Eastern Football Club as they revelled in this game of strange excitements, their hearts yearned for participation.

The Eastern had come into existence in December, 1872. They played on a piece of the wide space of ground known as the Fleshers' Haugh, the pitch abutting a small plantation or shrubbery, which served as dressing quarters. In those days the Fleshers' Haugh was on an elevation only slightly above the level of the river, but in many other respects it possessed the same features as it does to-day, and the playing ground which the Eastern F.C. made their own, and which the Rangers afterwards shared with them, may be visualised from the plan on page 11.

On this pitch, on 15th July, 1873, there was played a match between teams styled Argyle and Clyde respectively. These names did not represent organised clubs. The two sides were selected for the purpose of providing a game, and names were chosen in order to give the event some individuality. Nevertheless, this match has a historical value, for in the Argyle team there figured players who, later, took part in the inception of the Rangers, and who lived to become famous, not only as club exponents, but as representatives of Scotland in International contests. For that reason, the individual names of the players must be chronicled. Here they are :—

Argyle.—Moses M'Neil (*captain*) ; Peter M'Neil and Tom Vallance ; William M'Beth and J. Ryburn ; J. Yuill, Peter Campbell, W. Thomson, D. Smith, James Watson, and D. Forrest.

Clyde.—J. Rankine (*captain*) ; D. Armstrong and A. Herriot ; L. Herriot and W. Reid ; R. Hunter, H. Clunie, J. Clunie, A. Gray, J. Baird, and David Hill.

It is recorded in a news print of the period that the game was very exciting and ended in a draw.

Events afterwards moved rapidly. There were seven brothers M'Neil, members of a Gareloch family, who resided in Glasgow. The three eldest—James, John, and Alec—never were associated with football, but the other four—William, Harry, Moses, and Peter—gained celebrity in the game in later years. To William there fell the rare gift of a football from the son of a gentleman by whom his father was employed in the Gareloch. The generous donor was a Mr. M'Donald of the firm of Stewart & M'Donald, in Buchanan Street. When, shortly after the match between Argyle and Clyde, it was proposed to form a club with this football as the starting point, the younger enthusiasts expressed the view that William M'Neil was too old to be admitted to membership. Thereupon William picked up his ball, put it under his arm, and with the remark, " If you can't have me, you can't have my ball," brought the discussion to an end for that evening. But the young

ones were not to be foiled in their purpose in that manner.
Soon a meeting was held. It was proposed and carried
that a club be formed, and that, right on the spot, a
subscription be taken wherewith to purchase a ball. Then
arose the great question of the name to be given to the
club they were about to launch on an unsuspecting world.

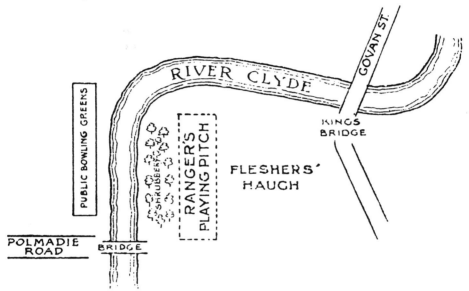

PLAN OF GLASGOW GREEN GROUND.

Moses M'Neil proposed that it should be called the Rangers
Association Football Club, and to the young minds the
name had an alluring appeal. It was adopted unanimously.
Mr. M'Neil has related that he had been reading C. W.
Alcock's " English Football Annual," and had been
attracted by the name he had seen belonging to an English
Rugby club. A few other necessary details having been
satisfactorily arranged, the lads dispersed with hearts
beating high and with visions of great sport and mighty
achievements.

That is the simple story of the beginning of the Rangers.

THE STORY OF THE RANGERS.

Of the hopeful young band who gathered round to discuss what, to them, was a subject of vast import, only Moses M'Neil and Tom Vallance are alive to ruminate upon the realisation of their glittering dreams. Harry M'Neil was at the christening, but he was not a member of the Rangers, preferring to join the Queen's Park. He became so famous as an outside left that he represented Scotland against England six times, and was only once on the defeated side. The trifling incident in which William and his precious ball figured was soon forgotten, and as a half-back he played a foremost part in the exploits which brought the Rangers into prominence among the great clubs of the period. It is on record that, on at least one occasion assistance was given by Harry M'Neil and William M'Kinnon, another distinguished Queen's Park forward, and also by J. Hunter and W. Miller, two noted members of Third Lanark, or 3rd L.R.V., as they were then called.

The first colours of the Rangers were royal blue jerseys, white knickers, and blue and white stockings. A few of the players, the dandies of the team, wore blue and white cowls on their heads, but these were discarded as time went on. For only one short period were the original colours laid aside. When the late Mr. Angus Campbell was honorary secretary in 1879-80, jerseys with blue and white hoops were adopted. Matters had not been going too well with the team. Mr. Campbell felt his responsibility. He was a true Highlander with a liberal strain of super-stition in his being. A change of colours might change the luck, so, at his suggestion, the old royal blue was packed away in the locker. Nobody was happy, however, until it was brought out again by a decree of a committee meeting of 1883. In royal blue the Rangers have played ever since.

The team to which the Rangers really owed their success

in surmounting the early and inevitable difficulties, which wrecked so many promising adventures in those early days, was :—

J. Yuill.

Tom Vallance and Peter M'Neil.

William M'Beth and William M'Neil.

M. M'Neil, Peter Campbell, George Phillips, Jas. Watson, D. Gibb, and John Campbell.

The formation was, of course, two half-backs and six forwards. The Campbells did not stay in the game so long as some of the others, but they were potent forces in keeping the club alive. Peter Campbell was " one of the prettiest and most poetic of dribblers, and on the touch line moved as graceful as a sylph." M. M'Neil, small but sturdily proportioned, was a terror to opposing defenders. The laws of the game for many years permitted a freedom of action which would make people turn up their eyes nowadays, and he believed in playing up—or down—to the laws. James Watson was a schoolmaster. He played a cultured sort of game and was always a valuable guide when a crisis arose in the affairs of the club. A crisis was an incident of recurring certainty. In 1890-91, he became president, and a few years ago his death, as the result of a scratch on the hand by a cat, was deeply deplored. William M'Beth was a Glasgow man and a friend of the M'Neil family, and he imbibed all the enthusiasm of the Gareloch natives.

1873—1876.

ALTHOUGH it was midsummer when the club was formed, nothing could cool the ardour of these youths from the Gareloch. Fixtures were arranged with the Eastern, Callander, Star of Leven, and the Rovers—the matches with the Rovers were called the " Wee Internationals." But the four great clubs of that period were Queen's Park, Vale of Leven, Third Lanark, and Clydesdale. Vale of Leven were first of the four to favour Rangers with a match on Glasgow Green. It resulted in a draw. Then Clydesdale came along and also had to be satisfied with a half share of the honours. Queen's Park were repeatedly asked for a fixture, but they " were sorry to refuse, as the Rangers had no private ground ; they would, however, be pleased to play them with their second eleven." During their first season, and also in 1874-75, the Rangers continued to play on Glasgow Green, but they were growing bolder with the knowledge that they were able to hold their own with the strongest clubs against whom they had been allowed to match their skill. They would not be satisfied until they had a ground of their own. But, while still making the best of the cheerless comforts of the Green, they joined the Scottish Football Association in time to take part in the Scottish Cup competition of season 1874-75. Thus the Rangers missed competing in only the first season's competition for the Cup. The Scottish Football Association had been formed in March, 1873, before the club came into existence. Rangers' first Scottish Cup tie was played in October, 1874, against the Oxford, on the Queen's Park Recreation Ground, and, as in the case of their first Glasgow Cup-tie, played in 1887, and their first League match, played in 1890, victory rested with them. The names of those who took part in the long-forgotten Cup contest ought to be reproduced :—

> **Rangers.**—James Yuill; Peter M'Neil (*captain*) and Tom Vallance; Wm. M'Beth and Wm. M'Neil; Moses M'Neil, David Gibb, Peter Campbell, J. Campbell, George Phillips, and James Watson.

> **Oxford.**—M'Kinlay; Galbraith and Smith; Fraser and Robertson; Martin, Leggat, Alexander, A. Peden, S. Peden, and W. Peden.

In those days the newspaper reporter was punctilious about the courtesies due to our gentlemen athletes who performed in public. So it is recorded that " the first goal was scored by Mr. M'Neil, who sent both the Oxford goalkeeper and the ball under the tape." Then " the second goal was taken very neatly by Mr. Gibb about seven minutes before time was called." And " although the Oxford wrought nobly to retrieve themselves, they were unable to score." In the second round the Rangers were drawn against Dumbarton on the Green, where neither side could bring forth a goal, but in the replay, at Dumbarton, Rangers went down by a goal to nothing.

Shortly afterwards the club bade farewell to the Green, not, you may be certain, without a pang of regret. Many cherished memories were woven about the old birthplace, and for years afterwards these were fondly debated by those to whom the early adventures were the richest incidents in their career. After nearly fixing upon a ground at Shawfield, the club secured their first private field at Burnbank, the site of which may easily be located in the plan on page 17.

Burnbank ground, which was occupied only during the

season of 1875-76, was opened by Vale of Leven, and the result of the match was a draw, 1—1. Only one Scottish Cup-tie was played there ; it resulted in a victory for the Rangers by 7 goals to 0 over 1st L.R.V. The second round tie was decided on Cathkin Park against 3rd L.R.V., who won by 2 goals to 0. This tie gave rise to an extraordinary incident, such as would be impossible in modern football. The Rangers won the first game by 1 goal to 0, but some bright intellectual drew attention to the fact that the winners had once kicked off the ball when their opponents should have done so. 3rd L.R.V. protested on this ground, got their replay and won.

We cannot leave Burnbank without recording one memorable event associated with the only Cup-tie played there. It was in the match against 1st L.R.V. that one of the most illustrious of Scottish players first pulled a Rangers jersey over his athletic shoulders. This was George Gillespie, then a bright-faced, boyish figure, with a merry eye, and with athlete stamped on every line and curve of his well-knit frame. He came from a little club called the Rosslyn, which played on the open pastures of Whiteinch, where he had as a colleague George Goudie, who became president of the Rangers (1882-83), and was a successful Glasgow merchant. As a half-back, George Gillespie made his debut, but it is as a back that we find him acquitting himself with distinction in the historic Scottish Cup Final of 1876-77 against the then mighty Vale of Leven, while, two seasons later, in the no less memorable Final, also against the Vale, he stood guard between the posts. At that time almost anything short of assassination was permitted by the rules. Gillespie, a stripling, partially broke down under the stress of the vigorous onslaughts in the three games which were necessary in the 1876-77 Final. But rather than forsake the sport, which was his heart's delight, he stepped back into goal and thus became the predecessor of the great James M'Aulay and Harry Rennie, both of whom served an apprenticeship in the outfield before becoming the last line of defence.

George Gillespie, as a Rangers player, kept goal twice against England (1881-1882), and against Wales twice (1880-1881), while as a Queen's Park member he was also capped twice against Wales (1886-1890), and against

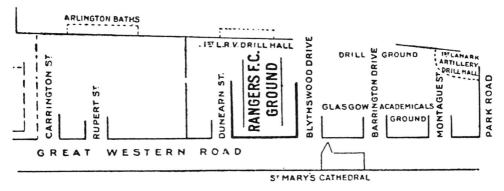

PLAN OF BURNBANK GROUND.

Ireland (1891). He was never on the losing side in an International. For eighteen consecutive seasons he took part in the Scottish Cup competition, beginning with the tie against 1st L.R.V., and finishing in the Queen's Park goal against the Hearts in season 1892-93. He resigned from the Rangers on 1st September, 1884, and his death took place in February, 1900.

In one other respect the Rangers' tenure of Burnbank was noteworthy. It was during this season (1875-76) that they were accorded the privilege of a first match with Queen's Park. Hampden Park was the venue, and the game was declared to be one of the finest ever played up till then. Queen's Park had a forward named J. B. Weir, renowned for his powers of fast dribbling, which was then practised more than it is to-day. He was opposed by Tom Vallance who, although only a lad, offered so strong a challenge with his speed and tackling, that he was marked out for International honours, which he duly received. Queen's Park won the match by 2 goals to 0, but the young Rangers left the field amid the ringing cheers of all who were present.

1876—1879.

Kinning Park—Two Cup Finals—Disputed Goals— The Mighty Vale—Reverse and Revenge—First Cup Won—The Two Captains—W. Struthers' Goals.

IT is now forty-six years since Rangers and Vale of Leven fought three stern battles in the first of the two disputed Scottish Cup Finals, yet to this day keen old sportsmen who witnessed the matches can be brought to a state of table-thumping and vigorous expletives if once launched upon an argument about the points of disagreement. This was in the year 1876, during which the Rangers moved into Kinning Park, where they became the possessors of a beautiful green playing pitch, formerly the property of the Clydesdale Club. The Clydesdale had then football and cricket sections, and when they left Kinning Park they went to Titwood Park, where they still exist as the Clydesdale Cricket Club ; the football section did not long survive, although during a brief career it was an influential force, being represented at the meeting at which the Scottish Football Association was formed, and contesting the first Scottish Cup Final with Queen's Park. Kinning Park ground is now the site of Anderson & Henderson's saw-mills, but it may be located by reference to the plan on page 21.

Rangers had now got together a fine young team, all animated with burning enthusiasm, and bent upon inscribing their name upon the Cup, then, as now, the irresistible lure. On their way to the Final the draw favoured them. Vale of Leven had a much more difficult journey; for in the third round, they had to encounter 3rd L.R.V., and in the fifth round they were opposed by Queen's Park, who had won the Cup in the three seasons for which it had been competed. Up till this fateful contest Queen's Park had been in existence for nine years and had never been defeated by a Scottish club. Their only defeat had been inflicted by the London club, the Wanderers, at the Oval, London, on 5th February, 1876; but on the 16th January, 1875, R. Paton, a Vale of Leven forward, had earned the coveted distinction of being the first Scot to score a goal against Queen's Park. So, in order to qualify to meet the Rangers in the Final of 1876-77, Vale of Leven had to make history. They made it. In the tie with Queen's Park, in the fifth round, at Hampden Park, the Vale won by 2 goals to 1 and thus became the first Scottish combination to lower the colours of the premier club. Here, at a glance, were the season's Cup achievements of Rangers and Vale of Leven previous to the Final :—

Rangers.			Vale of Leven.		
1st Round.	Queen's Park Jun. (H),	4–1	Helensburgh, -	-	1–0
2nd Round.	Towerhill (A), -	8–0	Vale of Leven Rovers,		7–0
3rd Round.	A Bye.		3rd L.R.V., -	-	1–0
4th Round.	Mauchline (A), -	3–0	Busby, -	-	4–0
5th Round.	Lennox (A), -	3–0	Queen's Park, -	-	2–1
Semi-Final.	A Bye.		Ayr Thistle, -	-	9–0

With Fame thus beckoning them, our young Rangers prepared for the Final with becoming zeal. Morning practice over, an adjournment was made to a cook shop, where eleven plates of ham and eggs and steaks were regularly laid upon the table. It happened frequently that only six or seven of the players were able to sit down to the feast ; still, the waiter never took anything back on the plates except the pattern. But if these youthful crusaders took themselves seriously no one else did. Here was a team, many of whose members were just emerging from boyhood. How could a forward line of striplings such as Moses M'Neil, Peter Campbell, James Watson and David Hill hope successfully to match their skill against Vale of Leven stalwarts like W. Jamieson, A. M'Lintock,

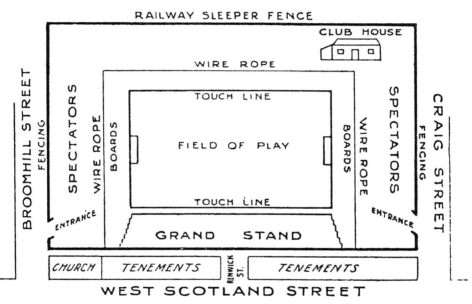

PLAN OF KINNING PARK GROUND.

and Andrew M'Intyre ? Absurd to think of it. All this and a lot more until the day of the Final arrived. Hamilton Crescent, Partick, the ground of the West of Scotland Cricket Club, was the chosen venue. When the Vale's men of iron walked on to the field, the spectators gave expression to their feelings of admiration. They were robust, rugged athletes ; and everyone admires a man of brawn. Then came the boy-men of the Rangers. Everybody took note of the contrast in physique. The debacle was just about to commence—so thought the waiting throng as the teams lined up thus :—

Rangers.—J. M. Watt; George Gillespie and Tom Vallance; Wm. M'Neil and Sam. Ricketts; D. Hill, W. Dunlop, A. Marshall, Jas. Watson, Peter Campbell, and Moses M'Neil.

Vale of Leven.—W. C. Wood; A. Michie and A. M'Intyre; W. Jamieson and A. M'Lintock; R. Paton, J. M'Gregor, J. M'Dougall, J. Ferguson, D. Lindsay, and J. C. Baird.

To some, of course, the sequel was a violent shock; but to the majority of the spectators it was an exhilaration. At all points the mighty men of the Vale found their experience, their physique, and their craft challenged by indomitable spirit and a natural ability which evoked wonder and, let us say, the expressed appreciation of the Rangers' opponents; for good sportsmen were the Vale of Leven, though, like others, jealous of their rights. Neither side could score, and so back to Hamilton Crescent went the rivals to fight it out again. This time each side scored. An extra half-hour was agreed upon. A few minutes before the half-hour had expired, a shot from a Rangers' forward was got away by W. C. Wood, the Vale custodian. Rangers claimed that the ball was through the goal. Excitement was running high. The claim was disallowed, and many of the spectators immediately invaded the field and the game had to be stopped.

Now, though this is a story of the Rangers, it would ill become us to seem to take sides in a matter of such historic value to the two contending forces. But Tom Vallance, who has extolled the merits of the Vale time and oft, declares that several impartial witnesses who were on a line with the goal saw the ball through by a yard. Sir George B. M'Leod, the great surgeon (regarded as one of the handsomest men in Glasgow), affirmed that he was standing behind the goal and that the ball actually came through and struck him. At that time there were no nets, and the spectators stood close up behind the posts. As a consequence, many disputes arose. From these two undecided matches Tom Vallance dates the beginning of a real enthusiasm for the game, which spread as the rippling rings when a stone is cast into the sea. For a third occasion the two teams had to get to grips, and now the scene of action was laid on Hampden Park. At a bound— two bounds, to be correct—the Rangers had become, if not famous, at least a team not to be despised.

An old chronicle relates that, on the day of the third, and what was destined to be the deciding, game, " cabs, 'buses, etc., swarmed to Hampden, and before the start there would be nearly 7,000 or 8,000 present." A crowd indeed ! Those who witnessed the match relate that it was worth going miles to see. But, gallantly as the Rangers fought to win, the fates were against them. James Watson, in running back to assist in the defence, put the ball through his own goal. At half-time the Vale led by this score, but early in the second half Peter Campbell equalised, and then Moses M'Neil put Rangers in the lead. Now heightened hopes and youthful ambition seemed likely to be realised. In a match where strength was most needed, however, the physique of the Vale men told. A second and equalising goal for them, scored by J. C. Baird, was but the warning signal of a third got by R. Paton. And so the Cup, for the first, but not the last, time went down the valley of the winding Leven.

But Rangers and Vale were to see more of each other in their quest for this Aladdin's Lamp. In the following season (1877-78) they were drawn together in the fourth round. A goalless draw at Kinning Park sent the Rangers to Alexandria, where they succumbed by 5 goals to 0.

Next season again they met in the final, and we shall hear more of that shortly. In 1883-84 Rangers adventured into the Vale's haunt to play in the sixth round, and again they bit the dust—score 3-0. Their last meeting in the Cup-ties was in season 1889-90. Rangers had moved into Ibrox Park two seasons previously, and this third-round tie was played there. It was drawn without scoring, and so Rangers went down the Vale to meet the usual fate ; but this was their best performance on the fatal venue, for they lost by only 3-2. Thus, in five Scottish Cup-ties with Vale of Leven the Rangers never once enjoyed the smiles of Fortune, although in the Final of 1878-79 they made what they regarded, and many others also regarded, as a just claim to victory. On their way to the 1878–79 Final the rivals cut through the opposition as here shown, the Rangers, be it noted, obtaining their first Scottish Cup-tie victory over Queen's Park by a goal scored by W. Dunlop :—

	Rangers.		Vale of Leven.	
1st Round.	Shaftesbury (H),	- 3–0	Alclutha, - -	- 6–0
2nd Round.	Whitefield (A), -	- 6–1	Renton Thistle,	- 11–0
3rd Round.	Parkgrove (H),	- 8–2	Jamestown, -	- 15–0
4th Round.	Alexandria Ath. (H),	3–0	Govan, - -	- 11–1
5th Round.	Partick (H), -	- 4–0	Beith, - -	- 6–1
6th Round.	Queen's Park (A), -	1–0	Dumbarton, -	- 3–1
Semi-Final.	A Bye.		Helensburgh, -	- 3–0

Of the history-making Rangers Final team of 1876-77 there still remained in the ranks George Gillespie, now, however, standing guard between the posts ; Tom Vallance with a new partner in brother Alec ; W. Dunlop, Peter Campbell, David Hill, and Moses M'Neil. The new men, in addition to Alec Vallance, were Hugh M'Intyre and J. Drinnan, the half-backs, and W. Struthers and

SCOTTISH CUP FINAL TEAM, 1876—1877.

Back Row—George Gillespie, William M'Neil, Tom Vallance, and J. M. Watt.

Middle Row—William Dunlop, David Hill, Peter Campbell, Moses M'Neil, and Sam Ricketts.

Front Row—James A. K. Watson and A. Marshall.

See page 19.

The late WILLIAM DUNLOP.

Played in the Scottish Cup Final of 1878-79 against Vale of Leven.
President, 1879-80.

Archie Steel, forwards. The teams as they lined up at Hampden Park were :—

Rangers.—Geo. Gillespie ; Tom Vallance (*captain*) and Alec Vallance ; Hugh M'Intyre and J. Drinnan ; W. Dunlop, D. Hill, W. Struthers, Archie Steel, Moses M'Neil, and Peter Campbell.

Vale of Leven.—R. Parlane ; A. M'Lintock and A. M'Intyre ; J. M'Intyre and J. M'Pherson ; J. Ferguson, J. M'Farlane, P. M'Gregor, J. Baird, J. C. Baird, and J. M'Dougall (*captain*).

Umpires—R. B. Colquhoun and W. C. Mitchell.

Referee—J. Wallace, Beith.

In after years it was a frequent saying of William Wilton that the Rangers never had much luck in Cup-ties. That word luck is a dangerous one to play with. It is double-edged and cuts. But its application here is surely justifiable. Twelve minutes after the start Struthers, a forward of a strong, bustling type, brought the ball down the field himself and finished by sending it through the goal out of the giant Parlane's reach. Then occurred the incident which had a unique sequel in the history of the Cup. Campbell and M'Neil took the ball down the left wing. It was centred right in front of goal, and, after some exciting head-work, Struthers again guided it past Parlane. The Vale raised an energetic protest against a goal being allowed on the ground of off-side against Dunlop. Referee and umpires supported the appeal amid a storm of dissent and counter-cheering from the spectators. Even then Rangers seemed likely to win. Until two minutes from the end they held their lead. Then Ferguson centred the ball in front of the Rangers' goal, and, in a loose scrimmage, it trickled just inside the post. George Gillespie apparently thought it would pass outside, and he was too late in getting down to it. The match was drawn, but the Rangers were not satisfied with the result. They lodged a protest with the referee, claiming the tie on the ground that their second goal was a good one. The Scottish Football Association decided against them, and ordered the tie to be replayed on a certain day. Vale of Leven appeared on the ground, but they found no one to play against. Convinced of the justice of their claim, the Rangers had resolved that they would play no more for the Scottish Cup that season. The Vale forwards ran from the one goal to the other and put the ball through, and thus, for the third year in succession, the trophy, which had hung by so slender a thread, was theirs.

Then ensued the most piquant part of the story. A week or two later Rangers and the Vale found themselves in the Final of the Glasgow Charity Cup, then only three years old. In the pavilion Tom Vallance and J. M'Dougall met face to face. " Well, Tom," said the Vale captain, " this is the conqueror." " It is," replied Tom. The tie was played as if it had been the Scottish Cup Final over again and Rangers won by 2–1, the exact score by which they had claimed to have triumphed in the Scottish Cup duel. This, the Charity Cup, was the only cup won by the Rangers in their first twenty years. A somewhat different story remains to be told of the second twenty years, as we shall learn in due course.

1879—1884.

Lure of England—Rangers' Losses—A Critical Period — Men of Mettle—Light Blue Again— Tom Vallance—William Wilton—J. K.'s Coup.

HAD the Rangers been able to keep together their fine young Cup team, what honours might not have fallen to them ! But the fame of this new force, which had arisen to challenge the might of Queen's Park and Vale of Leven, had been wafted across the Border. Already, as early as 1876, Peter Andrews, a once stalwart forward in the Eastern of Glasgow Green days, was playing for Heeley ; James J. Lang, a forward who had played for Clydesdale against Queen's Park in the first Scottish Cup Final, was in the ranks of Sheffield Wednesday; while James Love and Fergus Suter, of Partick, a little later joined Darwen. James Lang, a tough, alert old fellow, is still to the fore, and is usually on duty at the grand stand at Ibrox Park when Rangers are playing at home. He claims to have been the first Scot to go to England for the sole purpose of playing football, and he is supported in his claim by Mr. J. C. Clegg, who at that time was also a member of the Sheffield Wednesday team. Payment of players was not then permitted in England—it was not legalised there until 20th July, 1885, and in Scotland in May, 1893— but the Scots who traversed south were paid just the same. Everybody knew it, but no one could prove it.

Possibly it was inevitable that the Rangers should suffer from the lure of the English sovereign. Hugh M'Intyre was the first of the 1879 Cup Final team to bid farewell to his native hills. He became a Blackburn Rover, and, after a distinguished career with them, settled down in the town as hotel proprietor. Peter Campbell, as a result, no doubt, of Hugh's beguiling ways, played several games for the

Rovers, although never residing in Blackburn. Next to go was William Struthers, the hero of the 1879 Final. He chose Bolton Wanderers, in 1881, as being worthy of his assistance, and, in the same year, was the means of a Rangers' half-back, John Christie, entering the Wanderers' fold. These two old Rangers' men were famous in Bolton. They were in the Wanderers' team which won the Bolton Charity Cup in its first year (1882). In the first game of the Final, against Astley Bridge, which was drawn (3–3), Struthers equalised in the last minute, and in the replay, which the Wanderers won easily, he scored four goals. In addition to the departure of these celebrities, others of the old originals were gradually falling out of the ranks, some of them remaining to serve the club faithfully and well in an administrative capacity.

In the season of 1879-80 the Rangers were drawn against Queen's Park in the first round of the Scottish Cup. They played a goalless draw at Kinning Park, but in the replay at Hampden Park the Rangers went down by 5 goals to 1. It was no disgrace to be defeated by Queen's Park, for they were a great team then, and not only won the Cup in that season, but in the two succeeding seasons as well.

The season of 1880-81 found the Rangers doing better. They reached the sixth round with the loss of only one goal and the acquisition of 22, eleven of these being scored against the Clyde in the fourth-round tie at Kinning Park. But in the sixth round Dumbarton and " Fatal Boghead " was an insurmountable combination. For years afterwards Boghead Park possessed terrors for Rangers and all other clubs unfortunate enough to be sent there on a Cuptie mission. It was Dumbarton and Boghead Park which in the following season (1881-82) again sounded the knell of the Rangers' Cup hopes, and again it was in the sixth round. Dumbarton were at the zenith of their power.

They won the tie by 5-1 and went through to the Final, there to fall to Queen's Park after a drawn game. In the previous season they had also been defeated in the Final by Queen's Park, but at last, in 1882-83, that great Dumbartom team won the Cup, and surely none ever deserved the honour more. In three successive years they had cleaved their way into the last stage.

As bad luck would have it, the Rangers, in 1882-83, were drawn against Queen's Park at Hampden Park in the second round. They made a valiant bid to draw, at least, but were defeated, after a magnificent tussle, by 3-2. This was one of several critical periods in the Rangers' history. The enthusiasm of some of the members had abated. The financial affairs were in a serious condition. Mr. George Goudie, the president, at the request of the Finance Committee, extended a loan of £30, but at the end of the season the club was in debt to the extent of £100. It is impossible to overestimate the value of the service rendered to the club during these and later years by such devoted workers as—

JAMES M'INTYRE, as captain of the team and member of committee.

PETER M'NEIL, one of the originals, now on the committee and in 1886-87 appointed vice-president.

SAM. RICKETTS, one of the 1876 Cup Final team and a wise administrator, who became honorary secretary in January, 1887.

JAMES GOSSLAND, as member of committee, match secretary, and club secretary.

WALTER CRICHTON, as member of committee and secretary.

JAMES WALLACE MACKAY, as member of committee, club secretary, and match secretary.

JAMES WATSON, as member of committee, vice-president, and president.

ROBERT WHITE, as member of committee and honorary treasurer during three seasons.

ROBERT B. KERR, as member of committee and vice-president.

JOHN CAMERON, as player and captain of the team, member of committee, and three times vice-president.

THE STORY OF THE RANGERS.

T. C. B. MILLER, as member of committee and for five years honorary treasurer.

WILLIAM S. HAYS, as member of committee and honorary secretary.

GEORGE B. CALDWELL, as member of committee and vice-president.

DANIEL GILLIES, as member of committee and a warm friend of the club in many ways.

J. F. NESS, as member of committee and honorary treasurer in 1882-83.

A. YOUNG, first as a player, and, later, as member of committee.

GEORGE DENNY, as secretary of the Ibrox Eleven and member of the General Committee, and one who did much to recruit the team when good players were most required.

W. F. NESS, WILLIAM CORBETT, JAMES DUNCAN, WILLIAM FINDLAY, W. W. TAIT, and A. HENDRIE, all of whom did good work on committee.

These gentlemen were not all contemporary. The duration of their service differed according to the demands of business and other preoccupations. Each, however, in his own time and in his own way, gave to the club that loyal help without which the Rangers could not have survived those trying times. Somehow, the liabilities had a wicked way of out-distancing the assets. In the season of 1883-84 the membership was a round hundred. When at the annual meeting, in May, 1884, honorary secretary Gossland was able to report an accession of seventy-five to the roll those present would have thrown their hats up if they had not been already hanging up in the hall of the old Athole Arms Hotel. And note that those seventy-five new members were enlisted only as the result of hard work on the part of the committee, for which the latter were duly thanked in the minutes. Draw a contrast with to-day!

In those early '80's almost a complete transformation had taken place in the team. The eleven selected in March, 1883, " until further alteration might be rendered necessary," were :—

George Gillespie ; Charles Heggie and J. Duncan ; John Cameron and James M'Intyre ; Alexander Hamilton, D. Hill, A. M'Gregor, John Inglis, William Pringle, and James Gossland.

George Gillespie and David Hill were now all that remained of the 1879 Cup Final team, and in the following season both dropped out. To Queen's Park George Gillespie transferred his valued aid, and was succeeded in the Rangers goal by Wm. Chalmers, who, as we shall learn, helped to take the club into the semi-final round of the English Cup in the season of 1886-87.

But before we pass from the year 1883, let us record three notable events. In June, at a committee meeting, it was decided, after a long discussion, mark you, and on the motion of Mr. Sam. Ricketts, seconded by Mr. James Gossland, that the club revert to the old colours of Royal blue jersey and white knickers. These were the original colours adopted at the memorable meeting on Glasgow Green, but they had been dropped for a season or two under circumstances related in the first chapter.

The second notable event was the election to the presidency, at the Annual General Meeting, of Tom Vallance. This was an honour justified alike by his distinguished services as a player and the interest which, since the club's formation, he had taken in all that concerned its welfare. Only for one short period, in 1882, was his personal association with the club interrupted, and that was when he went to Assam, where indifferent health caused him to return home. At that time his playing days were supposed to have ended, but when he visited the old haunts at Kinning Park the lure of the sport proved irresistible, and he became one of the Ancients team of Rangers men who played many matches for charity. It was a fitting recognition of his work that he should have been asked to occupy the positions of president and captain. For six successive years Tom presided over the deliberations of the committee ; for the long period of nine seasons he was the general in command of the forces in the field.

THE STORY OF THE RANGERS.

That the Rangers owed much to Mr. Vallance for their ability to surmount early difficulties, the archives of the club eloquently testify. Without the spade-work which he, the Brothers M'Neil, the Campbells, and others performed, the Rangers probably would never have succeeded in reaching their present exalted position. He was the first of the club's pioneers to be chosen as one of Scotland's representatives against England. He played against the Saxon in 1877, 1878, 1879, and 1881. Only once in these epic struggles was he on the defeated side, while in his three matches against Wales, in 1877, 1879, and 1881, only one goal was surrendered by the Scottish defence. That he was a talented back, whether judged by the old or by the present-day standard, there is no room for doubt. Tall and spare, he administered many a shock to opponents who had not previously made his acquaintance, for he was big-boned and could take or give a charge with any man.

Like most of the lads who suckled the Rangers, Tom was an enthusiastic devotee of rowing before football cast its spell upon him. As an athlete, too, he gained considerable distinction. During the short time which he devoted to athletics he won over sixty prizes, and at the Queen's Park sports in 1881 he jumped 21 feet 11 inches, which stood as a record broad leap for fourteen years. But his leisure activities were not confined to the lighter realms of sport. He was a disciple of Art, and many works of high merit stand to his credit. On two occasions the Royal Scottish Academy recognised his genius by accepting pictures from his brush.

Born in the Vale of Leven, near Renton, Mr. Vallance, when budding into manhood, removed to Shandon, where the breezy waters of the Gareloch imbued him with a love for aquatics. Thus, by a process of strange chance, he was led on to the football fields of Glasgow Green, there and elsewhere to play a part in the weaving of the early chapters of the Story of the Rangers. As a sportsman of the best type he earned the respect of those whom he met in athletic rivalry, and he won the gratitude of his colleagues by the inspiration he brought to them in many a hard-fought fight. The club's followers regarded him with feelings that amounted to affection, which, at all times, has been the acid test of greatness.

The third notable event was the admission to club membership of William Wilton on 24th September, 1883, at the same committee meeting at which George Small and G. B. Caldwell were enrolled. Tom Vallance, as president, was the chairman ; as honorary secretary, Walter Crichton wrote and signed the minutes. A young man of keen perception and with progressive ideas, Mr. Wilton soon became recognised as one who could be trusted to maintain the fine traditions of the club. He played a little for one of the minor elevens, but it was as an administrator and organiser that he became a potent force. Six months after joining the club he was appointed secretary of the Shields Eleven, a post which he resigned in 1885 on being promoted to a place on the General Committee. He was also made a member of the Selecting, Finance, and Ground Committees, and, later, when a project was mooted for acquiring better and more commodious facilities than those afforded at Kinning Park, Mr. Wilton was one of the five appointed to make search for a new ground. This plan, however, did not mature, and it was not until 20th August, 1887, that the club opened the first Ibrox Park. At the annual general meeting on 27th May, 1889, Mr. Wilton was elected match secretary. Thus began a tenure of office which was interrupted only by his tragic death from drowning, in Gourock Bay, on

Sunday, 2nd May, 1920. He had been Match Secretary for ten successive seasons when, on 27th May, 1899, the club was incorporated as a Limited Liability Company and he was given the position of Manager and Secretary. When the Scottish League was formed in 1890, Mr. Wilton became the club's first delegate. He was also the first treasurer of the new body, which was destined to revolutionise the game in Scotland. At all times his opinions were respected as emanating from impulses which had the welfare of the great national game behind them. He was essentially a man of enterprise. To mark time meant to him retrogression. When Rangers were in first Ibrox Park he carried a scheme for a covered stand against the fears of the sceptics at a time when the funds of the club demanded the most careful administration. No point of detail was too trivial for his attention. What would have been petty things to most men received from him as much consideration as matters of apparently greater moment. He took especial pride in the part played by the club in fostering amateur athletics. It was due largely to his personal supervision that the running track was so perfected that many notable records were accomplished on it. The club hand-book, which has become an annual institution, was one of his pet creations.

Courteous yet firm in all his dealings, he earned the esteem of those with whom he might differ, while between him and his closer associates in the club there existed a bond of sincere attachment. In his manner there was a certain dignified reserve, not to be confounded with aloofness. It was always his object to raise the tone of football politics, and there is no doubt that he was successful so far as it was possible for one man's influence to be effective. His untimely death was a tragedy to all with whom he worked in an official capacity ; but there is a measure of consolation in the knowledge that the ideals for which he strove are still sought after by those who are left in custody of the cherished traditions of the club.

A club going through to the semi-final of the Scottish Cup nowadays may safely reckon upon filling the coffers to such an extent as to make the treasurer assume an expansive smile. In the season of 1883-84 the Rangers reached the semi-final, playing seven ties in all, and their total income from these was short of £90. In the season of 1919-20 they played the Celtic in the fourth round, at Ibrox Park, and the drawings at the gate, exclusive of tax, were £3,018. A comparison like that demonstrates, as nothing else can, the amazing advance in popularity made by this absorbing game of football. The semi-final tie of 1883-84 had piquant interest, for the Rangers were drawn against the Vale of Leven at Alexandria. This was the first meeting of the clubs in the Cup since the disputed Final of 1879, and, as showing the changes which had taken place since that memorable event, the teams may be given :—

> **Rangers.**—Wm. Chalmers ; R. Young and J. Duncan; J. M'Intyre and Chas. Heggie ; Alex. Hamilton, John Inglis, H. M'Hardy, John Christie, Jas. Gossland, and Wm. Pringle.

> **Vale of Leven.**—A. M'Lintock ; A. M'Intyre and J. Forbes ; J. Abraham and J. M'Pherson ; D. M'Intyre, R. M'Rae, D. Kennedy, W. Galloway, W. B. Johnstone, and M. Gillies.

John Cameron would have played had he been fit, but whether his presence would have averted defeat for the Rangers is doubtful. The Vale were still a powerful force, and their success by 3 goals to 0 was not wholly unexpected. The Rangers would always admit frankly that virtually their only chance lay in getting the Vale to Kinning Park, and, as it happened, they met only once there in a Scottish

Cup-tie, as has been chronicled already. The result then was a goalless draw, which was repeated when they came together at Ibrox Park in 1889-90 in the third round. The replay at Alexandria was their last trial of strength in the " Scottish."

Here I may as well tell you a story which has a connection with Kinning Park, and which, I think, does justice to the reputation for getting things done possessed by the S.F.A. Secretary, Mr. John K. M'Dowall. On 2nd February, 1884, there was due to be played a Glasgow F.A. trial match between teams of the North and South. This trial was to assist the selectors to choose a team to play Sheffield a fortnight later. You see how seriously an Inter-City match was then regarded. When Mr. M'Dowall and his confederates reached Kinning Park they found that the water from a burst pipe had flooded the field. The water had become frozen and the pitch was in ideal order for a curling match. Mr. M'Dowall took a rapid survey of the situation, and then as rapidly issued his instructions. An adjoining piece of ground was invaded, locks, bolts, and bars falling asunder under the persuasion of some good hearty kicks. " Geordie " Cameron then, and for years afterwards, the Rangers' groundsman, was called upon to improvise goal-posts. The solitary gate was opened just sufficiently to allow one person through at a time. Nobody got in without paying. A sum of £13 2s. 3d. was drawn, and the match was a great success. Tom Robertson, then a Cowlairs' player, and now a member of the Queen's Park Committee, had gone down to see the game, but was invited to play and agreed, thus making his first appearance in a representative match. The owner of the ground taken on " loan " remained blissfully ignorant of the purpose to which his property had been put by these football vandals.

Let me close this chapter by relating that away back in those old times Peter Weir was doing loyal and useful work in tending the ground. He is still serving the club by looking after essential little details, and nothing would please him better than that he should be permitted to remain in harness until the end.

1884—1887.

A Great Player Lost—Duels with Third Lanark—Link with Arbroath—Bid for English Cup—Into Semi-Final—S.F.A. Ban—J. R. Gow.

A DISCOURAGING experience befell the Rangers at the opening of the season of 1884-85. Alexander Hamilton, who had been one of their finest forwards during the preceding four years, went over to Queen's Park. This was a bitter loss, and was felt all the more keenly coming so soon after the departure of George Gillespie to Hampden Park. They were all amateurs then and free to answer the dictates of their pleasure. Still, one may be pardoned for merely stating that the experiences of Queen's Park in modern times are not without precedent. Moses M'Neil, in his very youthful days, also forsook the Rangers to play for Queen's Park, but he soon returned to his first love and never afterwards played truant. The measure of the loss sustained by the defection of Alexander Hamilton may best be gauged from the fact that, after joining Queen's Park, he played four times against England and once against Wales. He was the most brilliant right-winger of his day, possibly as accomplished a player as has ever worn the Scottish colours. James (" Tuck ") M'Intyre was elected captain of the Rangers team, which, as chosen for the first match of the season, was—W. Chalmers ; R. Young and R. Read ; J. M'Intyre and H. M'Hardy ; J. Cameron, J. Gossland, W. Pringle, J. Morton. Matthew Laurie, and A. Steel. Changes, however, had later to be made. J. Cameron returned to his proper place at half-back, A. B. Mackenzie came in as one of the centres (six forwards and two half-backs were still being played), while, later, Alec Vallance reappeared at back, and W. Corbett, A. Peacock, and T. Cook were in the attack.

There was great difficulty in finding an ideal forward combination, and the wonder is that the team made such excellent headway in the Scottish Cup-ties. Whitehill were defeated by 11 goals to 0 in the first round, but a more formidable task awaited the Rangers in round number two. They were called upon to attack the Third Lanark lions in their Cathkin den, and the team which undertook the job was—W. Chalmers ; A. Vallance and H. M'Hardy ; J. M'Intyre and J. Cameron ; W. Pringle. Jas. Morton, S. Thomson, A. B. Mackenzie, M. Laurie, and J. Gossland. In the Third Lanark team were Colin Campbell, a talented goalkeeper, and John Marshall, a strong, speedy right winger. When " Collie " Campbell's career was prematurely, but voluntarily, ended as the result of a foolish indiscretion on the part of a club official, the game lost a fine player. Although Third Lanark had much the best of the game, they had to be satisfied with a draw of 2–2. Alec Vallance inadvertently put the ball through his own goal, and the Rangers crossed over one down. Early in the second half Gossland equalised, but Third Lanark again took the lead through Connelly, and it was not until five minutes from the end that Morton made the scores level again. When the rivals met at Kinning Park for the replay the Rangers had Robert Read at back in place of A. Vallance, while Archie Steel took Thomson's position forward. As in the first game, Third Lanark had their Grand Old Man, as they loved to call A. Kennedy, at half-back. He was supposed to have retired, but he could not resist the magnetism of a Cup tie. Kennedy was one of those pioneers who played in the old Eastern on Glasgow Green before joining Third Lanark, and as early as 1875 he was capped against England. In this Cup-tie against the Rangers he showed all his old craft and was, indeed, reported as being the best player on his side. It was a magnificent contest in which neither team could score.

And so, having twice drawn, the two were finished with each other ; for, according to the rules which then controlled the competition, clubs drawing twice had to go into the ballot for the succeeding round and take their chance along with the clubs that had qualified. But then arose an extraordinary incident. The draw for the third round, by mere chance, brought them together again at Cathkin Park. This time the tie was given a quick despatch. Although not fancied to win, the Rangers played so well that they scored twice in the first half. Laurie got the first goal and T. Cook, one of the Shields Eleven, who had been drafted in at the last moment, registered the second. The third was scored by Morton after the interval, and thus ended one of the most remarkable ties in the history of the Cup.

But it was not the only extraordinary incident in Rangers' Cup-tie experiences during that season. In the fourth round they were sent to Arbroath, where they were beaten by 4 goals to 3. Rangers, however, lodged a protest on account of the pitch being only 49 yards 1 foot wide instead of the legal minimum of 50 yards. The S.F.A. acknowledged the justice of the protest in so far as they instructed Arbroath to have their field put right, but they threw out the Rangers' protest. Such an impossible decision could not be accepted, and although the next round of the ties was drawn with the Rangers excluded, they followed up their claim for a replay with both vigour and reason, and the Association were compelled to cancel their first ruling and grant the petition. When the Rangers returned to Arbroath the ground had

The late GEORGE GOUDIE.
President, 1882-83. Vice-President, 1883-84 and 1884-85.

THOMAS VALLANCE.

One of the Old Originals. Was Captain of the Team during nine seasons
and President from 1883 to 1889. Capped against England, 1877, 1878,
1879, and 1881.

See page 31.

been greatly improved and enlarged. It is recorded that in the first fifteen minutes the Glasgow men put on three points, all in dead silence. Arbroath got a goal early in the second half, but the Rangers replied with other five, and won by 8 goals to 1.

The sixth round brought the Light Blues against Renton, whom they had not met for several years. Although it was a finely contested match, weak goalkeeping caused the defeat of Rangers by 5 goals to 3. It is pleasant to know that after the fray the clubs "swore eternal friendship to each other." You may be sure that when the fine young Renton team went on to win the Cup by defeating Vale of Leven at Hampden Park in the Final none were more hearty in their congratulations than Rangers. Let it be noted that out of the Cup-tie with Renton the Rangers received the sum of £9.

In this season—on 25th January, 1885, to be precise— there was admitted to membership one who, in later years, became a distinguished associate of the club and a valuable asset to the playing strength of the team. I refer to John Robertson Gow. Nine months afterwards, his brother Donald, who became famous as a back both with the Rangers and with the greatest of all Sunderland teams, was also enrolled. "J. R." was a born athlete. Before he was seventeen years of age he won the hundred yards race at the Rangers sports from the 4½ yards mark, the time being returned as slightly under 10⅘ secs. He was a fine hurdler with an exceptionally graceful action. In 1893 he gained the proud title of Scottish hurdles champion, a distinction that also fell to another fine Rangers player, Alec Vallance. He came on the Committee in 1893, and only one year later he was promoted to the position of Honorary Secretary. In the following season again he became Vice-President, and during his occupancy of this office he once more took up the secretarial reins when a vacancy occurred in mid-season. From 1896 to 1898, which was one of the most successful periods in the club's career, he held the supreme post of President. Previously, of course, he had done splendid service as a player, and in this connection it is interesting to recall that, although not a left-footer, he played regularly on the left wing. In 1888 he was capped against Ireland and would, probably, have played against England also but for the fact that when the team was chosen he was suffering from an injury. Mr. Gow's progress in his official capacity was something of the whirlwind order, which really typified the man. Boiling over with energy, he was never at rest when the interests of the club were susceptible of improvement. He took a leading part in making the Annual Sports Meeting the best of its kind in Scotland. This was achieved by various devices, all of which reflected an enterprising mind and the precious gift of originality. On one occasion, some weeks before the sports meeting was due, an animated controversy broke out on the Glasgow newspapers regarding the relative merits of two famous men who were to compete at Ibrox Park. The public were roused to a high state of excitement over the correspondence, but nobody knew that Mr. John Robertson Gow had written all the letters himself. Necessarily, the newspapers were as ignorant of this fact as were the readers. His faith in the future of the club never wavered ; and although on occasion he might have seemed to be ahead of the times, there can be no doubt that during his period of official activity, he was a force that made for advancement in all directions.

To mark their appreciation of his " honorary services," the club presented him with a gold watch bearing an inscription, which testifies to the ungrudging spirit which actuated all his efforts. John Robertson Gow was a true Ranger. His ability to play games was a natural gift. At the age of thirty-five he handled a golf club for the first time, and very soon he was playing with a handicap of two strokes in his club's competitions. It is not surprising that his indomitable personality should have helped to secure for him a high degree of success in business life.

Many stories, some of them not strictly accurate, have been told regarding the Rangers' connection with the English Football Association and their participation in the English Cup-ties. At a meeting of the committee of 24th June, 1885, it was decided to join the E.F.A., and it was unanimously agreed that Walter Crichton should be the club's delegate. In the first round of the ties the Rangers were drawn against Rawtenstall. This tie, however, was never played. Rawtenstall insisted upon including professionals in their team, and on this ground the Rangers refused to meet them. A week or two later, the English F.A. fined the Rangers ten shillings " for infringement of rules." Which rule was infringed I have never been able to discover. Professionalism had been legalised in England on 20th July, 1885, and as Scotland was still wholly amateur, the intercourse between the clubs of the two countries was, for the time being, checked to some extent.

In the following season—1886-87—Rangers again entered for the English Cup, and this time had the distinction of playing themselves into the semi-final. Here is their record :—

1st Round.	Rangers, 1 ;	Everton,	- -	0	At Everton.
2nd Round.	Rangers, 2 ;	Church,	- -	1	At Kinning Park.
3rd Round.	Rangers, 3 ;	Cowlairs,	- -	2	At Kinning Park.
4th Round.	Rangers. Bye.				
5th Round.	Rangers, 3 ;	Lincoln City,	-	0	At Kinning Park.
6th Round.	Rangers, 5 ;	Old Westminsters,		1	At Kinning Park.
Semi-Final.	Rangers, 1 ;	Aston Villa,	-	3	At Crewe.

THE STORY OF THE RANGERS.

The team chosen for the tie with Everton was W. Chalmers; D. Gow and John M'Cartney; J. Cameron, James M'Intyre, and J. Muir; Jas. Buchanan, Matthew Laurie, C. Heggie, A. Peacock, and R. Fraser. It was recognised that a supreme effort would have to be made, and on that account the assistance of John M'Cartney was invited. Readers will recognise him as the same exuberant John who later played for Cowlairs and who became known to the present generation of enthusiasts, first as manager of St. Mirren and then of Heart of Midlothian. It will be noted that three half-backs were now the formation. By the time Rangers had disposed of Church and Cowlairs and entered the fifth round, they were the only Scottish survivors. Queen's Park, Renton, and Partick Thistle had fallen by the way. So well did D. Gow comport himself against Lincoln City at Kinning Park, that the English club offered to find him a job at £2 10s. per week if he would go to England. Imagine a present-day professor being offered such terms! John Forbes, the famous Vale of Leven back, partnered D. Gow in the tie with Old Westminsters and also against Aston Villa in the semi-final. The team against Aston Villa was—W. Chalmers; J. Forbes and D. Gow; J. Cameron, J. M'Intyre, and J. Muir; M. Laurie, P. Lafferty, Joe Lindsay (Dumbarton), A. Peacock, and R. Fraser. When the team went south for the match with the Villa there were great hopes that they would be the first Scottish club to bring the English Cup north. The Villa, however, were the superior side. There is a tale told of Chalmers, the Rangers' goalkeeper, having over-eaten at the dinner before the match, and being, consequently, unable to get about with his accustomed alacrity. This is not exactly an old wife's story. William was an excellent trencher-man, and Hugh M'Intyre, who had come along from

Blackburn to fraternise with old comrades, confessed, with some self-reproach, that it was he who, in a playful spirit, acted as agent to the goalkeeper's innocent little debauch. This was the last season in which Scottish clubs were allowed to compete for the English Cup. On 10th May, 1887, the Scottish F.A. having observed, with some alarm, the preference which our clubs showed for matches with English combinations, passed a rule—"That clubs belonging to this Association shall not be members of any other national association."

A curious feature was that while Rangers could go so far in the English Cup competition they were defeated by Cambuslang at Kinning Park in the third round of the Scottish Cup tourney. Some were daring enough to suggest that they were glad to be out of the home ties in order that they might concentrate upon winning England's bit of silver.

Before passing to a new chapter it should be recorded that on 28th January, 1886, the club joined the Scottish Amateur Athletic Association, and decided to hold sports in the following August. Mr. D. Gillies, who had for some years taken a close interest in the club, presented a gold and silver medal to be disposed of as the committee might think fit. As a token of the club's appreciation for long and valued services, Mr. Pringle received the gold medal. The cup won at the Edinburgh Exhibition tournament was given to John Cameron, than whom the club never had a more devoted player. He and James M'Intyre were for years a fine half-back combination. On committee he rendered faithful service, and in 1891 some slight recognition was made by his election to the vice-presidency, a post he occupied for three successive seasons.

1887—1890.

First Ibrox—The Christening—Hard Times—A Five-Game Cup-Tie—John Taylor—Four Wise Men—New Players—David Mitchell.

A HISTORIC milestone was reached in season 1887-88. The first Ibrox Park, with its eastern boundary in Copland Road, was opened on 20th August, 1887. For some years before this the officials, at various periods, had taken steps to secure a ground which would fulfil more adequately than did Kinning Park the growing requirements of the club. Obstacles and a sneaking fondness for the old field had prevented plans maturing, but when the factor appeared one fine day with an order that Kinning Park must be vacated by 1st March, 1887, the Committee had to get to business. Walter Crichton, who was now Honorary Secretary, had urged the suitability of the Ibrox district. He foresaw the spread westward of the city's teeming populace and the extension of the tramway car system in that direction. Almost all of Mr. Crichton's prophecies have been fulfilled, and no one could have felt warmer satisfaction when, on 30th December, 1899, the present Ibrox Park was opened, thus marking another milestone in the progress of the club. Away back in 1883, Mr. Crichton acted as Honorary Secretary for a short period. He was Convener of the Sub-Committee first appointed to secure ground at Ibrox, and when the club was incorporated in 1899 he was chosen as one of the Directors, and held that position for fourteen successive seasons.

Kinning Park was closed on 26th February, 1887, with a match between the Ancients and Moderns. Tom Vallance made a shrewd bargain with Preston North-End

46

to open Ibrox Park. The gate drawings amounted to £290, while £50 was taken at the stand. According to the bargain made, Preston North-End were entitled to only £50 of this. The match was not exactly a cheerful christening for Ibrox. Preston North-End, then known as the " Invincibles," had a magnificent team, which included several illustrious Scots, notably George Drummond, J. Graham, Sam Thomson, David Russell, J. Gordon, Nick Ross, and John Goodall, the greatest of them all. The Rangers' team consisted of W. Chalmers ; D. Gow and J. M'Cartney ; J. Cameron, J. M'Intyre, and J. Muir ; Hamilton Brown, Andrew Peacock, A. B. Mackenzie, W. Pringle, and R. Brand. For ordinary purposes this was quite a good combination, but Preston were not ordinary. At half-time the Rangers were five goals down, and after the North-End had added three more to one by Rangers, some of the spectators thought they had had enough and the match was prematurely stopped. Hamilton Brown became a Bailie of Glasgow and a director of the Clyde club.

This was another critical period in the history of the club. An early exit was made from the Scottish Cup competition, Partick Thistle giving them their quietus in the second round. The finances, owing to the expenditure on the new ground, required careful handling, and in this connection it is only fair that the contractors, Messrs. F. Braby & Co., should be given a word of praise for the consideration they extended.

But there was one consolatory feature. In the Glasgow Cup competition, which was commenced in this season, Rangers met Cowlairs in the semi-final, and an amazing sort of tie it proved. Five games, played " all over the shop," were necessary before Rangers qualified to meet, and be defeated by, Cambuslang in the Final tie at

Hampden Park. The games with Cowlairs were played at Gourlay Park (0–0), Ibrox Park (0–0), Cathkin Park (2–2), Barrowfield Park (Rangers 2–1), and Cathkin Park (Rangers 3–1). After the Barrowfield match, Cowlairs successfully protested against Brand for an alleged breach of the amateur rules. In these games Tom Robertson played for Cowlairs, so also did James MacPherson (a brother of John), William M'Leod, and John M'Cartney, who by this time had left Rangers and gone over to the rivals. Both clubs reaped from the ties what was then regarded as a rich harvest, and at the Rangers' annual meeting the income for the season was reported to have been £2,232, which, all things considered, was very satisfactory.

Before the season of 1888-89 opened, the Committee had decided to appoint a professional trainer, and the post was given to John Taylor, who by his zeal and capability helped to bring unprecedented honours to the club. His death, in 1897, was deplored by all who worked with him in the interests of the team.

But another bad season had to be tholed before the Light Blues started on the upward trend. 1888-89, which was notable for the visit of the Canadian team, who opened their tour at Ibrox with a draw (1–1), was the worst in Rangers' career. Of the 39 matches played, 13 were won, 19 lost, and 7 drawn, while 93 goals were scored and 108 lost. In the second round of the Scottish Cup, Clyde won at Ibrox (3–0) after a draw at Barrowfield (2–2), and in the third round of the Glasgow Cup, at Ibrox Park, Celtic, who had come into existence the previous season, won (6–1). The outlook was discouraging. Good players could not be found, and as an indication of the desperate measures adopted, Donald Gow was played at centre-forward.

But the silver lining was soon to appear. William

Wilton in 1889-90 became Match Secretary; John S. Marr was Club Secretary; Jas. A. K. Watson, Vice-President; John Mellish, President; and T. C. B. Miller, Treasurer. With a strong Committee to lend support, and with R. S. Craig as Secretary of the Swifts' XI., and George Denny as Secretary of the Ibrox XI., a more vigorous and more enterprising policy was pursued. William Chalmers, who had served the club well as custodian, resigned in August, 1889, and to succeed him D. G. Reid was secured. He was a Maryhill boy and was possessed of exceptional gifts, which made him a guardian of the fort who could be trusted. He stayed with the Rangers long enough to assist them to win joint League Championship honours in the first season of the competition. J. Hendry came along from Uddingston to partner Donald Gow at back, while another good back in Wm. Hay accompanied D. G. Reid from Maryhill. Robert Marshall left Partick Thistle to pull a light blue jersey over his broad shoulders. He was a right half-back of the rugged type, with inexhaustible energy and the proper temperament for " big " football.

James M'Intyre was the veteran of the team, one of the very old brigade who had stood by the club through thick and thin, through bad times and good times, always, as was said of him, coming up with a smile on his face. Cheery, inspiring, likeable " Tuck ! " Surely no club ever had a more loyal servant or colleagues a more heartening companion ! Worthy indeed was he of the honour bestowed by the Committee when in August, 1889, they made him a life member of the Rangers. And typical of the man were his few remarks when he stood up to accept from the hands of the president, John Mellish, the gift of life membership, which he has ever since cherished. In warm-hearted words, " Tuck " referred to his long

connection with the club, " and," he added, " whatever
may be the future of the Rangers, be certain of this, that
I shall ever seek in all circumstances to strive to do my
utmost for the prosperity of the club." He was still the
centre half-back, although, before the season ended,
Andrew M'Creadie arrived to keep brother Hugh company.
Andrew belonged to Girvan and played for Cowlairs before
making the short journey to the South Side. Hugh
M'Creadie had already been a season at Ibrox. After a
successful career with Rangers, he did service for Third
Lanark and Linthouse. There was a long-established
friendship between Rangers and the Linthouse.

For left half-back there came David Mitchell from
Kilmarnock to reinforce John Muir, another loyal clubman,
who gave ungrudging service in many capacities, one who
thought nothing of self, but always of what was best for
the " family." Tom Wylie, from Maybole, was the
outside right ; Hugh M'Creadie was his partner ; John R.
Gow was as elusive at centre as at outside left when he
played there ; James Henderson, from Dumfries, a strong,
dashing, inside left, operated along with John Allan, a
useful winger. It is interesting to recall that on one
occasion assistance was rendered by Malcolm Low, of
Kilbirnie, the father of James Low, who left the Rangers
a couple of seasons ago to play for Newcastle United.

Though that season of 1889-90 was only moderately
successful for the Rangers, it served as a period of constructive team work which was to bring rich results in
succeeding years. To gather these new players into the fold
was a task that required ingenuity, tact, and a seductive
charm which are natural to individuals only in rare cases.
Here the Rangers were fortunate in having these qualities
embodied in two of their committee members, Alec B.
Mackenzie and John M. Grant. John Grant was a school-

master. He had a pawky wit, a naïve way of asking a favour that swept away all inclination to refusal But behind his air of simplicity there lurked a real genius for estimating character. That was the secret of his success. It was a tribute to his qualities that he was elected a member of the original Match Committee of three in 1890, along with A. B. Mackenzie and William Wilton. This was a departure which the club never had reason to regret. These three knew their business and no one had cause to complain of non-fulfilment. Once, when the Rangers went to England for the annual tour, which was then an indispensable tit-bit in the season's programme, there was some alarm lest Robert Marshall, the half-back, would be spirited away by a certain Nottingham club. Scottish tourists had to watch their players with eyes of hawks, failing which they were likely to return home minus a lamb or two. At breakfast, on the morning after the match, William Wilton, assuming great concern for Marshall's safety, upbraided the worthy John Grant for being remiss in his vigil over the player. " Man, Willie, would you say that to me, and ma very collar nearly burstin' wi' anxiety for him ? " was the reply, made with a fine air of injured innocence.

The policy of progress which heralded the opening of this season of 1889-90 increased in strength as the term drew to a close. In April, 1890, William MacAndrew was enrolled a member, and two days later, at the annual general meeting, he was elected secretary of the Ibrox XI. Dugald MacKenzie became Vice-President, William Wilton was re-elected Honorary Match Secretary, and A. B. Mackenzie and John Grant were on the Committee.

I think that anyone who cares to explore the inner history of the Rangers will be able to satisfy himself that these five exercised a great and vital influence in laying the foundation of whatever eminence the club enjoys to-day.

THE STORY OF THE RANGERS.

Dugald MacKenzie became President in 1891 and retained
the honourable position until 1896. It was fitting homage to
one whose merits in respect of continuous length of service
were not excelled. In his salad days he played for the club,
and as late as 1889 he adventured into the field to do battle
against Third Lanark in the inter-committee matches,
which in those times were a pleasant, social kind of annual
foregathering. As president of the Scottish Football
Association, Mr. MacKenzie conducted business with an
easy dignity which won for him the respect and support
of councillors from all over the country. For several years
after retiring from business he devoted his time almost
exclusively to the interests of the club. Ibrox Park was
his home. When cycle-racing was at its zenith, it was
Dugald MacKenzie who went to England and brought to
Ibrox the most famous racers of the day, including Osmond
and Schofield, thus helping the club to maintain the
reputation long held as pioneers of athletic sports. As a
life member of the club, he was presented, in August,
1896, with a gold badge, a similar emblem of work well
done being also given to James (" Tuck ") M'Intyre, who
had been a life member since 1889.

When William MacAndrew was on Committee, in
1890-91, as secretary of the Ibrox XI., and again in
February, 1892, when he resumed that post upon the
resignation of A. S. Nisbet, the club required workers, not
ornaments. There was no time for applause. Every
man's shoulder had to be at the wheel, for it was do or
die, sink or swim for every Scottish club that desired to
remain in the first flight. The Rangers, like others,
discovered that it was one thing to get players, another
thing to keep them. Mr. MacAndrew's share in holding
control of all the vital strings was greater and more lasting
than those on the fringe of the official circle were aware.

But his co-workers knew, and at the annual meeting in 1892 he was unanimously elected honorary secretary in succession to J. C. Lawson, who for his honourable service received the warm thanks of the members. Mr. MacAndrew was secretary for two seasons. Stress of business compelled him to relinquish the office at the annual meeting in 1894, but in 1895 he came into harness again as honorary treasurer, and he occupied that position until 1899, when the club was incorporated, the legal work in connection with the flotation of the company being carried through by him. In that year he became secretary of the Scottish League, and the functions of that office he continues to fulfil. It was as treasurer, perhaps, that he did his best work for the club. The payment of players was legalised by the Scottish Football Association in 1893, and, consequently, the provision of close-season wages became a problem not easy of solution. But the treasurer solved it. Players who wanted a month's money in advance, and who got it, spent it and asked for more, were treated to a convincing little homily on the virtues of thrift, and told to apply again on the proper date. Our treasurer, with his keen, lawyer-like mind, knew exactly the value of a penny in swinging an adverse balance into the credit column. A good balance was the joy of his heart.

But though he was at all times jealous of the interests of the club, players and others often had reason to be grateful to him for personal acts of consideration. Incidents of later years showed that these were not forgotten. The club's greatest triumphs were achieved during Mr. MacAndrew's period of office. In 1896-97, the three cups—Scottish, Glasgow, and Charity—were won ; in 1897-98, the Scottish and Glasgow trophies were retained ; and in 1898-99, not a single point was lost in the League. These are recollections of which any man might be proud.

A. B. Mackenzie was a splendid type of the unselfish worker. His single purpose was to do what he could for the benefit of the club, and he laid down no terms. In his very young days he played for a club called the Pilgrims, and the Rangers sought his assistance in an emergency in 1881. It is curious that during his long connection with them as a player he should have been regarded as the ideal emergency unit, the " handy-man." He played in practically every position from goal out, and although he would have been the last to lay claim to any degree of brilliancy, there was such a rare motive of club loyalty behind his endeavours, that faith in his usefulness was deep and sure. He was appointed to the Committee in 1887, and from that year onward he continued without interruption to occupy a responsible position in the administration of the club's affairs. When the club was incorporated in 1899, Mr. Mackenzie was appointed vice-chairman of directors and for a number of years he sat on the Board. Whether as a delegate to the Scottish F.A., or as a committee member or president of the Glasgow F.A., Mr. Mackenzie made friends by reason of his sincerity and soundness of principle. For subtle manœuvre he had no use at all. He came to the point at once, and his words carried weight because they had a sense of reasoning and simple logic behind them. His death, in January, 1916, was deeply regretted, not only in Rangers circles, but also in the much wider sphere of Scottish football legislation.

Another earnest plodder was George Small, who was admitted to membership along with William Wilton on 24th September, 1883. For several years he was a devoted camp follower, and in 1889 his enthusiasm was recognised by his appointment to committee, in which he remained for four successive seasons. He returned to office after a year's absence, and continued to give the club devoted assistance, both in Committee and on the Board of Directors.

1890—1892.

The League Begins—Race with Dumbarton—
Joint Champions—How It Happened—Famous
Cup-Ties—John M'Pherson—A Discovery—His
Caps and Cups.

WE now enter upon season 1890-91, the first of the
Scottish League, which was to mark an epoch in
Scottish football. But before a ball was kicked
the Rangers had added three distinguished forwards to
their list. Neil Kerr, who was of Bowling, and who
played for Cowlairs, joined in May, 1890 ; John M'Pherson,
who had graduated from Kilmarnock to Cowlairs, was
enrolled on 25th June, along with David Hislop, an outside
left from Partick Thistle. The clubs comprising the League
were Rangers, Celtic, Third Lanark, Hearts, St. Mirren,
Dumbarton, Renton, Cowlairs, Cambuslang, Vale of
Leven, and Abercorn. Renton had taken the leading part
in agitating for its formation, and when the season opened
they were regarded as very likely winners. But they did
not finish the season as members. When they had played
five matches they came under the ban of the S.F.A., and
the points won and lost by them were cancelled. Their
offence was this. St. Bernards had been suspended
previously for a breach of the amateur laws, one of their
players, J. Ross, being alleged to have received payment
for his services. While they were under suspension, it
was against the rules for any club to meet them. A club
called the Edinburgh Saints immediately appeared on the
scene, but the S.F.A. declared the Edinburgh Saints and
St. Bernards to be one and the same. In spite of this
pronouncement, Renton met the Edinburgh Saints in
a match at Renton, and were consequently declared
professional and expelled from the Association.

The late JOHN MELLISH.
President, 1889-90.

The late JAMES A. K. WATSON.
President, 1890-91.

At that time the payment of players was known to be practised by most of the leading clubs, and what was called the Professional Committee of the S.F.A. was continually calling in the books for inspection. Club treasurers were invited to explain items of expenditure which the Committee could not understand. In one case the books could not be produced because they had been "lost in a fire." All this was merely an indication of the intense struggle for existence, and in this connection it is worth noting that only Rangers, Celtic, Hearts, St. Mirren, and Third Lanark have remained members of the League since the beginning.

But to get back to our story. The Rangers' first match in the League was played against the Hearts at Ibrox Park on 16th August, 1890, and the teams were :—

> Rangers.—D. G. Reid ; D. Gow and J. Muir ; R. Marshall, A. M'Creadie, and D. Mitchell ; T. Wylie, N. Kerr, H. M'Creadie, J. M'Pherson, and D. Hislop.

> Hearts.—M'Kay ; Adams and Roberts ; Begbie, M'Pherson, and Hill ; Taylor, Mason, Jamieson, Scott, and Baird.

Although the Rangers won this match by 5 goals to 2, they did not exhibit the quality of combination which enabled them to celebrate many a subsequent victory. The Hearts did not get the goals that day, but they showed qualities which ripened as the season advanced, so that when the ties came on they were at their very best, and the Scottish Cup, for the first time, was won for Tynecastle. For the development of Rangers team work, as distinct from individualism, John M'Pherson was primarily responsible. His was essentially a mind that strove for cohesion of effort, and there can be no doubt whatever that the many rare achievements in which he subsequently shared were largely attributable to his success in welding the component parts of the team into one harmonious whole.

I do not think that the story of how John M'Pherson was " discovered " as an inside forward has ever been told. In 1888, when he was a Kilmarnock player, his position was outside left. He knew no other. One fine morning a Kilmarnock official woke him out of a good sleep to tell him that he was wanted by the S.F.A. to play for the Improbables against Probables in the International trial match.

When John arrived at Ibrox where the trial was to be played, he found that the only other left winger available for the Improbables was Neil Munro, of Abercorn, who was also an outside artist. What was to be done ? It was agreed that Munro should play on the touchline in the first half and John in the second half. Walter Arnott was the Probables' right back and Robert Kelso, of Renton, the right half. William Sellar, a great forward, who played seven times against England, was the Improbables' centre. Before the game was very old the spectators—and the selectors—were raising their eyebrows in surprise. The inside left—a mere novice to the position—kept Munro and Sellar going so merrily that several things happened. Munro politely requested to be allowed to finish the game at outside ; Sellar got his cap against England ; " Sandy " Higgins, a Kilmarnock clubmate of M'Pherson's, who was the Probables' centre, complained that John had played Sellar into the International team and him out of it ; the Cowlairs representatives who were present swore they would have the new inside left in their team before many moons had passed, and they kept their oath. Although on occasion, when required, M'Pherson played afterwards at outside left, from that day onward he was regarded as an inside forward. But that trial match merely provided a glimpse of the versatility of the man. In after years, John M'Pherson played in every position, including goal, for the Rangers, and he never failed in any of them. But the most interesting sequel of all to that seemingly small matter of chance was that, in season 1888-89, M'Pherson and Munro were together again on the left wing in the Scottish team against England at the London Oval, where the Scots gained a brilliant victory by 3-2, after being two goals down in the first ten minutes.

M'Pherson's twelve years with the Rangers were crowded with glorious adventure. He was in three of the four teams that won the Scottish Cup and he had a share in the winning of five League championships. The Glasgow Cup was brought seven times to Ibrox during his period of service and the Charity Cup twice. He was capped thirteen times, his honours being : against England, 4 ; Wales, 2 ; Ireland, 2 ; English League, 3 ; Irish League, 2. The goals he scored for Rangers must have reached a colossal total, but, unfortunately, it is not possible to give an authentic record of his prowess as a marksman. Big and small football were all the same to him. He was in bed when word was brought to his home in Kilmarnock that he had been chosen to play against England in 1889. The household became agitated. John was shaken out of a sound sleep, heard the great news, turned on his other side and—promptly went to sleep again. He was not a great size of a man, but he was all whalebone and steel. His stamina was drawn from a rich fountain of natural strength which enabled him, more than once, to begin a fresh period of successful activity when it was supposed he should have been finished with football. He had marvellous control of the ball, and he would dribble right up to the feet of a defender before slipping the pass to a colleague. In front of goal he showed the footballer's sixth sense by making the weight of his shot balance with correct aim. If a sharp jab or mild angular push shot was required, he would beat the goalkeeper that way. He was seldom tempted into going for a spectacular drive just for the sake of making the thing look well. It used to be said of him that he " stole " his goals, but that was about the finest tribute that could have been paid him. His last match was against Hibernian in the Scottish Cup-tie of 1902. In 1907 he became a director of the club, and he has served on the Board ever since.

In the second match of the 1890-91 League against Cambuslang, the Rangers rattled up six goals, of which M'Pherson scored four. He could have made it five, but purposely kept out of the way of a long drive by Donald Gow, which went between the posts. Renton were next disposed of, at Ibrox, by 4-1, and with this excellent record to encourage them, Rangers entered their Scottish Cup-tie against Celtic. The match was played at Parkhead, and as it was the first meeting of the clubs in the national Cup competition, the teams are of some historic interest. Here they are :—

> **Rangers.**—Reid ; Gow and Muir ; Marshall, M'Creadie, and Mitchell ; Wylie, Kerr, H. M'Creadie, M'Pherson, and Hislop.

> **Celtic.**—Bell ; Reynolds and M'Keown ; Gallacher, M'Callum, and W. Maley ; Madden, M. Dunbar, Groves, Dowds, and Crossan.

Rangers were favourites to win the Cup. This tie was in the first round and they met the frequent fate of favourites. It was a tremendously exciting struggle, a fit introduction to the many thrilling cup-ties since played between the rivals. Forty minutes after the start, Madden, the most dangerous forward on the field, ran from mid-field, and, when well up, centred to Groves, who steadied for a moment, and then tipped the ball through the corner of Reid's goal That was the only goal scored, and so the Rangers passed out and the Celtic went on to be defeated in the sixth round by Dumbarton, who reached the final, there to fall to the Hearts by 1 goal to 0. Yet the Rangers in that season could beat the Hearts in both League fixtures, and at Ibrox treated Dumbarton to a 4-2 League defeat. But it was in the game with Dumbarton at Boghead that the Rangers sustained the first reverse recorded against them in the League. It was the club's fourth match in the competition, and the one in which they gave their worst display of the whole season. The only other defeat was inflicted by the Celtic, at Ibrox Park, after a draw had been secured at Parkhead.

Everybody knows that Dumbarton and Rangers tied for the championship and that they were left with joint honours, but everybody does not know how the latter condition arose. The two clubs ran almost neck and neck through the season until they met in their return match at Ibrox Park. This was Rangers' second last fixture and Dumbarton's last. Rangers had gained 27 points, Dumbarton 29. Up till then, Dumbarton alone had defeated the Rangers. It was a match, therefore, of tremendous import to both teams, for great was the desire to become first champions of the new League. Hugh M'Creadie had a broken rib and could not play, so W. Wilson was brought in from the Swifts eleven to play outside left. W. Hodge, who had joined from Linthouse in February, 1891, was Donald Gow's partner at back, and the team was—Reid ; Hodge and Gow ; Marshall, A M'Creadie, and Mitchell; Hislop, Henderson, Kerr M'Pherson, and Wilson. A ten-thousand crowd testified to the importance with which the match was invested. It was fought out at a furious pace, taxing the stamina of the players to the last ounce. Dumbarton's defence offered a magnificent resistance, but the fine working-up by M'Pherson and his judicious nursing of Kerr won the match for Rangers, who scored 4 goals to Dumbarton's 2. This was M'Pherson's first appearance after his marriage, which marked the first break in the bachelor ranks of the Rangers.

Thus, Dumbarton and Rangers became level with 29 points each. The championship hung upon the result of the Rangers' last match, which was against Celtic on the following Saturday at Ibrox. W. Wilson was left out of the team and John White, another Swifts player, was brought in as partner to Hislop on the right wing. Somehow, the Rangers never got properly into their stride. They fought the game out well in the first half, however, and at the interval each side had scored a goal. Andrew M'Creadie, in the second half, was very lame, but the others put in a little bit extra, and there were great hopes of a draw and the Championship when Reid allowed the ball to drop from his hands and roll over the line. This gave Celtic a 2-1 victory and left Rangers and Dumbarton equal with 29 points each.

There was nothing for it but a deciding match between them. They met at Cathkin Park, on Thursday, 21st May, 1891, and again there was a crowd of ten thousand. It was a Trojan struggle, and seldom, previously, had such intensity of excitement been witnessed. Rangers obtained a goal in the first minute, and playing dashing, clever football, became two goals up before the interval. The points, according to the way we judge these things nowadays, should have been fairly secure for the Rangers, but the Dumbarton players were of the bull-dog, never-say-die type. They made a brilliant recovery in the second half. Bell, who afterwards was with Everton and Celtic, gave them their first goal, and the equaliser was rushed through from a scrimmage. So, with the so-called decider over, Rangers and Dumbarton were still equal. What was to be done about it ? The great question was debated by the Scottish League Committee, and by the casting vote of the chairman, it was decided that the clubs should be joint champions for the season. The only other occasion on which a tie has occurred was in the season of 1904-5, and again the Rangers were concerned, this time along with Celtic, who won the decider at Hampden Park.

In that first season of the League the Rangers played 19 matches, including the deciding match which did not decide, but not including the match with Renton which was cancelled when the latter club were expelled from membership of the S.F.A. The players who took part in these and the number of games played by each are as follows :—

	Matches.			Matches.
David Mitchell,	19	Hugh M'Creadie,	-	13
Neil Kerr, -	19	Wm. Hodge, -	-	11
John M'Pherson,	19	John Muir, -	-	9
David Hislop,	19	Jas. M'Intyre,	-	9
Donald R. Gow,	17	Tom Wylie, -	-	4
D. G. Reid, -	16	A. B. Mackenzie,	-	4
R. W. Marshall,	16	John White, -	-	2
Andrew M'Creadie,	16	Wm. Wilson, -	-	1
James Henderson,	14	John Allan, -	-	1

All were awarded a badge except W. Wilson and J. Allan.

But there was one other remarkable feature of this very remarkable season. This was the Glasgow Cup third-round tie between the Rangers and Third Lanark. Five games were played, the fourth of the series being, however, a friendly—a " frost in every sense " as someone said at the time. In the second, third, and fourth games of the tie, Donald Sillars assisted the Rangers at back. He was a handsome athlete and very fast. A year later—in 1892— he played for Scotland against England, being then a member of Queen's Park. In 1894, at Celtic Park, he was at right back in the Scottish team against England and was opposed to Fred. Spikesley, then a famous left wing " flier " of the Sheffield Wednesday club. Those who witnessed that International tussle will not soon forget the thrilling duels of speed between them. Never had Spikesley been so effectively mastered.

The first of the four legitimate games in the tie was played at Cathkin Park, and it was the beginning of as thrilling a sequence of struggles as that generation of football enthusiasts had ever witnessed. Before the interval, the Rangers were two goals up, and shortly after the resumption they added a third, the scorers in order being Wylie, M'Pherson, Wylie. Third Lanark's outlook appeared to be hopeless. But they set to with a will, and at last Thomson scored. Eight minutes from the finish a second goal was rushed on in a scrimmage, and then, with only four minutes to go, a mighty cheer heralded the equalising goal shot by Thomson. The second game, played at Ibrox Park, was no less exciting. M'Pherson scored for Rangers in the first half and Johnstone equalised early in the second half. The teams went back to Cathkin Park for the third game which was played in a deluge of rain, but it could not quench the passion of players or spectators. It was now the turn of the Rangers to show whether they could play an uphill game. Third Lanark had a bleak sou'-wester in their favour, and before the interval arrived they were leading by three goals scored by Johnstone, Scott, and Burke. Twenty-five minutes of the second half had gone before Hislop reduced the leeway. With four minutes to play the Rangers were still two goals behind. Then Kerr whipped on a second, and from the centre kick the Rangers forwards swept down upon the Third Lanark defence and Wylie equalised.

People began to ask if the teams would ever be separated. The answer came quickly enough, for in the next trial of strength, at Ibrox Park, Third Lanark made no mistake. In a first half that throbbed with excitement, neither side could score, but only a few minutes after the change of ends, Lochhead put Third Lanark in the lead. Then Burke gave them a second goal, and although the Rangers scored once from a scrimmage, they had at last to surrender. It had been a wonderful tie and was the talk of the kingdom. Many people from England and Ireland watched the deciding game. It need not be doubted that a contributory factor to the defeat of the Rangers was the departure of Tom Wylie to Everton. He had played in all the games of the tie except the last one, on the eve of which the news that he had decided to join the Everton club fell like a bombshell among officials and players at Ibrox. That deciding match was mainly responsible for the penalty kick law being introduced in the following season. Smith, the Third Lanark back, had made such free use of his hands to stop the ball, that the need for a revision of the law governing free kicks was made very apparent.

The players who took part in the last of this series of games ought to have their names emblazoned in print :—

Rangers.—Reid ; Sillars and Gow ; Marshall, M'Intyre, and Mitchell ; Hislop, H. M'Creadie, Kerr, M'Pherson, and Henderson.

Third Lanark—Downie ; A. Thomson and Smith ; M'Farlane, Scott, and Lochhead ; Lapsley, W. Thomson, Johnstone, M'Innes, and Burke.

THE STORY OF THE RANGERS.

Tom Wylie later left Everton for Bristol, in which town he set up as a prosperous newsagent. Had the migrations stopped at him, the following season of **1891-92** might have been a better one for the Rangers. Unfortunately, Donald Gow, regarded as one of the best backs in the kingdom, went away to Sunderland on the princely terms of £70 down and £3 a week. David Hislop also took the professional ticket and joined Aston Villa. As compensation for these losses, David Haddow came from Albion Rovers to keep goal, D. G. Reid being retained as reserve ; Robert Scott changed over from Third Lanark to partner Hodge at back ; and M. Cullen, an outside right, left the Airdrieonians to don a light blue jersey. These were the new-comers when the season opened, but with things going badly, fresh efforts were made to improve the playing strength, not with a great measure of success it must be admitted. Five half-backs, variously distributed, were in the team which beat Renton in the opening League match. Marshall was the outside right and Muir operated along the left touch-line. But this victory was illusory. A defeat by 3 goals to 0 at Parkhead showed there was something very far wrong. The one satisfactory feature was the brilliant goalkeeping of Haddow, who declined an offer of £70 down and £3 a week from an English club. During the preceding season only two League defeats had been sustained. That number was equalled in the first three matches of 1891-92. This was disconcerting. All sorts of devices were tried in order to change the luck—a precious word that—but things went from bad to worse. A. B. Mackenzie, ever ready to answer the call, was brought out to play centre against Third Lanark, and he scored the team's two goals, which, however, were not enough, for Cathkin's darlings registered three. Dumbarton practically ended the Rangers' hopes for a big recovery,

66

for in the match at Ibrox, John Taylor rattled on three goals within five minutes, a feat that has, perhaps, never been equalled against the Rangers, and one which, on that account, deserves to be boldly recorded. Taylor was afterwards a pillar of the Everton team, which he captained.

Assistance was sought, and A. Tait, a good left back from Royal Albert, was glad of an opportunity to win his spurs in " big " football. He later joined Preston North-End, and afterwards had a distinguished career with Tottenham Hotspur, whom he assisted to win the English Cup in 1901. From Glenbuck Athletic came Robert Blyth, a fine right wing raider, who also, subsequently, took a southward express to join Preston North-End, and who is now an official of the Portsmouth club. Others who wore the Ibrox colours during the season were John Law, a Paisley Road boy, who was a very capable centre forward ; Frank Watt, a wing forward from Kilbirnie, who afterwards joined Queen's Park ; William M'Bain, from St. Mirren, a fine type of lad whose tragic death, as the result of an accident, before the season ended, caused sorrow among all his club-mates ; Tom Dunbar (brother of Michael), who left the Celtic to play left back for the Rangers, but who, after half a season at Ibrox, returned to the Parkhead fold. John Barker, an outside left from Linthouse, who, in 1893-94, helped to take the Scottish Cup to Ibrox for the first time ; and John Drummond, from Falkirk, one of the most famous of all Rangers' backs, who, like Barker, was in the first Cup winning team two seasons later, and in many other notable triumphs as well. Drummond joined the club in March, 1892, and played for them on 2nd April against Everton, at Goodison Park, the same ground on which he was destined to make his first appearance for Scotland against England just three years later.

THE STORY OF THE RANGERS.

Before the full strength of the team had been developed, the slide in the League was too pronounced to be retrieved. In that season the Rangers finished fifth in the race, *the only occasion in all their career on which they have had to be satisfied with so lowly a position.* That indicates a marvellous record of consistency. In itself, it would entitle the club to a place of honour in Scottish football history, should anyone ever tackle the writing of it.

Though doing so badly in a comparative sense in the League during that season, the Rangers reached the semi-final of the Scottish Cup for the first time since 1884. After defeating St. Bernards in the first round, they had three games with Kilmarnock in the second round, the deciding match being played at Westmarch, Paisley, where the Rangers won by 3 goals to 2. Annbank were disposed of at Ibrox in the third round, but to the accompaniment of a storm of wind and rain, Rangers took the knock-out blow from Celtic in the semi-final at Parkhead. The gate drawings amounted to only £180, an excellent index to the kind of weather that prevailed. Celtic, with the breeze, scored four goals in the first half, yet Rangers were beaten by only a two goal margin, the score being 5–3. More than that, they had two goals disallowed, which the players stoutly claimed were good goals. I put that down merely as a matter of history. The result stands. In the Glasgow Cup the Rangers defeated Third Lanark in the first round, received a bye in the second, and fell by 3–0 to Queen's Park in the third. But in the Charity Cup-ties, the Rangers got equal with the Hampden club, for, after two drawn games, they beat them by 7–1 at Celtic Park. A. B. Mackenzie returned to guard the Rangers' goal, and Donald Gow, up from Sunderland, also played. Celtic were encountered in the final, and once more victory rested with them, the score being 2–0. That, undoubtedly, was Celtic's year so far as concerned their trials of strength with their Ibrox rivals.

I might retrace a little to mention that in the club's last League match, which was against the Clyde at Ibrox, " General " M'Laren played for the latter club. He was called the " ould Gineral " then, for, by that time, he had a great football career behind him. He was one of the grand Hibernian team of 1887, which took the Scottish Cup to Edinburgh for the first time by defeating Dumbarton in the final at Hampden Park. The Hibernian half-back line was M'Ghee, M'Ginn, and M'Laren. They were a famous trio. M'Laren, like other noted Hibernian players, helped to lay the foundation of Celtic's early success.

There are just one or two points more before closing this chapter. In the committee match with Third Lanark, which was still the occasion of rare old rivalry, the Rangers team embodied the entire history of the club up till then. It was A. B. Mackenzie ; Tom Vallance (*captain*) and James M'Intyre ; John Cameron, D. M'Pherson, and D. Mitchell ; W. Wilton, W. MacAndrew, Jas. Watson, D. MacKenzie, and J. C. Lawson. And the " trainer " was John S. Marr. Despite the disappointing results obtained in the League and in the Cup-ties, the membership had steadily increased to nearly 600, and the finances were as sound as the Bank of England. There was a happy little gathering when the joint championship badges won in the previous season were presented to the players, and John M'Pherson, " a man of mighty deeds and not of eloquence," made his first speech. " Gentlemen, we are joint champions but we will not be satisfied till we become the real champions." Rangers had to wait other seven seasons before being " the real champions," and John was there again to accept his badge.

It was in May, 1892, that what was called the Great

Osmond Meeting, which did so much to popularise cycle racing, was held at Ibrox Park. It was at Ibrox, also, that the first professional cyclists' sports were held, in August, 1894, when 14,000 spectators were roused to a high pitch of enthusiasm by the thrilling contests in which took part such world-renowned racers as Schofield, Harris, Edwards, Wheeler, Banker, Farman, Barden, Lumsden, Hewson, and Perheyen. They came from England, America, and the Continent.

1892—1893.

THE season 1892-93 was one of light and shadow. For the first time in their career Rangers won the Glasgow Cup. They also fought their way into the final of the Charity Cup. In the League competition they had the Championship plum virtually stolen from their lips by Celtic who, finishing strongly, secured the prize with 29 points against Rangers' 28. In the Scottish Cup competition the light was dominated by the shadow. After romping through Annbank at Ibrox Park, they went to Boghead for the second round tie. Rangers had never won a match of any kind there, and so the wiseacres looked gloomy and shook a doubtful head. It was a game that pulsated with excitement from start to finish. Wm. Hay had come up from London to partner John Drummond at back, and there is no doubt that the strong, determined defence of these two, coupled with magnificent goalkeeping by Haddow, shattered the power of the pounding Dumbarton forwards and paved the way for the victory which was sealed when M'Pherson scored the only goal of the match. Thus a little bit of history was made. The Boghead spell was broken after twenty years of desperate striving.

Then the shadows. The tie with St. Bernards at Edinburgh, in the third round, appeared to offer comparatively slight danger. Unfortunately, the players approached the contest with the mistaken belief that the opposition could be easily dealt with. They overlooked the fact that in their own forward line there was an element of uncertainty caused by the necessity of playing an inexperienced lad at centre. Duncan Clark, who had come out of the Swifts XI., was making his second appearance in the first team, and though a capable leader in ordinary games, the bigness of the occasion affected him in a way that minimised the cohesion of the attack in general. In addition, St. Bernards were of sterner mettle than Rangers had bargained for, and the end of it was that the Light Blues left the Capital beaten by 3 goals to 2.

The early exit from the Scottish ties was the more vexatious since, in their triumphal progress through the Glasgow Cup tourney, the team had displayed a standard of consistent cleverness which had not been excelled at any time in the history of the club. Proudly wearing the scalps of Northern, Linthouse, Queen's Park, and the old Glasgow Thistle at their belts, they went forward to meet Celtic in the final round, at Cathkin Park. Such a supremely correct display was given by Rangers against their greatest rivals that the names of the men who achieved a glorious 3–1 victory deserve to be set forth :—

Haddow ; Hay and Drummond ; Marshall, A. M'Creadie, and Mitchell (*captain*) ; Davie, H. M'Creadie, Kerr, M'Pherson, and Barker.

Thus another spell was broken. For the first time Celtic were compelled to bow the knee to a Rangers eleven, and the success was enhanced by the fact that the Glasgow Cup was won for the first time. Working in almost perfect harmony, the Rangers were three goals in the lead before their opponents could strike a retaliatory blow. It is interesting to recall that in this match Tom Dunbar made his first appearance for the Celtic since his association with Ibrox was severed.

Only a League conquest was needed to compensate fully for the Scottish Cup disappointment. A splendid

The late WILLIAM WILTON.

Honorary Match Secretary from 1889 to 1899. Manager and Secretary from 1899 to 1920.

See page 33.

DUGALD MACKENZIE.

Vice-President, 1890-91. President, 1891-92, 1892-93, 1893-94, 1894-95
and 1895-96.

See page 52.

endeavour was made to obtain it. Unique in the fact that they were undefeated in their first 15 matches, Rangers went to Boghead Park on 25th April with high hopes of repeating their memorable Scottish Cup-tie feat. But this time Dumbarton were on their toes, and Rangers, showing signs of long-sustained strain, fell a prey to the lusty, sweeping tactics of the opposing forwards. Though beaten, there was still a chance left to win the Championship. But that chance disappeared in the next game, which was against Celtic at Parkhead. Rangers were again defeated, and though they won their concluding match, they could amass only 28 points against 29 for Celtic.

Donald Gow had returned from Sunderland and played in four of the five Glasgow Cup-ties, missing the final owing to an injury.

The League match against Heart of Midlothian on 18th March, 1893, at Tynecastle, was notable for the first appearance in the Rangers team of Nicol Smith, perhaps the greatest right back who has played for the club during the last twenty years. Here began the great combination of Smith and Drummond who, without doubt, formed the most distinguished back division ever possessed by the Rangers. Nicol Smith, or " Nick," as he was affectionately called, belonged to Darvel, the small but not unimportant Ayrshire town. Robust in build, and speedy, he could tackle with great power, and his recovery was such that opposing forwards could never completely shake him off, though they might, by subtle passing, evade him for the moment. In front of goal his height served him well, for he was as sure with his head as with his feet. Big and strong as he was, no one could say that he ever put his physical attributes to a mean advantage. A vigorous shoulder charge he revelled in. He was brave, too, and

F

never did this quality reveal itself in such striking fashion as in his first match for Scotland against England at the Crystal Palace in 1897, when he was opposed by the famous Everton left-wing pair Milward and Chadwick. Nick played four times against England. He was one of that magnificent Scottish eleven which defeated the Saxon at Celtic Park, in 1900, by 4 goals to 1. This was the occasion when the Scots wore Lord Rosebery's racing colours, and his lordship watched the game from the pavilion balcony. Against Wales and Ireland, also, Nick did duty four times, while for the Scottish League he played against the English League on six occasions and thrice against the Irish League. It is not easy to say in which of these matches he played his finest game, but the late Dan Doyle, of Celtic fame, who was his partner in the Scottish League team of 1898 at Birmingham, would have it that Nick never excelled his display in that engagement. That was the match in which the Scottish League team included seven Rangers' players, the others being Matthew Dickie, Neil Gibson, James Miller, R. C. Hamilton, John M'Pherson, and Alec Smith. Nick was in his twelfth season with the Rangers when, in December, 1904, a fatal illness overtook him. He died on 6th January, 1905, in the full flush of manhood, mourned by all followers, not only of the club, but of the game. No more popular man ever wore the light blue of Ibrox. His last match was against Third Lanark, at Ibrox, on 19th November, 1904.

At the same Committee meeting at which Nicol Smith was made a member of the club, there were also enrolled James Steel, who had played for Linthouse ; Douglas Dick from Morton ; and Robert Reid, a Govan boy. Of these three, only Steel became a regular member of the first eleven, and he was one of those who helped to bring the Scottish Cup to Ibrox, for the first time, in 1894.

A momentous decision was made by the Scottish Football Association at the annual meeting in May, 1893. *The payment of players was sanctioned.* For several years previous the abuse of the amateur laws had been a public scandal. It was known far and wide that players had received money from practically every club that could afford to pay. Officialism was steeped in hypocrisy on that question. People at home laughed at the assumption of amateur purity ; Englishmen sneered at it. Many of those who were directing the affairs of Scottish clubs hailed the new order with relief. With professionalism, open and unashamed, came security of possession of players. In preceding years the practice of one club taking a player from another had been known by the progressive titles of drafting, grafting, and poaching, but the proper term in nearly all cases was unadulterated theft. Players had now to be registered. Clubs could begin the season safe in the knowledge that men engaged could not leave them unless by mutual agreement. Thus, stability was assured and the whole fabric of football placed on a basis of honesty and candour.

The terms offered to, and accepted by, the Rangers players in the first season of professionalism were £2 per week when playing in the first eleven and £1 per week when standing as reserve or playing in the second eleven. Under these terms the team, as we shall see, went forth to win the Scottish Cup for the first time since the Rangers were formed on that sunny summer evening of 1873.

1893—1894.

**The Cup at Last—After Twenty Years—A
Glorious Final—Celtic Conquered—Rejoicings—
Alec Smith—Record Service—His Many Honours.**

THIS season of 1893-94 will ever be a red-letter one
in the annals of the Rangers. Fifteen years
previously they had fought the final of the
Scottish Cup with Vale of Leven. They claimed, indeed,
that they actually won the Cup then, and, as we have
seen, their faith in the justice of their claim was the motive
which impelled them to decline to replay a game which,
officially, was declared drawn. During the long intervening years they had doggedly struggled to reach the
final. Never once had they succeeded. But now their
time was come. There were some who had been associated
with the club almost from its birth. Who could grudge
them their thrill of pleasure when, on the Second of
February, 1894, the team came off the sward of Hampden
Park victors over their greatest rivals, the Celtic, and
winners of the trophy which, for twenty years, had been
the beacon of their hopes ? When the season opened, the
club had seventeen players registered as professionals.
These included D. Haddow, N. Smith, J. Drummond,
Donald Gow, Robert Marshall, A. M'Creadie, R. Scott,
N. Kerr, J. M'Pherson, Robert Blyth, H. M'Creadie, John
Gray (from Albion Rovers), James Steel, and David Boyd
(who was a Troon boy and a junior International forward) ;
he had, moreover, gained some eminence with Abercorn.
The signing of Boyd led to a sharp dispute with the Bury
club, who claimed that he was their player. Some indiscreet
words were used towards the Rangers by certain officials

of the English club, but when the latter realised that they had erred, they lost no time in making honourable amends. Mr. H. S. Hamer, the secretary, wrote a letter of full apology. It was left to the player to decide whether he would play for the Rangers or for Bury, and he chose Ibrox. He had, in fact, signed a professional form for Bury, who had paid him sums of money, and in respect of these circumstances, they, unquestionably, had a real grievance. But there was some looseness at that time in the practice of signing, and possibly Boyd did not realise the gravity of his action. Blyth was a wanderer returned. Since he departed from Ibrox, he had played for Cowlairs and Middlesbrough, and now he did not remain long a Ranger but went south again to play for Preston North-End. Donald Gow stayed only until October, and then asked to be released. He returned to Sunderland where, it was said, his heart lay. Donald was ever a dreamer, with the mystic strain of the far Highlands in his blood; the elusive gleam could lure him into new haunts.

Now, it is a curious feature of this season that while the Scottish Cup and the Glasgow Cup were won with a goal record of 22-3 in the one case and 13-1 in the other, the achievements in the League were, on the whole, commonplace. The Hearts twice beat the Rangers for points; the Celtic, Third Lanark, Dumbarton, and St. Bernards each accomplished the feat once. Fourth position on the championship table was the best the Rangers could secure. Yet, in the League, they obtained the most decisive victory of their career over the Celtic, whom they defeated at Ibrox Park by 5 goals to 0. *This stands as the record win for either club over the other in their sixty-six League engagements.* The players who effected this historic feat were the same who, later, triumphed over Parkhead's

77

forces in the Cup Final. Twelve thousand people watched the Rangers forwards in that memorable League match play a game which, for sustained brilliance of combination and overpowering finish, had seldom been witnessed. The £360 taken at the gates was a record for Ibrox Park. The first goal was scrimmaged through ; Barker got the second, Gray headed the third, and Rangers led by 3–0 at the interval. M'Pherson, working his way through the Celtic half-backs practically at will, brought the score to four, and Barker capped the day's sensation with a fifth goal. Such was the enthusiasm aroused among the club's supporters that seven brake loads went to Renton for the succeeding match. The first League reverse was sustained at Tynecastle in the eighth match played. But Marshall was lame practically throughout the game, and Barker had to be carried off injured. From that point, hopes of winning the League were, if not abandoned, at least not seriously entertained. Cups, and nothing but cups, was the slogan.

Deeming discretion the better part of valour, Whitefield scratched in the first round of the Glasgow Cup. Rangers had a bye in the second round and found braver opponents in the third. Pollokshaws came to the scratch and refused to run away while eleven goals were being piled up against them at Ibrox. In the semi-final, Celtic were received, also at Ibrox, and took their exit from the ties with a 1–0 defeat. The final was played against Cowlairs at Cathkin Park, and by a goal to nothing Rangers won the Glasgow Cup for the second season in succession. Now the full power of concentration of the club was devoted to landing the greatest prize of all. Would the Scottish Cup become a Rangers possession at long last ? Players and officials bent themselves to the task before them. Never was greater enthusiasm shown. It was the old Kinning Park

days over again. "Can you do it, boys?" was the
question asked by anxious officials. And the "boys"
replied, "We can try." Not a very heroic declaration,
but the significance was in the steady glance and the firm-
set jaw. They were men with the pride of club in their
veins.

Intense was the interest in the result of the draw for the
first round. It was Rangers v. Cowlairs, at Ibrox. That
proved easy going. Old Cowlairs, with a wonderful
record of adventure behind them, were fallen on evil
days. Most of their former mighty men were wearing
the colours of rival clubs or they had grown old or had
voluntarily quitted the game. Rangers took eight goals
from them and then ceased the slaughter. In the second
round, Leith Athletic, then members of the First Division
of the League, and who had taken a point off the Rangers
at Leith, proved to be of sterner metal. They finished
an exciting contest at Ibrox only two goals to the bad.
But the narrowness of the victory put Rangers on their
guard for the third round tie with Clyde, at Barrowfield
Park. The match was played under conditions very
similar to those which prevailed at Shawfield in 1923
when the teams met in the first round. The similarity
did not end there. Smith and Drummond both went
lame just as M'Candless did on 13th January last, and the
score was 5 goals to 0, or only one more than the total
compiled by the Rangers at Shawfield. Strange how
history repeats itself! Steel had three of the goals to
himself, but the finest of the five was John M'Pherson's.
So far so good, but the real test was to come. The semi-
final draw brought Queen's Park to Ibrox, and Queen's
Park were the Cup-holders, they having defeated Celtic
in the final of the previous season. Let me give you the
team which played the Rangers to a draw that day, for

they were names that were famous then ; some of them are famous yet :—

> A. Baird ; D. Sillars and A. Freeland ; J. Gillespie, T. Robertson, and D. Stewart ; W. Gulliland, T. Waddell, J. Hamilton, D. Berry, and J. A. Lambie.

This was not Queen's Park's strongest team, for W. Sellar and W. Lambie were unable to play. Waddell scored after 35 minutes, but a minute after the restart, Boyd headed the equaliser. Rangers had a claim for a second goal, scored by Barker, disallowed, and so the teams had to get to grips again on the following Saturday at Hampden Park. During the week, Boyd, while working as a ship carpenter on a vessel, fell from a plank into the hold 20 feet below, and he was thus unable to take part either in the replay or in the Final against Celtic. Hugh M'Creadie came in as partner to Steel on the right wing, and right worthily did he qualify for a cup-winners' badge. Queen's Park made several changes, W. Lambie being played at centre and W. Sellar at outside left, while with Robertson and Gillespie injured, R. M'Farlane and a young player named Lang, who had gone over from the Rangers Swifts, were placed in the half-back line. A heavy wind was blowing in favour of the Rangers in the first half, and, as luck would have it, Nicol Smith got home a great, long punt from mid-field, 25 minutes after the start. This was quite all right, but when Haddow helped a ball into his own net from a corner kick by Gulliland, the Rangers' stock went down with a thump. For ten minutes of the second half the outlook was as dark as a starless night. Then suddenly the Rangers forwards sprang into their stride, and with all-along-the-line passing of brilliant precision, they broke the defence of the lion-hearted Sillars and his partner. M'Pherson shot a second goal from his favourite range, 20 yards out, and a third was "stormed" some minutes later. Stamina and skill won the day, and the Rangers were in the Final. Meanwhile, Celtic had already carved their way there, and here were the records of the rivals when they lined up at Hampden Park on Saturday, 17th February, 1894 :—

Rangers.				Celtic.		
Cowlairs,	-	-	8–0	Hurlford,	- -	6–0
Leith Athletic,	-		2–0	Albion Rovers,	-	7–0
Clyde,	-	-	5–0	St. Bernards,	-	8–1
Queen's Park,		-	1–1	Third Lanark,	-	5–3
Queen's Park,		-	3–1			
			19–2			26–4

The teams as they stood to attention on a pitch soaked by continuous rain were :—

Rangers.—Haddow ; Smith and Drummond ; Marshall, A. M'Creadie, and Mitchell (*captain*) ; Steel, H. M'Creadie, Gray, M'Pherson, and Barker.

Celtic.—Cullen ; Reynolds and Doyle ; Curran, Kelly, and Maley ; Blessington, Madden, Cassidy, Campbell, and M'Mahon (*captain*).

Referee—John Marshall (Third Lanark).

Five of these Celtic stalwarts had played against England—Doyle, Kelly, Maley, Campbell, and M'Mahon. It was a team worthy of the highest respect. They were the favourites. But the speed and stamina of the Rangers players rose superior to all pre-conceived notions of how the game should go. It was said that the pace was the severest ever seen in a Scottish match. The confessed plan of the Celts was to rush their opponents at the start, and they succeeded to an extraordinary degree. But the defence was just as extraordinary. Drummond and Mitchell seemed like men inspired. The Celtic right wing in vain strove to wear them down. Nicol Smith, young then, but strong as a lion cub, and fearless of reputations, electrified the crowd by his duels with the renowned " Sandy " M'Mahon. Andrew M'Creadie, cool, watchful, and tenacious, fell back or swung forward to force the game as the ever-changing conflict dictated. The rival forwards, with concentrated dash, threw themselves upon the defence to be broken like the waves on a rocky shore. When the interval arrived with neither side able to show a single emblem of mastery, the spectators plunged into a discussion of second-half prospects. The team that could stand the pace would win. Such was the con-sensus of opinion, and events proved it right. For fifteen minutes of the second half the furious struggle continued, neither side yielding an inch. But then came the turning point. A free kick was awarded Rangers. Mitchell placed the ball beautifully in front of goal, Hugh M'Creadie pounced upon it, and his shot went spinning into the net out of Cullen's reach. Rangers never looked back. Within a quarter of an hour of their initial success they were three goals in the lead. With the ball at his feet, Barker went careering for Cullen's bastion, skipping over all the opposing legs which aimed at dispossessing him. Reynolds was charged out of the way and a vicious shot from close range shook the back of the net. Nothing now could stay the whirlwind onslaughts of those machine-like Ibrox forwards. The Celtic defence wavered, fought back manfully, and then had to surrender to a slip shot by M'Pherson. That was not the end, however. M'Mahon, plucky as ever, forced a free kick off Nicol Smith and Maley scored. A goal, at anyrate, was allowed, but the Rangers defence would never agree that the ball was over the line when Haddow held it.

From all over the United Kingdom and from Ireland came telegrams of congratulation upon the club's first

Scottish Cup triumph. Over the counter of a Birmingham telegraph office was handed a message bearing the words— " Good old Rangers. Congratulations from Sunderland F.C.—Donald." What would Donald Gow not have given to have been one of the. " good old Rangers " who won the victory that day ! " Tuck " M'Intyre addressed the winners at the finish thus : " Well, boys, you have got the Cup and I have got the hiccup." Mr. J. B. Sliman, President of the Scottish F.A., spoke of the pleasure it afforded him in handing over the Cup to such a club as the Rangers, a club which for twenty years had nobly struggled in pursuit of what had been attained that day. In accepting the trophy, Mr. Dugald Mackenzie, the club president, said that he could ill conceal the pleasure he felt in receiving the Cup. No former president of his club had had similar good fortune. Many years had elapsed since he had hopes of seeing the " Light Blues " Scottish champions. Although during all that time they had been as sleuth-hounds after their prey, time and again it had doubled and evaded them until that day, when they had safely secured it. The presentation took place at a jolly social function in the Alexandra Hotel. Celtic's officials and players were strongly represented and paid many warm-hearted compliments to their victors. And the Rangers had an opportunity of paying compliments in return on the following Saturday, for the teams met at Parkhead in the League, and Celtic won by 3 goals to 2. The pitch was in a dreadful condition, and Celtic wanted the match postponed, but Rangers, being in arrears with their fixtures, preferred to play. Celtic had M'Ilheny and Divers in place of Maley and Campbell, and the Rangers had the assistance of Johnstone, a Kilmarnock boy, to substitute Mitchell, who had been injured in the final. Haddow was hurt in the course of the game, and this probably was responsible for the loss of two of the goals. But on the season's exchanges, as the following results show, the Rangers had a clear advantage over their greatest of all rivals :—

Friendly,	at Parkhead,	Rangers 3 Celtic 2
League,	at Ibrox,	Rangers 5 Celtic 0
Glasgow Cup,	at Ibrox,	Rangers 1 Celtic 0
Scottish Cup,	at Hampden,	Rangers 3 Celtic 1
League,	at Parkhead,	Rangers 2 Celtic 3
Friendly,	at Parkhead,	Rangers 1 Celtic 1
		15 7

It only remains to be said that for winning the Cup the players were each given a bonus of three guineas, and that John Taylor, the trainer, and George Cameron, the groundsman, were not forgotten. Nicol Smith and Robert Marshall each received a marriage present. At the annual meeting, Mr. John S. Marr gave some striking comparisons to show the progress of the club. In 1889 the income was £1,240 ; in 1894, it was £5,227—a quadruple increase in five years. How puny these figures appear alongside present-day compilations !

The closing days of season 1893-94 were marked by two incidents deeply affecting the club in opposite ways. On Saturday, 12th May, 1894, there was laid to rest one of the staunchest clubmen who ever donned light blue. William Pringle, whose name has frequently occurred in these memoirs, could trace his connection with the Rangers to the year 1878 when he played his first important match against the Clapham Rovers, at London, as a substitute for James Campbell, one of the old originals. Pringle was a most valued member of the team during a lengthened period. Quiet and unassuming, he was genuine to the core ; there was no humbug about him. His popularity with the club can be gauged from the fact that upon his retirement from active service he was made a life member, which was a rare honour.

The other incident was the first game played by Alec Smith for the Rangers, on Monday, 30th April, 1894. Notts County, who were holders of the English Cup, were the visitors to Ibrox Park, and the match became a sort of International test, a championship of the world affair, as some people loved to call these bouts between cup-holders of the respective countries. From the Notts County cup team only J. Hendry was an absentee. Mitchell, Andrew M'Creadie, and Barker stood down from the Rangers' side, the position usually occupied by Barker being allotted to Smith, the recruit. Rangers won by 3-1, their goals being scored by Hugh M'Creadie, M'Pherson, and Boyd, while Logan got Notts County's goal. Great men in the English team of that time were Toone in goal, Watson and Dunnley, the right wing ; and Shelton at half-back. Before Alec Smith signed for the Rangers, he was invited to join Kilmarnock, whose terms were 12/6 for a win, 10/ for a draw, and 7/6 for a defeat. No bargain was struck, although he played for Kilmarnock in one match against Sunderland, at Roker Park, which constitutes his debut as a senior. Mr. Charles Smith, for years the guide, philosopher, and friend, was at outside right in this match. Sunderland, a day or two later, offered a more handsome inducement—£2 a week, which was advanced to £2 10/. But James Miller, who was then a Sunderland player, had counselled his young county cousin to hold out for the terms which the regular Sunderland team received. They were paid £3 a week and the captain 5/ extra. The brothers Henderson, who were Sunderland's emissaries, would not " come " the additional 10/ and the negotiations ended. Alec was busy working in a Darvel lace mill a day or two later when Nicol Smith walked in and said, "Alec, you are wanted at Ibrox to play a trial for the Rangers against the Notts County." That is how Nicol and Alec became senior clubmates just as they had chummed it together in the Darvel junior team which Alec assisted to win the Ayrshire Junior Cup shortly before joining the Rangers. Thus, also, began a period of service which was to establish a record for a Rangers player. *Alec Smith was in active service for his only senior club during twenty-one seasons.*

A probationary period in the second eleven was followed by his installation at inside right as partner to John Cowan, but when John Barker departed, he became the recognised outside left, and as such shared in the club's greatest triumphs. Standing 5 ft. 7¾ ins., and weighing round about 11 st. 4 lbs., this Darvel boy had imbibed the strengthening breezes that come over the Loudon Hill. He was a composition of bone and muscle and could run for a week, as the saying goes. In that glorious season of 1896-97, he took a prominent part in the winning of the three cups. In the four successive seasons, from 1898 to 1902, in which the Rangers captured the championship of the League, he played in sixty-nine of the seventy-four matches, surely a standard of consistency which any player might envy. Season 1898-99 was the one in which the Rangers won every League match, and Smith did not miss a game. His opinion of the 1896-97 team was expressed in these words : " The Rangers team showed the most brilliant football of any I have ever known. The 1898-99 team was a marvellously good side, but for purity of football, easy, confident, swinging combination, I think our three-cup team was the better." His representative honours numbered thirty-four, another record for a Rangers player. He played seven times against England, seven times against

Ireland, six times against Wales, ten times against the English League, three times against the Irish League, and once against the Southern League. He was in the Scottish team of 1900 that beat England by 4 goals to 1, and he regarded that eleven as the most brilliant International side of which he was ever a member. Other Rangers men who played on that memorable day at Celtic Park were Nick Smith, John Drummond, Neil Gibson, and "Jacky" Robertson. Harry Rennie was in goal, Alec Raisbeck at centre-half, Jack Bell and Bobby Walker on the right wing, R. S. M'Coll at centre, and John Campbell, the once famous Celt, at inside left. Smith would very probably have been capped against England in 1899, at Birmingham, but he was just then recovering from a broken collar bone. As a player, he was of the absolutely dependable order. A storehouse of energy, he could not get enough of the ball. He had a little trick of slapping his hands together as a signal to his partner to send him the pass. Another characteristic was his habit of tucking his jersey inside of his knickers, and when he was impatient he would run his thumbs round the inside rim of his breeks. He could send across a low centre at terrific speed and with a swerve which made it difficult for a goalkeeper to judge the flight of the ball. A true Ranger in every sense of the word, his popularity with all classes was demonstrated by the presentation to him of a public testimonial and, also, when he took his last benefit on 6th January, 1913. In the team of International players which met the Rangers before a great crowd at Ibrox Park, there was present the "Welsh wizard," William Meredith, who played for Wales in fifty-one International matches. When he and the Darvel Ranger shook hands on the field, a mighty cheer arose, homage at once to two men who had played the game as men should. Sportsmanship knows no distinction of nationality. Alec Smith played his first representative match against the Irish League in 1897. Sixteen years later, which is more than the average of a man's playing career, he assisted the Scottish League to a brilliant victory over the English League.

CANADIANS AT IBROX PARK, 8th SEPTEMBER, 1888.

RANGERS, 1, CANADIANS, 1.

See page 48.

FIRST TEAM TO WIN THE SCOTTISH CUP, 1893-1894.

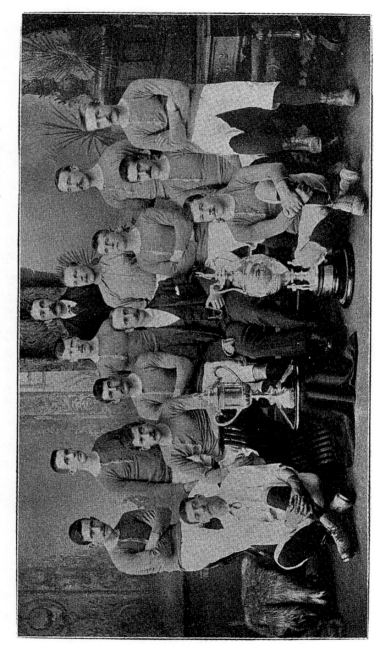

J. Taylor (*Trainer*).

Back Row:—H. M'Creadie, J. Steel, N. Smith, D. Haddow, D. Mitchell.

Sitting—A. M'Creadie, D. Boyd, W. Wilton (*Secretary*), J. Drummond, J. MacPherson, J. Barker.

Front Row:—R. Marshall, J. Gray.

Scottish Cup.   Glasgow Cup.

See page 70.

1894—1896.

Neil Gibson—Famine of Honours—Cups Lost— Famous Inchview Tie—Goalkeepers Galore—David Haddow's Departure—Good Team Spoiled.

IT is a curious thing that, between the club's maiden Scottish Cup triumph of 1893-94 and the famous sequence of conquests from 1896 to 1902, there should intervene a period so barren of honours as were the two seasons of **1894-95** and '**95-'96**. The circumstance is the more remarkable from the fact that during these latter years there became associated with Ibrox one or two of the most noted players who ever enlisted in the club's service. One of these was Neil Gibson, who made his debut against Dumbarton at Boghead Park on 1st December, 1894. He came from Larkhall, which has produced several distinguished exponents of the game, but none who surpassed him or gained greater distinction, although it might be right to place on a similar pedestal his famous fellow-townsman, Alec Raisbeck. Neil Gibson's progress was almost a romance. In his first season with Rangers, and when he had been with them a matter of only three and a half months, he was chosen to play for Scotland against England at Goodison Park. That was the last match in which Scotland was represented by a team composed wholly of players from Scottish clubs. A severe drubbing shattered the long-sustained opposition to the playing of Anglo-Scots, and ever since the selectors have been impartial in their radius of choice.

For six successive seasons Gibson retained his place in the Scottish team against England, and for eight consecutive years he played against the English League. He was with the Rangers during the most successful period of their career—when they won the three cups in 1896-97, and when they secured the League Championship four years in succession—1899-1902 inclusive. Gibson was a slim, fair-haired boy when he joined the Rangers, and he developed more on the lines of a clipper craft than a warship. He had a jaunty, elastic style of moving over the ground, was never flurried, and could turn a ball in almost any position. His specialty was a little juggling trick which he used most effectively as a defensive measure. If the ball was too high to be reached with the head, he would allow it to fall behind him, and before it touched the ground, he would bring it back over his head with the back of his boot. So sure was he in the execution of this stratagem that he frequently brought it' off in front of his own goal. At first it seemed a reckless thing to attempt, and it gave the club's followers the shivers ; but scarcely ever did he fail in his intention. Just as Alec Smith signed a League form for Bolton Wanderers and never played for them, so Neil Gibson signed for Everton and never played for them either. The only thing binding about such a signature was that the player could play for no other English League club in the event of his deciding to cross the Border.

Another fine player who joined the club in December, 1894, was David Crawford, a stylish back from St. Mirren, who played many splendid games during the several seasons he was at Ibrox. He returned to St. Mirren in 1903-4, and after his playing days were over, he co-operated in the formation of the Clydebank, of which he became a director. In exchange for Andrew M'Creadie, Sunderland gave the Rangers Wm. Gibson, but after a season or so, the two of them changed over again. John Pray, of Falkirk, was also secured as a half-back, but after a little while he went to Bury. So also did Archie

Montgomery, who during this season was reserve to Haddow, and proved himself a very capable custodian. Montgomery returned to Scotland after a successful career with Bury and became manager of Albion Rovers, a position he occupied at the time of his death in 1921. He was succeeded by Wm. Reid, another ex-Rangers player.

Harry Gardiner, a half-back who had been with Bolton Wanderers, was also signed. John Cowan, an outside right, and brother of the more famous James of Aston Villa, came from Preston North-End. The season was opened with a flourish. Four League matches were won off the reel, but then things began to go wrong. The individual talent was there all right but not the necessary power in combination. Rangers' first meeting with the Celtic that season at Parkhead brought about their first defeat, and the score, 5-3, was sufficient to show that there was a vital defect somewhere. Five more defeats were sustained in the League, the championship of which was won by the Hearts, who had a magnificent team ; they finished five points in front of Celtic who, in turn, were four points better than Rangers. As Scottish Cup-holders, the Rangers were regarded as fortunate to be drawn at home in the first round against the Hearts, but they never looked like saving the tie. Hogg and Chambers were the Hearts' scorers and Cowan got the Rangers' goal. This stands as the Hearts' only Scottish Cup victory over their Ibrox rivals, as the record of their meetings in the Cup reveal :—

1894-95,	First Round,	at Ibrox,	Rangers 1	Hearts 2
1898-99,	First Round,	at Ibrox,	Rangers 4	Hearts 1
1902-03,	Final,	at Parkhead,	Rangers 2	Hearts 0
1903-04,	First Round,	at Ibrox,	Rangers 3	Hearts 2
1921-22,	Third Round,	at Tynecastle,	Rangers 4	Hearts 0
			14	5

THE STORY OF THE RANGERS.

The Glasgow Cup, which had been held for two seasons, had likewise to be surrendered, although not until the team had gone through to the final again. Queen's Park and Third Lanark were disposed of in the first two rounds, and then the Rangers went down to Inchview to meet Partick Thistle in the semi-final. Up till then the two clubs had met seventeen times in all kinds of matches, and Thistle could claim eight victories against the Rangers' six ; there had been two draws. It was said that the Rangers "could not play the Thistle." In this game at Inchview, the Thistle set the whole town talking by winning by 1–0. Smith, in goal, was the hero of the hour. He had great big hands and he used them to the best advantage. The Thistle scored after 25 minutes, and hung on to their lead despite terrific assaults by the Rangers forwards, led by James Hamilton, of Queen's Park, who was playing as an amateur. The Thistle centre was Wm. Paul. The left wing was Wilkie and Campbell, who subsequently became Rangers players after a term with Blackburn Rovers. But the Thistle were not to contest the Final, after all. Rangers discovered that Smith, the big-handed Thistle goalkeeper, had committed an infringement by playing in a five-a-side tournament for Duntocher Harp in the preceding August, after having signed for the Thistle. They lodged a protest, got a replay, and won by 5 goals to 3. Then came the final with Celtic, at Cathkin Park. The winning of the toss was an important factor. " Sandy " M'Mahon guessed the coin for Celtic, who took a stiff breeze behind them and scored twice through Divers in the first half. It was not one of the Rangers' happy days. The first goal, which was hotly disputed, unsettled them. Neither Nick Smith nor Drummond was confident. Still, it was only marvellous goalkeeping by Dan M'Arthur that enabled Celtic to retain their lead. In after years, M'Arthur played some wonderful games for his club, but possibly never a better one than this. By the turn of the year Neil Gibson had become a regular member of the first team and Alec Smith was the recognised outside left. David Crawford's merits were also more fully recognised, and he was more frequently in the team, for not yet had Nicol Smith's powers fully ripened. While the First Eleven was unable to supply any silver plate for President Mackenzie's sideboard, the Swifts Eleven afforded the members some consolation by winning the Kirkwood Shield and the Glasgow Reserve Cup.

But for the loss of David Haddow, who went to Motherwell, and later to Burnley, where he was known as '' The little Scotch marvel,'' the following season of 1895–96 would probably have been one of real progress. Gray and John Cowan also left, the former to play for Clyde and the latter to join his brother James in the ranks of Aston Villa. David Mitchell was offered terms which he declined, but before the season was very old, the Committee was petitioned by a section of the membership to re-engage him and the veteran came into harness again. Among the new players were James Oswald, a centre forward, who came from Third Lanark. He had played against England in 1889 and 1895. Rangers could have had him as a junior, but here he was at last still with some good football in him. The first goalkeeper tried was Murdoch, a recruit from Kilmarnock Athletic, but he soon gave place to Wilson, a bandsman in the H.L.I. stationed at Maryhill Barracks. Next came J. M'Leod, of Dumbarton, who had played against England in 1892, but he too failed to solve a problem which was the despair of committee and followers alike. Then arrived John Bell from Slamannan, but he stayed only until the Scottish Cup-tie with Hibernian was played and lost. Holding himself responsible for the Rangers' defeat, he dressed himself without uttering a word, walked out of Ibrox and was never seen there again. Even pay day did not lure him to the ground. He was a big-hearted chap but terribly sensitive. Next on the swelling list of custodians tried and found not up to standard was M'Allan, of Parkhead Juniors, but he, in turn, was displaced by M'Leod, again restored to favour. James Yuille, who had played some good games for the Swifts eleven, stood guard between the posts on occasion. The goalkeeper difficulty was like an Old Man of the Sea hanging round the necks of the officials. It was solved at last, but not until the season was practically at an end, and the evil had been done. Rangers finished second in the League to Celtic, were beaten by Queen's Park in the first round of the Glasgow Cup, and lost to Hibernian, at Ibrox, in the third round of the Scottish Cup. That the blame for this latter reverse did not all belong to goalkeeper Bell is evident from the fact that the Rangers failed to convert two penalty kicks. This was the first time Rangers and Hibernian had met in the Scottish Cup. They have crossed paths four times since then, and the record of their combats is :—

1895-96,	Third Round,	at Ibrox,	Rangers 2	Hibernian 3
1896-97,	Second Round,	at Ibrox,	Rangers 3	Hibernian 0
1901-02,	Semi-Final,	at Ibrox,	Rangers 0	Hibernian 2
1903-04,	Second Round,	at Edinburgh,	Rangers 2	Hibernian 1
1913-14,	Third Round,	at Edinburgh,	Rangers 1	Hibernian 2
			8	8

" Soldier " (Tom) Miller, from Hamilton Barracks, was a more than useful forward during that season. The half-back line gave a good deal of trouble until David Mitchell was reinstated. A young player named Russell, from Aston Villa, was tried at left half, but was not a success. The season ended on a sombre note. True, the championship of the Glasgow League, instituted to maintain interest during the closing weeks, was won, but this competition never set the grass on fire, and it died an early and unlamented death. Better times were coming, however. A brilliant Rangers epoch lay immediately ahead.

1896—1897.

Greatest Rangers—Three Cups Won—A Wonderful Boy—Pulverising Attack—A Dundee Thriller—Record Following—Nineteen Caps.

WAS the 1896-97 team the finest that ever championed the cause of Rangers? On what basis can this question be decided? That the players who wore the colours during that season played football as brilliant as any ever witnessed on this side of the Border will be readily admitted by those privileged to watch them in most of their matches. They won the three Cups, a feat never before or since equalled by a Rangers team. It is true they finished only third in the League, but it is equally true that the vital points were lost early in the season before there was time to develop that wonderful harmony of inter-action which swept everything before it in the cup-ties. Naturally, there is forced upon us a comparison between the Three-Cup team and the side that won all the League engagements of 1898-99. Alec Smith, who was a member of both, has told us that the Three-Cup team was the better in the sense that it was capable of touching a higher level of brilliance in combination. I think he is right. I saw the 1896-97 team in nearly all their important matches, and, with a sincere desire to be strictly impartial, I would unhesitatingly say that no Scottish team was ever more capable of expressing the science and intricacies of the football game. The most difficult things were made to appear simple. Each man had his place and kept it, and all worked together like a piece of well-oiled mechanism.

Matthew Dickie had been secured from Renton in April,

1895, and he came to Ibrox to solve at once the goalkeeper problem which had cost the Rangers some bitter experiences. N. Smith, Drummond, and D. Crawford were retained as backs, supplemented by Alec Miller, from Dumbarton. Gibson, M'Creadie, and Mitchell were the half-backs. The great accession of strength was in the forward line, for here were installed R. Crawford, who had been a shining light in the Clyde ranks ; James Miller from Sunderland ; ex-Guardsman Tom Hyslop, from Stoke ; and Peter Turnbull from Blackburn Rovers. John M'Pherson, James Oswald, and Alec Smith were the others at command. Before the season was very old, however, something occurred which was to have an important influence upon the club's fortunes. On the Glasgow Autumn Holiday the Rangers met Blackburn Rovers in a friendly game at Ibrox. On the Rovers' right wing was Thomas (Tommy) Low, who had been taken from the junior Parkhead club on trial. He was opposed to John Drummond, and it is safe to say that John had never had to do a more lively bit of man-hunting. Tommy's dodgy runs and accurate centres were largely responsible for a substantial Rovers' victory. When the match was over, William Wilton said, " We must sign that boy," and sign him he did. As Low was, in fact, only a boy, it was agreed that the partner best suited to him would be M'Pherson. They were played together in a League match at Ibrox Park in October, and they were such a successful right wing that for the remainder of the season they never were separated except when circumstances compelled a change. This boy Low had an extraordinary record ; it was, indeed, almost romantic and perhaps unique. Coming into the team when about three months of the season had gone, he gained Scottish, Glasgow, and Charity Cup medals, was capped against Ireland, and assisted the Scottish League at Ibrox to achieve the first victory over the

English League on which glorious occasion he scored one of the goals, and M'Pherson, his partner, the other two.

Lightly built and clean cut, Low would have had precious little chance in a rough-and-tumble duel. His manner on the ball was rather jaunty, even ladylike. How did he avoid physical disaster ? Well, he got John M'Pherson as a partner to help him to avoid it. That was in the plan. John, whenever possible, drew away not only the half-back but the back as well, and then threw out the pass for the swift-footed boy winger to race for goal. But Low could not hope to be always convenienced in this fashion. He had to go through the mill often. He soon learned to take care of himself and he had no more effective defensive measure than an instinctive sense of knowing when an opponent was going to charge him. On such occasion, if he was going full speed with the ball, he would tip it ahead and slightly curve away from his enemy without slackening his pace, so that the man of evil intent generally charged the air and didn't like it. In successive seasons, Low obtained Junior and Senior International honours.

With the coming of " The Boy," as he was called for a long time, the recognised line of attack became Low, M'Pherson, Miller, Hyslop and Smith. Some of the football these five played entranced the spectators. They could begin at the centre of the field, and by the mesmerism of their combination, lay the ball in the net without having permitted an opponent to touch it. Think of some of the scores amassed during that season ! Against the Hearts, 5–0 ; against Third Lanark, 5–1 and 6–1 ; against St. Mirren, 5–1 ; against Abercorn, 9–2 and 6–1 ; against Clyde, 7–2 ; against Celtic, 4–1 and 3–0. In the three Cup finals the total scoring was 13–3 in the Rangers' favour. The season's aggregate for the team was 166 goals.

Into the Final of the Glasgow Cup the team went prancing. Third Lanark, at Ibrox, in the first round, failed to stand up to a bewildering burst of forward play and were defeated by 5-1, which was not so staggering as the 6-1 reverse inflicted upon them by the Rangers a week or two later in the League. A bye in the second round and a 3-0 victory over Linthouse in the semi-final brought the Light Blues once more into the arena of Hampden with their old friendly enemies, the Celtic. Twice before had they met in the Final—in 1892-3, when Rangers won, 3-1, and in 1894-95, when Celtic were victors by 2-0. Now it took two games to decide the issue, and in the end the Rangers had the Cup. In the first game the teams were splendidly matched. Each disputed the goal scored by the other. Low tapped the ball into the net before Dan M'Arthur could recover, after having been charged down, and M'Mahon headed the equaliser from a position which many considered was off-side. But it had been a thrilling, throbbing contest between two clever, determined teams and a draw was its value. The teams which played in the first game were :—

> Rangers.—Dickie; N. Smith and Drummond; Gibson, M'Creadie and Mitchell; Low, M'Pherson, Turnbull, Hyslop and A. Smith.

> Celtic.—M'Arthur; Mechan and Doyle; Russell, Kelly and Battles; Blessington, Madden, King, M'Mahon and Divers.

Before the day of the replay arrived, Nicol Smith's brother died and he asked to be allowed to stand down. This was a bad blow, for David Crawford was injured and could not take Smith's place. It was decided, on the advice of Donald Gow, to put Hyslop at right back on the understanding that if he was not comfortable there, M'Pherson would change places with him, John having previously partnered David Crawford, with some success, against the Hearts, at Tynecastle. The re-arrangement meant the bringing in of Jas. Miller, who was only recovering from an illness, and so the Rangers' prospects were not at all encouraging. The entire team, however, played with great courage and gained a very fine victory. Skill triumphed for, unquestionably, Celtic were physically the stronger side. Hyslop stood the test at back, and the half-backs gave the nimble forwards superb support. To the Rangers this success was specially welcome by reason of the fact that it was their first against the Celtic since February, 1894. Before the season ended, they could claim two more victories over their Parkhead rivals, for in the League match, at Ibrox, the Rangers won by 2–0, and in the Charity Cup they romped home by 4 goals to 1. Groves assisted the Celtic in this League game, but he broke down and had to retire. As the League match at Parkhead, earlier in the season, was drawn, the Light Blues could reasonably plume themselves on the results of their encounters with the " old enemy " during 1896-97. They met seven times, and the Rangers had four wins and three draws.

Before the Scottish Cup-ties began, the League championship was beyond the reach of the Rangers. They had scored 61 goals in seventeen matches, which was an easy best in the competition, but repeated changes in the defence, caused by injuries, had contributed to the loss of four games. So it was agreed to concentrate upon winning the Scottish Cup, and never did enthusiasm and grit carry a team to a more auspicious triumph. The New Year was opened with a third successive victory over the Celtic in a Glasgow League match, at Ibrox, where the " gate " was only a few pounds short of the record for a Scottish League match up to that date. The pulse of the club's supporters was quickened. On every lip was the question, " Would the Cup be won for the second time ? " The team, with all the men now tuned up to concert pitch, and imbued with a burning desire to emulate the Cup victors of 1894, prepared themselves with the zeal of Spartans. Miller had settled down in centre, and on his flanks he had two beautifully moving wings in Low and M'Pherson, right, and Hyslop and Smith, left. In the first round tie against Partick Thistle, at Inchview, M'Pherson had to stand down with a dislocated shoulder caused by an accident in the gymnasium, and Oswald came in. The Thistle put up a plucky fight but were beaten by 4–2, Hyslop getting two of the Rangers' goals and Gibson and Nick Smith (from a free kick) one each.

It was in the three succeeding ties that the forwards attained a standard as near perfection as they could ever hope to approach. Hibernian were a good team then, for Breslin and Raisbeck were in the half-back line ; Robertson and M'Farlane were a capable pair of backs, and for the second-round tie with the Rangers, at Ibrox, Storer, of Liverpool, was brought north to guard the goal. But on a frost-bound ground, the Rangers half-backs and forwards took command right from the start and won even more convincingly than the 3–0 score suggests. Nick Smith, Miller, and Gibson were stars that twinkled.

Thus far events had worked out well for the realisation of the club's Cup aspirations, but when the draw for the third round demanded a visit to Carolina Port, Dundee, everybody knew that the greatest test had come. Carolina Port had proved a fatal spot for the Rangers on more than one occasion, and the Dundee team contained such famous names as Hillman, Kelso, Keillor, and Burgess. On the appointed day the Rangers journeyed north, but the ground was in such a dreadful condition that only a friendly match was played. It was refereed by genial John Cameron. On the following Saturday, when the Rangers again travelled, they took with them the largest following that had ever accompanied a Scottish club. It was a stormy day, and when Captain Drummond won the toss and decided to play with the hurricane in his favour, a great stroke of luck was thought to have befallen the team. But a brilliant defence by Hillman and Kelso held the Rangers forwards at bay until the interval. With not a goal on the register, the loyal band of enthusiasts from Glasgow gave the team up for lost. The task before them seemed now hopeless, for the hurricane continued to drive down the field and the Light Blues had to turn and face it. The sequel was dramatic. Scarcely had the second half begun when Gibson beat Hillman with a tremendous drive. Almost immediately the ball was rushed into the Dundee net again, following a free kick. Hyslop then went striding through to crash on a third goal, and Low, a minute or two later, raced clear of the defence to let Miller in for a fourth. Four goals within seven minutes ! ¡This was one of the most thrilling achievements of that illustrious combination of players. When the situation was most desperate then was the time which they chose to reveal all their inherent genius. Dundee showered congratulations upon them. Hillman said, " I couldn't help it, but I hope you win the Cup."

Still another journey had to be undertaken in the semi-final. Five train loads of supporters went with the team to Greenock where Morton fell easy victims. The score was 7-2. Rangers had the ball in the net ten times. Harry Rennie played at right half-back for Morton and, as is well known, he later became a talented goalkeeper, in which position he played for the Hearts, Hibernian, and Rangers, and also for Scotland.

Thus, for the fourth time since they were formed, the Rangers were into the Final of the Scottish Cup, and their opponents were their old and respected rivals, Dumbarton, who had beaten in succession, Raith Rovers (2–1), Leith Athletic (3–2), St. Bernard (2–0), and Kilmarnock (4–3). On Saturday, 20th March, 1897, the teams faced each other at Hampden Park in this order :—

> **Rangers.**—M. Dickie ; N. Smith and J. Drummond ; N. Gibson, A. M'Creadie and D. Mitchell ; T. Low, J. M'Pherson, J. Miller, T. Hyslop and A. Smith.

> **Dumbarton.**—J. Docherty ; Dan Thomson and Andrew Mauchan ; Alec Miller, John Gillan and Albert Sanderson ; Lewis Mackie, Wm. Speedie, Robt. Hendry, Wm. Thomson and John Fraser.

Alec Miller, who was at right half in the Dumbarton team, had begun the season as a Rangers player and was transferred on loan to his old club, none of those concerned having ever given a thought to the possibility of events taking this peculiar turn. Fraser, who was on the Dumbarton left wing, is the same " Jack " who, later, set up a famous partnership with Alec M'Farlane in the Dundee team. He is now on the managerial staff of the Chelsea club. The Dumbarton right wing, Mackie and Speedie, were known as The Midgets, but they were as clever as they were small. Speedie was a brother of the more renowned Finlay Speedie, who became a great Rangers forward ; at any rate, forward was his favourite position, but he was versatile from top to toe and could play anywhere. On the same day that the Final was played at Hampden Park, Scotland met Wales, at Wrexham, and it was a striking indication of the playing resources of the Rangers that James Oswald, one of their reserves, was thought good enough to play in the International team.

Now, although Rangers won the Final by 5 goals to 1,

the team, as a whole, fell short of their season's Cup-tie standard. It is difficult to explain why this was so. True, eight trains unloaded their freight of lusty-lunged Dumbarton followers in Glasgow, and in the matter of vocal power, the Ibrox votaries were relegated to second place at Hampden, but the Light Blues should have been indifferent to all that. The score was more one-sided than was the play, and the victors were among the first to say so. Against such a fine old club as Dumbarton they bore no animus. They were ancient rivals, but they loved each other as foemen worthy of their steel. Miller gave Rangers the lead after 35 minutes, and Hyslop followed with a second goal eight minutes after the interval. With 25 minutes to go, Dumbarton scored from a free kick and then almost equalised. There was a critical period here, during which Dumbarton seemed likely to swing the game round. Then a tornado struck them. Within five minutes the Rangers rattled on other three goals and the Cup was won for Ibrox for the second time in the club's history. Thus, as in 1893-94, the Scottish and Glasgow trophies rested on the president's sideboard. Would the team prove equal to the task of adding the Charity Cup to his possessions ?

Before the first of the ties against Celtic became due, there was sworn in at Ibrox a player destined to take a distinguished part in the club's great campaigns of the five succeeding years. This was Robert (" Bobby ") Neil. He was a centre half-back who had joined Hibernian in June, 1894, and who had later done fine service with Liverpool. He made his debut for Rangers in a Glasgow League match on 8th May, 1897, against Clyde, at Barrowfield Park. Rangers won by 7–0, and although the game was not one to unfold the abilities of a player keen upon making an impression, it was apparent to all that Neil had come to stay. He was retained in the team for

JOHN ROBERTSON GOW.

Honorary Secretary, 1894-95 and 1895-96.   Vice-President, 1895-96
President, 1896-97 and 1897-98.

See page 41.

THE THREE-CUP TEAM, 1896-1897.

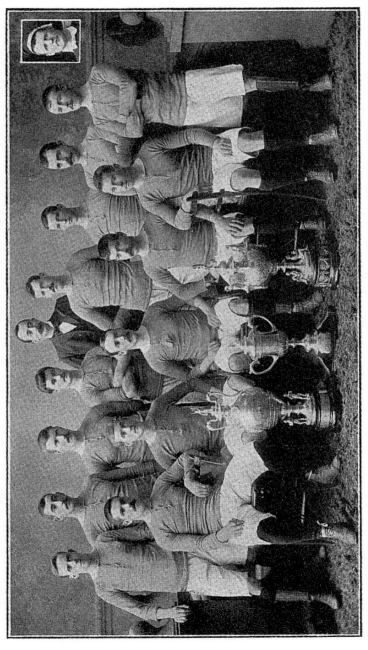

J. Muir (*Committee*).

Standing—T Low, M. Dickie, N. Smith, J. Miller, T. Hyslop, A. Smith, J. Oswald, R G Neil.
Sitting—J. MacPherson, N. Gibson, D. Mitchell, A. M'Creadie, T. Turnbull.

Inset—J. Drummond.

Glasgow Cup.   Scottish Cup.   Glasgow Charity Cup.

See page 96.

the Charity Cup-tie with the Celtic at Hampden Park,
Andrew M'Creadie going out.   In the Celtic team were six
new men from England.   Two of them were real Englishmen, Jas. Welford, a back, and J. Reynolds, a half-back,
both from Aston Villa.   John Campbell, who had played
for the Celtic against Rangers in the 1894 Scottish Cup
Final, and who had since been in Aston Villa, was wearing
again the Parkhead colours.   Geo. Allan, from Liverpool,
was in the forward line ; Wm. Orr, from Preston North-
End (now manager of Airdrieonians), was at half-back ;
and Henderson, Preston North-End, was on the left wing.
For their moderate display in the Scottish Cup Final, the
Rangers made ample amends in this Charity tie.   It was,
in fact, one of the four best games played by the team
during the season.   The forwards developed perfect
combination and seemed to get goals whenever they sought
them.   Low, M'Pherson, Miller and Alec Smith each
scored.   Reynolds converted a penalty kick for Celtic.
But the Rangers victory was not untinged with sadness,
for on the morning of the match there passed away John
Taylor, the club's trainer, who had done noble work in
fitting the team for their arduous contests.   In a benefit
match for his widow, the Rangers played against eleven
Internationalists and beat them by 4–0, this being another
of the four best games played by the team.   The other
two were the Scottish Cup-tie at Dundee and the return
" friendly " with Blackburn Rovers, in which Tommy Low
did for the Light Blues the same as he had done for the
Rovers when he played for them at Ibrox in the match
which made him a Ranger.

Third Lanark, who had defeated Queen's Park in the
semi-final, were expected seriously to challenge the
Rangers' Three-Cup ambition, but they went down by 6–1
before another overpowering burst of forward play

featured by the " 110-ton shots " of big Tom Hyslop, who by crashing on the last goal of the six, earned the distinction of having scored the first and the last goal of the season in competition matches.

That is how Rangers won the three Cups in **1896-97** and this, in tabloid, was their way of doing it :—

Scottish Cup.		Glasgow Cup.		Charity Cup.	
Partick Thistle (A),	4–2	Third Lanark (H),	5–1	Celtic	
Hibernian (H),	3–0	A Bye.		(Hampden),	4–1
Dundee (A),	4–0	Linthouse (H),	3–0	Third Lanark	
Morton (A),	7–2	Celtic (Cathkin),	1–1	(Hampden),	6–1
Dumbarton (Ham.),	5–1	Celtic (Cathkin),	2–1		
	23–5		11–3		10–2

Here are some captivating features about this memorable season's achievements. " Bobby " Neil won a Charity Cup badge after being a fortnight with the club. John M'Pherson, regarded as something of a veteran when the season opened, played a luminous part in all the Cup-ties ; it was said of him at the end of it that he could " run, dodge, score, and last a game as well as the youngest and smartest forward in the country." The club's revenue was a record for Scotland ; there was a credit balance of £2,314. But the most striking proof of the talent possessed by the team is contained in the list of International honours awarded the individual members. Here it is :—

v. England.	v. Ireland.	v. Wales.	v. English League	v. Irish League.
N. Smith.	M. Dickie.	J. Oswald.	N. Smith.	N. Smith.
N. Gibson.	J. Drummond.		N. Gibson.	N. Gibson.
J. Miller.	N. Gibson.		T. Low.	J. Miller.
T. Hyslop.	T. Low.		J. M'Pherson.	A. Smith.
	J. M'Pherson.		J. Miller.	

Against England, who were beaten by 2–1 at the Crystal Palace, Hyslop and Miller were Scotland's scorers. At Ibrox, against the English League, beaten for the first time by a Scottish League team, Low (1) and M'Pherson (2) divided the goals between them. M'Pherson and David

Mitchell were first reserves for the match with England. Miller was chosen to play against Ireland, but was too ill to travel. In the International trial matches, ten of the Rangers team took part, the one omitted being Nick Smith, who was, at the time, indisposed. Seven goals were scored in the two trials, five of them by Rangers players. Of that fine team, four, alas! have passed the Great Divide. Nicol Smith, as previously recorded, died of enteric fever in January, 1905. James Miller, a beautiful forward, of whom it was said that he could make the ball talk, returned to Sunderland in 1900-1. He helped them to win the English League Championship in 1901-2, and afterwards went as trainer to Chelsea. He died in the south of England of galloping consumption. A rare companion, with the heart of a boy and as fond of fun, " Jamie " held a firm place in the affections of everyone at Ibrox. Not a giant for strength, he relied for his success solely upon the expertness of his footwork. He had a dainty touch and seemed to go straight through the defence simply by tip-tapping the ball from one foot to the other. It was just art. At the time of his death, R. C. Hamilton was playing for Fulham, and he was able to attend the funeral.

Robert Neil remained with the club until the close of season 1903-4, and then went into business as a restaurateur in Glasgow. He died a young man, and his death was deeply regretted by all his old colleagues who best knew and understood him. Andrew M'Creadie, whom Neil succeeded, was a centre half-back of a similar mould. In the ordinary course, he should have remained longer in the game, but his brief sojourn in Sunderland appeared to unsettle him. As one of the 1894 team which first won the Scottish Cup, he will always be remembered with a sincere fondness by those who were following the fortunes of the club at the time.

1897—1898.

The Cups Again—Almost Three—Beaten by a Hair— R. C. Hamilton—A Scorer—Nick Smith's Greatest— Records.

LITTLE did any Rangers adherent think, when the season of **1897-98** dawned, that the Three Cup triumph would come within a hairsbreadth of being repeated. The word hairsbreadth is no imaginative term, for, as the story will reveal, it was *just the hair of a man's head that frustrated the Rangers in their enticing quest.* During the summer months a number of new players had been signed. The most prominent was R. C. Hamilton, of Elgin, who had come to Glasgow to study at the University for the teaching profession. He had hoped to play for the Rangers, but Queen's Park were first on the scene with an invitation, and he became, for a season, a powerful unit in their forward line. Now he was a Ranger after all, and as such he gained the highest honours within the reach of any Scottish player. J. Yuille, a goalkeeper, also came over from Hampden, but he was an old Ranger and so was merely returning " home." All the members of the Cup-winning team were available, also David Crawford, Peter Turnbull, and James Oswald. Some other useful players, including Robert Glen, from Renton, a back, were in reserve, and James Wilson was the new trainer.

You who read these lines will perceive a touch of irony in the statement, cold and truthful though it be, that at the start of this season of 1897-98, players and officials were thinking more of the League Championship than of cups. For seven long and weary years, as the sad tragedienne says, in melodrama, the Rangers had sought to add a League flag to their laurels, but never had they been able even to equal the partial success of their first attempt when they divided championship honours with Dumbarton. Twice—in 1893 and 1896—they had finished second, and now, once again, they were to be satisfied with the position of runners-up. Yet they suffered only two defeats in the League—against Celtic, at Ibrox, and at Dundee. Celtic, whom they could beat in the Glasgow Cup and in the Charity Cup, won the Ibrox League game by 4-0. That was rather a dismal day for the Light Blues, but its lesson was not entirely overlooked.

In the early part of the season, injuries to Nick Smith, Neil, Mitchell, and Hyslop prevented the team gaining the rapid momentum which had been its characteristic of the previous year, yet on the day the Glasgow Cup was won (28th November, 1897) the record was 18 matches played, 14 won, 3 drawn, and 1 lost ; the goals scored numbering 74 and those lost 18. Within a period of sixteen days the Rangers met Hibernian, Hearts, Third Lanark, Celtic, and Partick Thistle, and the only match lost was that one to Celtic. The first match of the season was at the opening of Meadowside Park, of which Partick Thistle were pardonably proud, for in general equipment it was far superior to old Inchview of beloved memory. Neil had the distinction of scoring the first goal of the new campaign, and in that same match Hamilton signalised his debut as a Ranger by registering two goals with his long, screaming shots for which he became famous. Six feet or so in height, he travelled fast by means of a raking stride, and the swing of his deadly right foot when he went for the shot usually caused the ball to describe a long rising curve which finished when the top of the netting stopped it. M'Pherson, Miller and Hyslop exploited Hamilton's scoring powers with all the craft at their command, and he was soon

piling up a fine and large total of goals. After nine continuous seasons at Ibrox, Hamilton went to Fulham, with
whom he spent the season of 1906-7. He then returned to
the Rangers, and later, played for the Hearts, Morton, and
Dundee, being capped against Wales in 1911, while a
member of the Dens Park club. We shall hear more of
him.

When the draw for the first round of the Glasgow Cup-
ties sent the Rangers to Meadowside, Partick Thistle saw
themselves with a chance to obtain revenge for their
defeat at the christening of the ground, but an even worse
fate befell them. In a 6-0 score Miller claimed four of
the goals and Hyslop two. Two days later Rangers were
at Tynecastle drawing with the Hearts in the League ;
five days later, again, they were at Cathkin Park defeating
Third Lanark by 3-0 ; and then, with only an interval of
two days, they had to meet the Celtic in the League, at
Ibrox. Little wonder if the team was tired. A League
record crowd of 30,000 witnessed this match, in which
M'Mahon (2), King and Russell got the Celtic goals. But
the Rangers recovery was quick and convincing. Before
Celtic were encountered once more, in the semi-final of the
Glasgow Cup, Partick Thistle were defeated in the League
at Meadowside by 5-1 and Clyde by 8-1, at Barrowfield,
and by 7-0 at Ibrox.

This Glasgow Cup semi-final tie with Celtic will rank as
one of the most remarkable contests in which the two
doughty champions of Parkhead and Ibrox have ever
engaged. Three games, and an extra half-hour in the last
of them, were required to decide the superiority of the
Light Blues. In the first game, at Celtic Park, the
drawings totalled £1,149, not staggering figures perhaps,
as present-day money goes, but a record then, nevertheless,
for the United Kingdom. Who that was present at the

match will forget the dramatic finish ! M'Pherson scored for Rangers after 31 minutes, and five minutes later Hamilton headed a second goal just as Orr, the Celtic left half-back, was leaving the field injured. Until a few minutes from the end Celtic were still two goals down. Thousands had left the field satisfied that the issue was decided. But a wonderful rally by the Celtic "ten" caused a marvellous transformation. Gilhooly, a nimble and elusive forward, who played on the right wing, ran through to score, and almost as the whistle went, Russell, the centre half, beat Dickie for a second time. The evening papers came out, and many people who had been at the match rubbed their eyes in bewilderment. But it was a draw, sure enough. When the replay, at Ibrox, came round, Rangers found themselves without the assistance of Nick Smith, Hyslop, and Miller, and with both Neil and Mitchell still feeling the effects of their old injuries. Orr could not play for Celtic. Still, it was a magnificent tussle, full of intense life and well-directed energy. From a penalty kick, Neil opened the scoring for the Rangers and Gilhooly equalised before the interval. In the second half, Alec Smith, from close in, shot with such terrific force that the ball went between the posts and clean through the net, but the referee was not satisfied that a goal had been scored, and so another draw was the result. The spin of a coin gave the third game to Ibrox again, and once more it was a battle royal. At the end of ninety minutes the score stood 1-1, and it was unaltered with twenty minutes of the extra thirty minutes gone. Then stamina told, and the Rangers rattled on two more goals. The great men on the winning side were Drummond and Alec Smith, but all the half-backs—Gibson, Neil, and Mitchell—played well, and had a great share in strangling the clever Celtic attack before it could burst in on Dickie. Meanwhile, Queen's Park, who had defeated Cameronians, 10-0, and Third Lanark, 4-2, awaited Rangers for the Final, at Cathkin Park. The teams were :—

Rangers.—Dickie ; Crawford and Drummond ; Gibson, Neil, and Mitchell ; Low, M'Pherson, Hamilton, Miller and Smith.

Queen's Park.—K. Anderson ; J. Ritchie and J. Gillespie ; J. Allison, A. J. Christie, and D. Stewart ; W. Stewart, H. Butler, R. S. M'Coll, D. Berry, and W. A. Lambie.

Queen's Park were a team composed mostly of young players whose natural cleverness could not effectually combat the strength and unity of purpose of their opponents. The Rangers half-backs were at their best, and both wings worked in perfect harmony. Neil began the scoring from a penalty, M'Pherson notched a second goal after beautiful leading play by Miller, and, after the interval, Alec Smith and Hamilton took the total to four. Thus Rangers won the Glasgow Cup for the fourth time and so equalled a record cherished by their Celtic rivals. *Scottish Sport*, the leading athletic paper of the period, had offered a gold medal to be awarded to the player in the Final who received the greatest number of votes signifying that he was regarded as the outstanding player in the match. The medal was won by Alec Smith. But the team, as a whole, played a magnificent game, such a game, in fact, as had featured their triumphal Cup record of the previous season. Still, the winning of the Glasgow Cup did not bring complete happiness. At the half-yearly meeting of the club, Mr. Wilton told the members that the ambition of the players and officials was to win the League championship. It was a fight between them and the Celtic, and the pair were due to meet in their return game, at Parkhead, on New Year's day. Before that fateful day arrived, Rangers, in successive matches, had beaten St. Mirren, at Ibrox, by 9–0 ; Hibernian, at Edinburgh, by 5–0 ; and Dundee, at Ibrox, by 5–0. Celtic were undefeated, but had lost two points in drawn games. The Rangers had been once defeated—in the Ibrox match with Celtic—and had drawn with the Hearts. It was necessary for the Light Blues to win at Parkhead in order to have a fighting chance. Interest in the match was at fever heat in the two camps. A new British record for a sixpenny gate was established and a mighty struggle was in progress, with every prospect of a thrilling finish, when a section of the crowd invaded the field and the game had to be abandoned. The score was then standing 1–1. Gilhooly, after eight minutes, scored for Celtic from what Rangers claimed was a palpably offside position. So strongly did Nicol Smith, the captain, feel the injustice of the decision that he ran down the field to appeal to his old sporting comrade Dan Doyle, but the referee was the judge, and he would not budge. However, Hamilton shortly after headed the equaliser from Alec Smith's corner kick, and then the Rangers proceeded to bombard the Celtic goal, whereupon some hundreds of people came over the railing and refused to go back despite the earnest supplication of the Celtic officials. Thus were the Rangers hopes of a victory and the Championship disappointed. Before they met Celtic again in the rearranged fixture, the Light Blues were defeated at Dundee by 1–2 and this sent the championship to Parkhead.

There was nothing for it but to go out for the Scottish Cup again, and so brilliantly had the team been playing all season that few doubted their ability to retain the trophy. Already they were being talked about as " the Team of the Year," and the suggestion was made of a challenge match between them and the best team in England. But the difficulty was to decide which was the best team in England. The defeat at Dundee, while of vital importance, did not sully the team's record, for N. Smith and Hyslop were unable to play and Low, injured early in the game, had to retire and leave the other ten to fight it out. Besides, Dundee were a strong, vigorous force with Hillman (goal), Kelso and Burgess (backs), and Battles and Longair (half-backs) in their defence. They could reach the semi-final of the Scottish Cup, while in the League they lost at Celtic Park only by a penalty kick goal.

In looking back upon that season's Scottish Cup exploits one can see how generously good fortune was mixed with bad. Nicol Smith, owing to a series of mishaps, did not play in any of the ties until the Final, but the club was lucky to have so good a substitute as David Crawford, who played in all the ties except the Final. Hyslop was also an invalid for several weeks, off and on, and Hamilton was studying closely ; on the day of the Final he had to sit a three hours' examination. It was, therefore, fortunate, that the first and second rounds gave the team little trouble, Polton Vale leaving eight goals at Ibrox and Cartvale twelve. Neil Kerr and Andrew M'Creadie both played against Cartvale. Queen's Park were expected to have proved a difficult hurdle to get over, but the Rangers team came away with one of their dazzling displays at Hampden Park and won easily by 3-1. The real test was yet to come. When the draw for the semi-final brought Third Lanark to Ibrox, the Rangers knew it had come in very truth. Third Lanark had provided the sensation of the ties by defeating Celtic and Hibernian in successive rounds. They were a splendidly balanced side, big and strong in the rear and skilful in attack. In the game at Ibrox they scored after twenty minutes. They seemed to be going straight to victory when a penalty was awarded them, but Johnstone failed with it, and in the second half Alec Smith equalised with a beautiful shot. Again, in the re-play, at Cathkin Park, victory was within the grasp of the " Warriors." Until eight minutes from the end they led by 2-1. Rangers seemed doomed to defeat, for Neil had missed two penalties, but a last desperate rally brought the equaliser, and so, just as in 1885, a third game was necessary to separate the old rivals. It was such a desperately-contested tie between opponents who showed tenacity of the best bull-dog type, that the players who took part in the third and deciding game, at Cathkin Park, deserve any little fame we can give them here :—

> **Rangers.**—Dickie ; Crawford and Drummond ; Gibson, Neil, and Mitchell ; Kerr, M'Pherson, Hamilton, Miller and Smith.

> **Third Lanark.**—Milne ; Barr and Gardiner ; Simpson, M'Cue, and Banks ; Gillespie, Beveridge, Smith, Hannah, and Johnstone.

In seven minutes the Rangers were a goal to the good, M'Pherson snatching a chance which would have been neglected by nine out of ten. Then the Rangers half-backs withstood a vigorous counter-attack, and in the second half a converted penalty kick by Gibson made victory secure. This protracted battle had kept Kilmarnock waiting for the Final. On the way there they had defeated 6th G.R.V. (H), 5-1 ; Leith Athletic (H), 9-2 ; Ayr Parkhouse (A), 7-2 ; and Dundee (H), 3-2. They were a dashing, bustling company, and though not greatly fancied to win the Cup, they gave the Rangers a sultry afternoon at Hampden Park, on 26th March. It was not until well on in the second half that Alec Smith shot the first goal after an enormous expenditure of effort by the entire team. The second goal, and the last, was the outcome of a long dribbling dash by Hamilton, who finished by planting the ball in the net. The teams which played that day were :—

> **Rangers.**—Dickie ; N. Smith and Drummond ; Gibson, Neil, and Mitchell ; Miller, M'Pherson, Hamilton, Hyslop and A. Smith.

> **Kilmarnock.**—J. M'Allan ; Thos. Busby and Robt. Brown ; David M'Pherson, George Anderson, and John Johnstone ; Robt. Muir, David Maitland, Jas. Campbell, Wm. Reid, and Robt. Findlay.

In the two teams there were sixteen Ayrshire players, Kilmarnock having nine and Rangers seven. Mitchell and John M'Pherson were ex-members of Kilmarnock, while M'Allan and David M'Pherson (John's brother) had each had a season with the Rangers reserves. In the Rangers team there were only two changes from the victorious Cup Final eleven of the previous year. Neil was at centre-half in place of Andrew M'Creadie, who had suffered more or less from an injury all season and made only a few appearances ; Hamilton was in the forward line, and Low was held as reserve.

With the Scottish and Glasgow Cups in this manner held in custody for another season, it only remained to extend the success to the Charity Cup. But nothing recedes like success—when your luck is out or you don't deserve to win. In the first round of the Charity Cup-ties, Rangers came up against Celtic at Cathkin Park. Miller and Hamilton scored the goals which took the Light Blues into the Final with Third Lanark. Recollecting the stormy passage they had experienced in the thrice-played Scottish tie, they took the field with their nerves on edge. That, and the fact that they were a bit stale, may have affected their play. There is no necessity to look for excuses. We are seeking for explanations. As a matter of fact, the team never had played with so little sparkle all season except in the Scottish Cup Final. Third Lanark, who now had J. Smith at left half-back and Banks at centre forward, took their chance ; they were reinvigorated by the discovery that their opponents could be beaten. Late in the game, Barr placed a free kick from which the ball was sailing into the net without touching anyone (at that time a goal could not be scored direct from a free kick), but up jumped " Blood " Hannah, and the ball, just touching the hair of his head, became qualified. Dickie was content to have seen it go behind him before it touched Hannah's hair, but after it had done so he had no time to try to avert the score. Thus Rangers were baulked of the distinction of winning the three cups two years in succession. But they added the championship of the Glasgow League to their laurels. In practically their last match in the competition they met Celtic, who led at half-time by 3-1, but lost by 4-3. That was the real fighting Rangers. The team's Cup record for the season was a fine one despite the Charity Cup defeat. It was as follows :—

Scottish Cup.		Glasgow Cup.		Charity Cup.	
Polton Vale (H),	8-0	Partick Thistle (A),	6-0	Celtic	
Cartvale (H),	12-0	A Bye.		(Cathkin),	2-0
Queen's Park (H),	3-1	Celtic (A),	2-2	Third Lanark	
Third Lanark (H),	1-1	Celtic (H),	1-1	(Cathkin),	0-1
Third Lanark (A),	2-2	Celtic (H),	3-1		
Third Lanark (A),	2-0	Queen's Park			
Kilmarnock		(Cathkin),	4-0		
(Hampden),	2-0				
	30-4		16-4		2-1

The record of all matches played was—34 won, 5 lost 8 drawn, 179 goals scored, 49 goals lost.

THE STORY OF THE RANGERS.

It was in this season that the Rangers had paid to them one of the greatest compliments ever conferred upon any club eleven in connection with an International match. We are dealing, of course, with the period dating from the time the game was properly organised by, first, the Scottish F.A., and then by the Scottish League. To meet the English League team, at Birmingham, seven Rangers players were chosen—Dickie, N. Smith, Gibson, Miller, Hamilton, M'Pherson, and A. Smith. The only non-Rangers forward selected was clever Pat Gilhooly, of the Celtic. Dan Doyle was Nick Smith's partner at back, and Harry Marshall, of Celtic, and Pat Breslin, of Hibernian, were at half-back, along with Neil Gibson. The Scots won by 2–1, and Hamilton scored the two goals. It was one of the teethiest games played between the two Leagues, a real do-or-die, last-ditch affair. Big, generous-hearted Dan Doyle, in speaking later of it, dilated in glowing terms on Nicol Smith's magnificent back-to-the-wall display. Doyle would not budge from his conviction that his Darvel comrade-in-arms had never excelled himself as he did that afternoon on the Aston Villa enclosure. Gibson also rose above his club form. He had a great English wing to watch in Athersmith and Wood, and it is doubtful if ever he tackled with such smashing effect a wing of such undoubted quality. But the whole team showed an iron determination, being actuated by a desire to show that the maiden victory of the League in the previous season was no mere chance thing. Against England, at Celtic Park, four Rangers were capped— Drummond, N. Smith, Miller, and A. Smith. Miller scored Scotland's goal. Scotland was beaten in that match largely owing to an unhappy incident which is better forgotten. The Rangers players were not concerned in it. The individual honours obtained are shown in the following lists. On the day Scotland met Ireland the Rangers were playing the Scottish Cup Final, and so no Irish caps were conferred upon them. It is worth recalling that when the noble seven were away helping to beat the English League, a Rangers team met Third Lanark in a Scottish League match and drew 0–0. The championship had been won by Celtic by that time.

v. England.	*v*. Wales.	*v*. Anglo-Scots.	*v*. English League.	*v*. Irish League.
J. Drummond.	N. Smith.	N. Smith.	M. Dickie.	R. C. Hamilton.
N. Gibson.	J. Miller.	J. Drummond.	N. Smith.	A. Smith.
J. Miller.		N. Gibson.	N. Gibson.	
A. Smith.		R. Neil.	J. Miller.	
		J. Miller.	R. C. Hamilton.	
		A. Smith.	J. M'Pherson.	
			A. Smith.	

Another financial record was created by the club. The income was £13,273 and the credit balance £4,534. Even to-day these would be regarded as acceptable figures by most clubs.

1898—1899.

The Greatest Record—18 Played, 18 Won—Thrilling Escapes—A Match Winner—In Three Cup Finals—Campbell's Goals—Celtic Battles.

TO the alluring question, " Which was the best team the Rangers ever had ? " there will always be forthcoming different answers from equally competent authorities. The **1896-97** team which won the three cups has been awarded the badge of supremacy by those whose opinion commands the highest respect. On the other hand, the **1898-99** team provides its champions with a powerful weapon wherewith to meet the challenge. *For this team accomplished a record in the League competition never previously nor since equalled.* It is a record which, in the matter of hard, actual results, may possibly never be equalled. On the question of intrinsic value, there is no immediate necessity to dilate. An instructive discussion could be carried on for a long time regarding the comparative merits of the achievements of teams which have represented the club, and there would be found many ready to acclaim certain of the more modern combinations of the Ibrox forces as second to none. It would, for instance, be impossible to deny the merit of the League record of the **1920-21** team which, in the course of a campaign of 42 matches, suffered only one defeat ; or of the **1919-20** team which sustained only two reverses in a like number of engagements. But whatever may be the opinions or prejudices of individuals, nothing can deprive the **1898-99** team of the unique distinction *of having gone* *through an entire League competition without losing a single point.* Looked at from any angle, it is a performance brilliant in the extreme, testimony at once to the endurance, the enthusiasm, and the skill of the players who accomplished it, and to the inspiring influence wrought by the men in the committee room. On the day when the Rangers completed the record by defeating Clyde, at Shawfield Park, R. C. Hamilton, the captain, speaking at the tea party which always followed the matches played in Glasgow, said their success was due largely to the splendid *esprit de corps* that had animated the team. They were heart and soul for the club, prepared to fight out every match to the last second ; and, indeed, the story of their victories shows that without indomitable courage this wonderful record could never have been created. That the Championship was not supplemented by a single cup may be attributed, in part, to the strain imposed by the making of the League record. In that season the Rangers reached the finals of the Scottish, Glasgow, and Charity Cups, a feat in itself of some merit. They had previously had their full share of cups, and as we have learned, their hearts were set upon winning the League. They began the season as holders of the Scottish and Glasgow Cups, and would have liked well enough to have kept a grip upon both, but the double pleasure of being sole League Champions, for the first time, and the custodiers of a world's record was ample consolation for the loss of the trophies.

Before the season opened, Tom Hyslop had left Ibrox to return to Stoke, but he came back, a married man, in time to don Light Blue again in a Glasgow League match just before the end of the term. Turnbull went to Millwall and Glen to Hibernian. To make good these losses, several new players were signed. The most important acquisition

I

THE STORY OF THE RANGERS.

was John Campbell, who was accompanied by his old Partick Thistle comrade, John Wilkie. These two had been earning some fame in the ranks of Blackburn Rovers. The Rangers knew them well, for had they not played a devastating part in the memorable Glasgow Cuptie of 1894, at Inchview, when a Thistle victory was followed by a Rangers protest and a win in the replay ? Two young brothers, John and Andrew Sharp, from Dalzell Rovers, both forwards, were also newcomers. Andrew was a smart right winger and played in five of the League Record matches. To John Campbell, the outside right position was allotted, for though Tommy Low was still available, he had not developed as it was hoped he would ; during the season he was occasionally brought out of the second eleven for more or less important games, but he did not play in any of the League matches. The League was comprised of ten clubs. Eighteen matches were played, and the Rangers players who shared in the making of **The Record** were :—

Player.	Position.	Matches.
M. Dickie,	Goalkeeper,	18
N. Gibson,	Right Half-back,	18
R. G. Neil,	Centre Half-back,	18
R. C. Hamilton,	Centre Forward,	18
A. Smith,	Outside Left,	18
D. Crawford,	Right or Left Back,	17
J. Campbell,	Outside Right or Left,	16
J. Miller,	Inside Left,	16
J. M'Pherson,	Inside Right,	15
N. Smith,	Right Back,	13
D. Mitchell,	Left Half-back,	13
J. Drummond,	Left Back,	5
J. Miller (Elgin),	Left Half-back,	5
A. Sharp,	Inside Right,	4
J. Wilkie,	Inside Right or Left,	3
J. Sharp,	Outside Right,	1

Sixteen players, it will be observed, took part in one or more of the eighteen matches. But for injuries, the number would have been reduced. Nicol Smith, who, for one so big and strong, was peculiarly unfortunate, came by a mishap before the opening League game was played, and he missed the first five matches. David Mitchell was absent from the last five, also on account of injury, and this made an opening for a very capable half-back who was known as " Elgin " Miller, in order to distinguish him from the more famous forward of the same name. The recognised League team was :—

Dickie,

N. Smith, **Crawford,**

Gibson, **Neil,** **Mitchell,**

Campbell, M'Pherson, Hamilton, **Miller,** **A. Smith.**

They were a light brigade, as a whole, for only Nicol Smith exceeded 12 st. But they played football of a brilliant type when they were in normal form. It was what the Americans call airtight. When they began the season they had no notion whatever of making a record. At that time it was generally believed that the wonderful performance of Preston North-End in the English League competition of **1888-89**, and the equally great feat of the Celtic in the Scottish League of **1897-98** would stand unequalled for ever. The North-End team had gone through the English League without defeat, losing only four points in drawn matches ; Celtic had also avoided defeat and had lost only three points in drawn games. Not until the Rangers found themselves winning match after match did the dream come to them of possessing an absolutely untarnished record. Once the flash had entered their minds, the players braced themselves for a mighty effort. In more than one of their engagements they had to fight to the last gasp. But for the impulse which was driving them on, they would probably have given up the game as lost. In only one contest could they be said to have enjoyed real good luck. That was in the Easter Road match with Hibernian, which was Rangers' eleventh fixture of their schedule. Here is **The Record** fully compiled :—

	Home.	Away.	Total Goals.
Celtic,	4–1	4–0	8–1
Hearts,	3–1	3–2	6–3
Third Lanark,	4–1	3–2	7–3
St. Mirren,	3–2	3–1	6–3
Hibernian,	10–0	4–3	14–3
St. Bernards,	5–2	2–0	7–2
Clyde,	8–0	3–0	11–0
Dundee,	7–0	2–1	9–1
Partick Thistle,	6–2	5–0	11–2
	50–9	**29–9**	**79–18**

First Match.—To Hamilton fell the distinction of firing the first effective shot of the campaign. The opening match was with Partick Thistle, at Ibrox, and " R. C.," as he was briefly designated, had three of the Rangers' six goals. Nick Smith did not play in this match nor in the four succeeding ones. As soon as he had fully recovered from an injury, he came in to partner Crawford, and the pair were afterwards only once separated, again owing to injury, but this time to Crawford.

Second Match.—The second match was with St. Mirren, at Paisley, and it was a good performance to win there by 3–1, for the Saints had then one of the most powerful sides they have ever possessed. Patrick, who played against England in 1897, was in goal. Greenlees, Bruce, and M'Avoy were a trio of big, able half-backs who could stop the most expert combination of attackers ; and Chalmers, Orr and Wylie—to mention only three of the forwards—were renowned for their power of penetration. It was the Rangers' half-backs who exercised the deciding influence. Gibson, Neil and Mitchell were a relentless force when they settled down ; never during this season did they excel the display which they gave at Love Street.

Third Match.—There were serious misgivings when the team went to Edinburgh for the third match. Drummond could not play, and, no reserve back being available, it was decided that M'Pherson should partner Crawford. In the Hearts team were George Livingstone, the Rangers' present trainer ; Charles Thomson, at centre forward, the position in which he aimed at making a name for himself ; Robert Walker, just entering upon a long and brilliant career ; Harry Marshall, at centre half-back, in which position he finished the season in Celtic's Scottish Cup winning team ; and Harry Rennie in goal. Rennie had been a half-back when he first played with Greenock Morton, but on 15th May, 1897, he tried his 'prentice hand as a custodian against Kilmarnock, and in goal he remained ever afterwards to the profit of himself and the benefit of his country, which he represented three times against England. Handicapped as they were, the Rangers found this strong Hearts team very difficult to overcome. " Cocky " Taylor, the Tynecastle outside right, who was an extremely clever forward, beat Dickie early in the game. So severe was the pressure on the left side of the Rangers defence, where the Hearts sought to find a weak link in M'Pherson, that it seemed impossible to avoid further loss. When things looked their worst, however, Hamilton raced away with the ball and did not ease up until he had shot it into Rennie's net. Once level again, the Rangers never looked back. Wilkie, who had taken the place of Miller for the day, scored a second goal before half-time, and shortly after turning round, Hamilton went dashing in to score a third. The Hearts made a brave fight, and before the end, Livingstone converted a penalty kick, but a grand bit of defence by Crawford, and crafty strategy by M'Pherson, prevented a point being wrested from the Rangers. It had been a desperate struggle. Possibly the winners had no greater credit by any of their subsequent victories. With Nicol Smith, Drummond, and Miller standing down, the chances were all against them. The " little bit extra " triumphed over a fundamental handicap.

Fourth Match.—At full strength again for the match with Third Lanark, at Ibrox, Rangers won very easily. The " Volunteers " were without Gardner, Smith, Beveridge, and Hannah. With the breeze behind them in the first half, Rangers rattled on four goals before the interval, Hamilton getting two, M'Pherson the third, and Neil the fourth from a penalty kick. Third Lanark scored once in the second half.

THE STORY OF THE RANGERS.

Fifth Match.—St. Bernards were encountered at Logie Green, on the Edinburgh holiday, two days after the match with Cameronians, in the first round of the Glasgow Cup. Hamilton and Neil (from a penalty kick) were the scorers of Rangers' two goals. St. Bernards played a dashing, clever game but could not score.

Sixth Match.—Against the Celtic, at Parkhead, The Record was regarded as in grave danger. In the previous season, Rangers had not scored a single goal in the League against their east end rivals. There was tremendous interest in the fixture, and 46,500 people were present. Nicol Smith made his first appearance for the season in a League game, and Crawford changed over to left back; he was playing so consistently well that Drummond had to give way for him. In the Celtic team was J. Fisher, an outside left from Aston Villa, who had played for King's Park, East Stirlingshire, and St. Bernards before crossing the Border. He was small but fast and dodgy. He never, however, came quite up to the reputation which he took with him when he joined Aston Villa. For this match, Peter Somers stood by as reserve. He was just a lad then, but a few years later he became an indispensable unit in the Celtic forward line. Within five minutes, Rangers were a goal in the lead. Campbell was dribbling in on M'Arthur when he was brought down inside the penalty area, and Neil, one of the most deadly penalty kickers the game has known, netted. Celtic struggled with volcanic energy to restore equality, but the magnificent defence of Crawford and Mitchell against Bell, and the success of Neil against Campbell, the Celtic centre forward, enabled the Light Blues to retain their lead until the interval. The second half had a dramatic opening. In less time than it takes to tell, the Rangers forwards swept in a body through the Parkhead defence, the ball moving quickly from one to the other with that perfect precision which had been a characteristic of the 1896-97 line of attack. Alec Smith forced a corner, placed it beautifully in front of goal and M'Pherson headed past M'Arthur. Rangers never looked back after that. A third goal was scored following a free kick placed by Crawford. A little later, M'Arthur left his goal to deal with Alec Smith, who was coming in with the ball at full speed. When the custodian was well on his way, Smith gave the ball a sharp push to Campbell, who sent it spinning into the net. Four goals up, Rangers went easy until the end. The sting of the

Ibrox 4–0 reverse of the previous season was drawn and they were one important step nearer to the Championship.

Seventh Match. — Two days after the Parkhead match, Rangers were at Cathkin Park playing Third Lanark in the first of the returns. A disaster almost befell them here, for, after leading at half-time by three goals scored by Campbell, M'Pherson, and Campbell again, they were nearly caught napping by a great rally by the Third Lanark forwards. First Devlin, and then M'Whinnie scored, and until the end there was a thrilling tussle. The Rangers won with little to spare.

Eighth Match. — By defeating the Hearts, at Ibrox, Rangers practically swept a rival for the Championship out of their path. Only Hibernian were now to be feared, for, like the Light Blues, they were undefeated, although they had lost a point to Clyde at Shawfield Park on the day the Rangers defeated the Hearts for the second time. Knowing the vital significance of the Ibrox match, the Hearts husbanded their resources for a supreme effort. Michael was at centre forward, and this was rightly regarded as adding dash to the attack. He was the sort of centre who gave opposing backs not a moment's relief from worry. Staggered by the opening whirlwind raids, the Rangers defence had to surrender after ten minutes, the ball being rushed past Dickie who made a gallant effort to save. It really seemed as if the Rangers had met more than their match, for George Livingstone and Blair, on the Hearts left wing, were playing up to Gibson and Nick Smith with an almost overpowering skill and strength. A rapid change occurred, however. Alec Smith got the ball pushed out to him and away he went on one of his tearing runs. First he eluded Begbie, then Allan, and at the right moment centred to Hamilton, who had galloped through the centre and gave Rennie little chance to save. Level at the interval, the Rangers struck a shrewd blow less than a minute after changing round. M'Pherson took a short run through and swept the ball ahead for Hamilton to race between Allan and M'Cartney and beat Rennie a second time. Not yet were the Hearts finished. Several times they were on the point of equalising, but Dickie was on one of his great days and could not be beaten. Gibson, Neil and Mitchell, with twenty minutes to go, began to exercise a dominating influence, and, thanks to the way in which they cut through, to throw extra weight upon the Hearts defence, the latter wavered for one fatal moment, and after some exciting exchanges round Rennie, Campbell rammed the ball into the net.

Ninth Match.—For the match at Dundee, Wilkie took Miller's place at inside left. Dundee had several changes since last Rangers met them. Hillman was succeeded in goal by Stewart, Davidson was a resourceful back, and Leckie, Gerrard and Keillor were a sound half-back line. Before the game was very old, M'Pherson was injured and was off the field for a period. Fired with the ambition to be the first to lower the colours of the undefeated Rangers, the whole Dundee team played with surprising vigour and indomitable courage. It was rapier against broadsword. The crowd cheered Dundee to the echo as the defence turned aside the thrusts of the Ibrox forwards. At last Hamilton got the ball past Stewart, but before the interval, W. M'Donald, a clever little Highlander who played at inside left, equalised. Tense was the struggle in the second half. Up till the last quarter of an hour Dundee bravely held their own. Then M'Pherson threw off the effects of his injury, and he and Campbell began to work in on Stewart. A corner was forced, and when the ball came over, Neil dashed into the crowd and banged the ball into the net. On this same day the Hearts defeated the Hibernian, at Tynecastle, by 4–0. It was the Hibernian's first defeat and Rangers were now three points ahead of them. But they had not yet begun to dream of an unsullied record.

Tenth Match.—Before Rangers met Partick Thistle in the return game, at Meadowside, they had defeated Celtic, at Parkhead, in the semi-final of the Glasgow Cup, and thus qualified to meet Queen's Park in the Final. Another important event had taken place, the Hearts defeating Hibernian, at Easter Road, in their return match and so making the Rangers' championship prospects exceedingly bright. Partick Thistle gave little trouble, the match merely providing Miller and Campbell with an opportunity to exhibit their artistry. Five goals were piled up.

Eleventh Match.—Now came the great test, the most throbbing, most dramatic match the Rangers have ever played. When they faced Hibernian at Easter Road, both knew that the Championship might depend upon the result. But besides the championship stake, there was also the record of successive victories to be preserved by the Rangers. A defeat for them would be a humiliation, a draw a disaster. As the match is historic, we must give the teams :—

Hibernian.—M'Call ; Nelson and Glen ; Breslin, Handling and Robertson ; Gemmell, M'Guigan, Reid, Atherton, and Porter.

Rangers.—Dickie ; N. Smith and Crawford ; Gibson, Neil and Mitchell ; Campbell, M'Pherson, Hamilton, Miller and A. Smith.

When the referee, James Adams, the old Hearts back, stepped on to the field, he had to raise his cap in acknowledgment of the cheers which greeted him. The incident was piquant in view of what happened later. Within 22 minutes, Rangers were two goals down. They had never had such an experience during this season, and there can be no doubt the awesome sensation startled the team. They had been playing well, the forwards combining beautifully right up to goal, doing everything but score, in fact. But there was little venom in the attack. When the Hibernian forwards burst upon Smith and Crawford, they came with their batteries fully charged. Mitchell and Crawford were taken aback by the speed with which Gemmell and M'Guigan went past them, and when Gemmell, with a short, sharp cut-in and smashing short-range shot, left Dickie helpless, there was such a scene of enthusiasm among the Hibernian supporters as had never been witnessed in the Capital. A thunderous roar proclaimed the scoring of the second goal, also by Gemmell, the procedure leading up to the earlier success being repeated almost exactly. Well was it for the Rangers that they had players in their ranks who had grappled with problems as difficult as this. Up went sleeves, and grim was the visage of every forward as they lined up once more. No more short, dainty passing. No searching after the picturesque. It was goals or a smashed record. The change of style, the wide passes and the quick, long centres threw the Hibernian defence out of gear. Nelson was in difficulties, Glen rushed over to assist, missed his kick and in sped Miller with the ball to notch a fine goal. This happened just before the interval, and a minute after the resumption, Rangers were level. Campbell, Hamilton, and A. Smith took the ball right through the Hibernian defence without allowing a defender to touch it, and the left-winger stopped running only when he had given it the scoring touch. Events followed thick and fast. Rangers were playing like a winning team, but the Hibernian defence steadied again, and their forwards, waiting their chance, broke through once more and Gemmell completed a puzzling movement by scoring his third goal and giving Hibernian the lead for the second time. It was the only match, League or Cup-tie, in which Rangers lost three goals in that season, and it was a great personal triumph for Gemmell to score all three. The situation was now more perilous than ever for the Light Blues, but when Hamilton restored equality at 3–3, the excitement was feverish. Stamina and nerve were now brought into play. Rangers bombarded the Hibernian goal without effect until a minute only remained to play. Then away over in the corner Robertson and Campbell were seen to be struggling for possession of the ball. At that time the penalty area extended right across the field. Robertson got hold of Campbell's jersey about the neck and seemed to try to throw him. Captain R. C. Hamilton dashed over to Referee Adams and claimed a penalty. This was immediately granted, and, without demur, the Hibernian players fell out to allow the kick to be taken. Neil, as coolly as walking to church on Sunday, placed the ball on the spot, stepped back, and then, striding up to it, smote it into the net. The teams were lining up when the whistle sounded, leaving Rangers winners of a contest which can never be forgotten by those who witnessed it. What followed has really nothing to do with our story. Referee Adams had to escape as best he could from an angry section of the crowd whom the Hibernian officials tried to pacify. Before meeting Hibernian, Rangers had suffered their first defeat in the Glasgow Cup Final with Queen's Park, who won by 1–0, but we shall deal with that event later.

Twelfth Match.—A pleasant relief from the tension of Easter Road was the match with Clyde, at Ibrox. Andrew Sharp played his first game for the League team, taking the place of M'Pherson. He scored two of the eight goals, Miller registering three, Gibson two, and Watson, the Clyde back, who afterwards played for Sunderland, Middlesbrough, and Scotland, putting the ball past Donnelly, his own goalkeeper, for the eighth time. With six matches to play, Rangers required only five points to make certain of the Championship.

Thirteenth Match.—Although, in the end, St. Bernards were beaten decisively, at Ibrox, they caused the Rangers real anxiety. The strain was telling. Continued success demanded a price. It was not now the Championship that lured, but **The Record** which had become a real live possibility. The Saints, by the same dashing tactics which had profited the Hibernian, snatched a goal in the first half and held on to their lead for fifteen minutes of the second half when Hamilton equalised. Fifteen minutes from the end the Saints scored again. The depressed Rangers followers were resigning themselves to. catastrophe when the match-winner, Campbell, jumped into his most dazzling form and within ten minutes rapped on four goals. It was the greatest piece of individual paralysing brilliancy that had been exhibited by a Rangers player.

Fourteenth Match.—With a 7–0 victory over Dundee, at Ibrox, the championship was sealed for Ibrox, for on the same day the Celtic defeated the Hearts who had supplanted Hibernian as challengers. Dundee had been through troublous times. On the verge of spontaneous collapse, they had all but decided to give up the ghost when the League came to their assistance and enabled them to carry on. " Elgin " Miller played his first League match at left half for Rangers and remained in the team until the fixtures were completed.

Fifteenth Match.—When the Hibernian came to Ibrox for the return, everybody had the Easter Road drama in mind. What a change was there ! The same goalkeeper, backs and half-backs were playing for Hibernian ; the same forwards for Rangers. Note the result. Within twenty minutes, Rangers were in the possession of five goals. Other five were added in the second half. Alec Smith had four, Hamilton two, and Miller, M'Pherson, Campbell, and Neil one each, Neil's being from a penalty kick. Another penalty was awarded Rangers, but Neil was merciful and invited Campbell to take it ; he obligingly failed to score. Yet M'Call performed wonders in the Hibernian goal. The whole Rangers team just struck a game which was without a flaw. They could do nothing wrong. Probably no team on earth could have stood up to them that day. They were like full-blooded race-horses trained and tuned to the minute. And Hibernian, a good young team, were the unfortunate ones.

Sixteenth Match.—Worse conditions could not be imagined than those in which the game with St. Mirren was played at Ibrox. Both teams suffered, perhaps to a different extent, but that is immaterial. Rangers had to struggle hard to win, for in the first minute Chalmers scored for St. Mirren, and after A. Smith had equalised, Orr again gave the Saints the lead. Campbell once more came to the rescue of his side, for he levelled the scores before the interval and got the winning goal in the second half. Thus was a sensation averted and chief credit was owing to Gibson, Neil, Campbell, and Alec Smith who, as was said at the time, worked " like ten men." Those big, strong St. Mirren half-backs were terrible fellows to circumvent.

Seventeenth Match.—Only one day elapsed between the punishing ordeal with St. Mirren and the return with Celtic, at Ibrox Park. This was really the only obstacle that had to be feared, for the next and last match was with Clyde, at Shawfield, and no danger was anticipated there. Celtic had Bell playing on the left now and Gilhooly was in his old place at outside right. Battles returned to the fold, was at centre half, and Davidson at right back with Storrier. A fiery opening by the Parkhead forwards almost broke the Rangers defence in the first few minutes, but very soon an entirely new aspect was given to the game. Some fine concerted play by Miller and Smith carried operations up to the Celtic defence, where Hamilton received the pass and scored with a shot that went swinging away from M'Arthur. Irresistible now, the Rangers forwards seemed to slay with an enchanted sword. Campbell scored a second goal with a beautiful shot from the touchline. The one-sided nature of the play had its disadvantage, for in a breakaway Bell cleverly raced in on Dickie and scored Celtic's only goal. To this, Rangers replied with more of their marvellous effectiveness, and five minutes from the interval Hamilton shot a third goal. He also scored a fourth goal in the second half from a Campbell centre, and so, happy and confident of completing **The Record** on which they had set their hearts, Rangers went forward to meet Clyde in the last and

Eighteenth Match.—Terrible conditions prevailed at Shawfield Park, and neither team got a chance to play good football, but Rangers put their superior skill to sufficient purpose. Alec Smith scored after ten minutes and Miller registered a second goal before half-time. A third goal came as a result of a penalty converted by Neil.

That, in brief outline, is how the greatest of all League records was contrived. Nine of the best teams in the country had been defeated on two occasions. For a stretch of four and a half months, the Rangers team had to keep in prime condition and play under varied conditions which became an agency, sometimes, more in favour of their opponents than of themselves. They had to finish up with three matches in eight days, one of these matches regarded as the crucial engagement of the schedule. Twenty-two years have passed since **The Record** was achieved. It stands in splendid isolation.

But what of the Cup-tie adventures of the team in this memorable season of **1898-99**? As has been related, in passing, the Rangers fought the finals of the three cups and lost them all. In the Glasgow Cup they had a curious experience, for having drawn with Celtic, at Ibrox, in the semi-final and winning the replay at Parkhead, they went down before Queen's Park in the Final by a mere goal. The victory over Celtic at Parkhead was regarded as one of the best ever gained against them. Alec Smith had taken ill and could not play, so Low was brought in at outside right and Campbell transferred to the left, being given his old Partick Thistle colleague as a partner. Divers played along with Bell on the Celtic right wing. In nine minutes Hamilton scored but Gilhooly equalised. Before the interval, King and Divers, in turn, failed with a twice-taken penalty kick, a failure that cost Celtic dear, for in the second half Campbell dropped over a rainbow centre which Hamilton met in front of M'Arthur and converted into a goal. On their way to the Final, Queen's Park had beaten Partick Thistle (6–1) and Third Lanark (2–1). They were a fine young team who had been able to give a satisfactory answer to the question, " Can Queen's Park live ? " which was frequently on the lips of the " candid friend " round about that period. In the

Final the side that opposed the Rangers full League eleven were :—

> K. Anderson ; J. Gillespie and D. Stewart ; J. H.
> Irons, A. J. Christie, and J. F. Templeton ; W. Stewart,
> T. A. Bowie, R. S. M'Coll, D. Berry, and R. A. Lambie.

People who had seen all the Glasgow Cup finals declared this one to be the best ever played. It was, at anyrate, a rare ding-dong affair. Long before Queen's Park got their goal, the Rangers might have had the Cup safely landed, but their shooting was the one glaring weakness. But when once the Hampden forwards became confident, they played with admirable vim and cleverness. W. Stewart and Tom Bowie were an elusive wing, and it was from that quarter the goal came in the second half. Stewart sped up the wing and centred. Dickie made to fist the ball but only partially got it and it struck Nick Smith and rebounded into the net out of the goalkeeper's reach. Thus the Glasgow Cup went back to Hampden Park, which had not housed it since 1889. And it was well and truly won. This was Rangers' nineteenth match of the season and their first defeat.

Much of the history of the club's interests in the Scottish Cup competition of that season centred in the first-round tie with the Hearts, at Ibrox. An incident which appeared, at the time, to be of no particular concern to them, very probably cost them the Cup. Harry Marshall, the Portobello boatman, who was the Hearts centre half-back, should have played in the tie at Ibrox but didn't. When the Hearts were defeated, they offered Marshall to St. Bernards who declined the offer, preferring to go into the ties with their own players. Whether Marshall would have joined St. Bernards is another question. As a matter of fact, he joined the Celtic in time to play against St. Bernards in the second round, and he had possibly more to do with the defeat of Rangers in the Final than any other single player. Had Marshall played for the Hearts against the Rangers he would, of course, have been ineligible to serve any other club in the ties and possibly he would have helped the Hearts to avoid such a heavy defeat as they sustained at Ibrox, for it was considered that he could hold Hamilton better than any centre half-back then playing. In three minutes Gibson scored, the referee adjudging the ball to be over the line before Rennie got hold of it. Neil followed with a second goal from a penalty kick, Hamilton got a third, and Gibson a fourth from a free kick—all within forty minutes. Of the incidents of an unpleasant second half only brief mention is necessary. Hogg, and then Begbie, the Hearts half-backs, had to go to the pavilion shortly after the resumption. Begbie, as captain, called upon the remaining nine to follow him, but they wisely declined, and near the finish of the game, Albert Buick, then budding into a fine half-back, scored for the Hearts, who from first to last were out of luck.

In the second round Rangers defeated Ayr Parkhouse, at Beresford Park, by 4–1, Hamilton getting three of the goals and Campbell one. Alec Smith sustained a broken collar bone in this match, his first serious accident since joining the club in 1894. Fortunately their third-round tie gave no difficulty, for Clyde, at Ibrox, were easily dismissed by 4–0, Low, M'Pherson, Gibson, and Hamilton being the scorers. It was fortunate for Rangers that International matches delayed the semi-final round since they were fated to challenge the St. Mirren lion in the Love Street den. The delay afforded Alec Smith time to recover and he was able to resume. Nick Smith had to stand down with a chill, and St. Mirren also had a change at back, Bennie giving way to T. A. Jackson, who played against England five years later in a blizzard International at

Celtic Park, in which Bloomer scored the only goal. This was the first time St. Mirren had reached the semi-final, and had they gone a stage further instead of having to wait until 1908, none could have grudged them the pleasure. In a thrilling first half, Rangers were fortunate to get the only goal scored by M'Pherson from a back pass by Hamilton. Chalmers equalised with a glorious shot early in the second half, and the Saints were bidding well for a win when Gibson placed a free kick towards Patrick. Had the Saints goalkeeper left the ball alone it would have gone into the net untouched. He fisted it out and Miller, meeting it, banged it into the net and won the tie.

Thus once more, Rangers and Celtic were face to face in the Scottish Cup Final. Celtic's victims were—6th G.R.V., 8–1 ; St. Bernards, 3–0 ; Queen's Park, 2–1, after an unfinished game, 4–2 for Celtic ; Port-Glasgow Athletic, 4–2. The Final was played at Hampden Park and the teams were :—

> **Celtic.**—M'Arthur ; Welford and Storrier ; Battles, Marshall and King ; Hodge, Campbell, Divers, M'Mahon, and Bell.
>
> **Rangers.**—Dickie ; Smith and Crawford ; Gibson, Neil and Mitchell ; Campbell, M'Pherson, Hamilton, Miller and A. Smith.

Hodge, the Celtic outside right, had joined Celtic from Port-Glasgow Athletic in the previous January, and was a good, serviceable player. He took an important part in this Final, for he scored the second goal ten minutes from the end, the first being notched by M'Mahon early in the second half. Rangers did not play up to their usual standard. Hamilton could not get away from Marshall, and the other forwards were thrown out of gear, simply because they had accustomed themselves, and with good

GENERAL COMMITTEE, SEASON 1896-1897.

T. Deans.

J. Cameron.

Back Row—D. M'Pherson, P. Nimmo, J. Macintyre, J. Walker, A. B. Mackenzie, G. Small, J. M'Lean, J. Muir.

Sitting—W. Wilton (*Secretary*), J. Henderson (*Vice-President*), J. R. Gow (*President*), D. MacKenzie, W. MacAndrew.

Glasgow Charity Cup.   Scottish Cup.   Glasgow Cup.

See page 96.

.The late JAMES HENDERSON.

President, 1898-99. Chairman of Directors from 1899 to 1912.

See page 130.

reason, to depend upon their centre picking up their passes. In accepting the Cup on behalf of the Celtic, the late Mr. J. H. M'Laughlin paid the Rangers a striking tribute. " If," he said, " they looked back to the history of the Rangers, there was no club in Great Britain who could boast of a record like theirs. They struggled on till they became, four years ago, certainly the premier club in Scotland, and from that time to this day they had been about the best team in the British Isles."

The rivals were not finished with each other yet. In May they met in the Charity Cup Final, and again the Light Blues went under by 2–0. M'Mahon scored the first goal and a shot by Peter Somers was helped through by Gibson. Somers played at inside right to Hodge and David Russell, returned from Preston North-End, was at centre half again for Celtic. That the score was against the run of the play may, I think, be fairly stated. But that has happened before, and has happened since in matches between the clubs. So Rangers had been in nine consecutive cup finals and had five victories and four defeats to show as :—

1896–97,	-	Three Finals,	-	Won Three Cups.
1897–98,	-	Three Finals,	-	Won Two Cups.
1898–99,	-	Three Finals,	-	Won No Cup.

The record of their **1898-99** Cup exploits are best shown thus :—

Scottish Cup		Glasgow Cup		Charity Cup	
Hearts (H),	4–1	Cameronians (A),	4–0	Third Lanark	
Ayr Parkhouse (A),	4–1	Celtic (H),	1–1	(Hampden),	4–1
Clyde (H),	4–0	Celtic (A),	2–1	Celtic (H),	0–2
St. Mirren (A),	2–1	Queen's Park			
Celtic (Hampden),	0–2	(Cathkin),	0–1		
	14–5		7–3		4–3

THE STORY OF THE RANGERS.

Honours secured in **1898-99** were :—

v. England	v. Wales	v. Ireland	v. English League
N. Smith.	N. Smith.	M. Dickie.	N. Smith.
N. Gibson.	N. Gibson.	N. Smith.	N. Gibson.
J. Campbell.	J. Campbell.	N. Gibson.	J. Campbell.
R.C.Hamilton.	R.C.Hamilton.	J. Campbell.	R.C.Hamilton.
		R.C.Hamilton.	J. M'Pherson.

Against the English League, Campbell scored the Scottish League's only goal. Against Ireland, Hamilton scored four goals and Campbell one. Against Wales, Campbell scored two. They were fond of doing their country a good turn.

Another record. In 1898-99, the club's turnover amounted to £15,800, an enormous sum for those days. There was a profit of £1,200 and a credit balance of £5,785. Confidently, then, a new ground scheme was embarked upon, and thus we have Ibrox Park as it is seen to-day.

Before the new season of **1899-1900** dawned, the club whose flag had braved the "battle and the breeze" for twenty-six years had ceased to exist. It was the Rangers Football Club no more. On 27th March, 1899, the members, at a special general meeting, resolved to adopt the principle of limited liability. At another special general meeting, on 10th May, 1899, that decision was confirmed and the first Board of Directors appointed. It was now the Rangers Football Club, Limited—not, perhaps, an impressive change on paper, a mere word, in fact, added to the old and cherished title, but to those who had faced the battles and the breezes, there was a real sense of pathos in the passing of the old order. Yes, there was something in a name. But it was the compulsion of events. The great and growing popularity of the game had created vast changes, and this was one of them. At the last annual meeting of the Club, held on 30th May, 1899, William

Wilton, the honorary match secretary, was appointed manager and secretary. His was the only name put forward. Round after round of cheering greeted his election. Such trust as this ovation indicated was well bestowed, for as we have already related, Mr. Wilton retained his onerous post until the day of his death. To the first Board of Directors, William MacAndrew was one of those appointed, but in the same week as the last annual meeting of the Club was held he was chosen by the Scottish Football League to be their first paid secretary, and such he has remained ever since. The vacancy thus created on the Board was given to John S. Marr, who died in March, 1906, after having given the club devoted service for a long period of years.

During the season of **1898-99**, Mr. James Henderson had been president of the club. He was returned to the Board of Directors at the top of the poll, and at the first Board meeting, on 1st June, 1899, was unanimously appointed chairman. His tenure of that office was not interrupted until his death on 10th May, 1912. Mr. Henderson was a fine type of Scotsman, genial, kindly, and unassuming. His success in business was a romance, and the qualities which had enabled him to attain it characterised all his actions both as President and Chairman of Directors of the Rangers. He was prudent and far-seeing, not too hasty in coming to a decision, but firm once he had made up his mind upon what was right. In the public life of the city he took a deep and human interest. As a representative of Kingston Ward, he entered the Glasgow Town Council in 1903, and rose to the position of Senior Magistrate. He was made a Bailie in November, 1907. As one who, from his earliest days, had fostered a love for athletics and football, he exercised all his influence to keep sport clean. Manliness in a player he appreciated above all things.   He was one of the oldest members of the Queen's Park Club, and the fact that he insisted on retaining this membership along with that of the Rangers, prevented him, at one time, from accepting a seat on the S.F.A. Council.   As chairman of the Scottish League, he earned the confidence and respect of those with whom he collaborated in the work of that important body, while as chairman of the International League Board, the ambassadors from the sister countries paid homage to his shrewdness and integrity.   Men of the high character and steadfastness of James Henderson are a bulwark to whatever enterprise they may lay their hand.

1899-1900.

Another Championship—One League Defeat—
" Jacky " Róbertson — A Scoring Half-back—
Two Cups Won—A Great Sequence.

HAVING gained their ambition by becoming sole possessors of the League Championship, the desire to retain it was equal only to the wish to recover one or all of the lost cups. Nobody underrated the task which lay in front of the team, but nobody regarded it as impossible after the dazzling League achievement of the previous season. That this optimism was well founded, results eloquently proved. The League Championship was retained, the Glasgow Cup was won, so was the Charity Cup, and it was only in the semi-final of the " Scottish " that a very disappointing display led to defeat by the Celtic, whom the Light Blues had earlier conquered in the Final of the Glasgow Cup, and later vanquished in the Final of the Charity Cup. The only reverse sustained in the League was also from the Celtic, at Parkhead, and so Rangers had the distinction of having completed two arduous League campaigns with only a single defeat against them. Such consistency was a marvel to all beholders. But the strain was very trying, and it is not surprising that the team should strike a purple patch such as they encountered in the Scottish Cup-tie with their old and respected rivals of Parkhead.

In the previous season the reserve team had won all the competitions for which it had entered, but, despite this, the committee decided to disband it. Several of the young players found fresh quarters, but their new clubs willingly agreed to the stipulation that Rangers might have first call upon them at the end of the season. Low went to Dundee, Finlayson to Grimsby, " Elgin " Miller to Port-Glasgow Athletic, and Goudie and M'Dougall to Partick Thistle. But to offset these losses, Dunlop, a centre or left half-back, was secured from Sunderland, while, of course, Tom Hyslop, back from Stoke, was also available. On the very threshold of the new season one of the most brilliant players who ever wore the club's colours was signed. This was John T. Robertson, known as " Jacky." A Dumbarton boy, " Jacky " had crossed the Border to play first for Everton, and then for Southampton. He had played for Scotland against England in 1898 when a member of the Everton team, and again in 1899, when with Southampton. Rangers had tried to secure him during the close season and had failed. He had agreed to remain another season with Southampton, but the Ibrox officials tried again, and on 14th August, 1899, the transfer was carried through. Everton, who held the League rights, received £250 and the proceeds of a match, played later, while Southampton got £50 for the surrender of the Association transfer. I have said that Robertson was one of the Rangers' greatest players. He was one of the greatest players of all time. After joining the Ibrox staff he was capped five times against England, six times against Wales, three times against Ireland, five times against the English League, and once against the Irish League. He was thus the recipient of 22 International honours. In his first season with the Rangers he played against England, Wales, and the English League, the matches with Ireland and the Irish League being regarded as beneath his calibre, by which no offence is implied to those good sporting Irishmen. He captained the Scottish team against England on three occasions, a distinction equalled or excelled only by two other players, also half-backs—

Charles Campbell, of Queen's Park, and Charles Thomson, of Hearts and Sunderland. These two each led the Scots against the Saxon in five engagements. Robertson was almost as good a forward as he was a half-back. He figured, with success, at outside right and centre forward in the Rangers team in emergency. But as a left half-back he had no equal either in England or Scotland during his association with the Rangers. Strongly built, though not tall, he tackled with great power, and he seldom parted with the ball without first taking it up the field like a forward. He was a dead shot, too, as may be guessed from the fact that in season 1903-4 he scored 17 goals for the club, and in another season 15. His 1903-4 achievement was celebrated by the presentation to him of a gold watch. In International matches he scored five goals, which may be a record for a half-back, although I cannot swear to that. " Jacky " had an easy style of sweeping past those who tried to stop him. His muscles always seemed to be newly oiled. He could head a ball as far, and with as sure direction, as many players could kick it, especially if running in to meet a return from an opposing back. Power dwells with cheerfulness, the philosopher says, and " Jacky " was the soul of good humour. He had a laugh that was a tonic for those who heard it, and when he left to become manager of the Chelsea club, that merry laugh was missed at Ibrox. After Chelsea, he played for Glossop, then he went to the Continent as coach to a club, and afterwards returned home to work at his trade. It is difficult to say what was his greatest game, but taking the character of the opposition into account, he probably never equalled his display against England at Celtic Park, in April, 1900, when he captained the magnificent Scottish team which defeated the Saxon by 4 goals to 1. He was a sixth forward that day, in the best sense of the term, for he collaborated to perfection in the plan set for the Scottish attack, which was to feed R. S. M'Coll with the ball and let the then famous Queen's Park centre score the goals. M'Coll scored three in the first 25 minutes.

When the season of **1899-1900** began, there was general speculation as to how far the team would carry their spotless League record of 1898-99. In the opening game, against Third Lanark at Cathkin Park, the forward line was kept pretty much in the old order, both Miller and Hyslop being included, while David Mitchell held the left half-back position. Mitchell played in only two League matches that season, for in the club's second engagement, against Clyde at Shawfield Park, Robertson· made his debut and was never afterwards out of the team except when injured or engaged in International games. Third Lanark were beaten by 5–1, Campbell scoring two of the goals, and Miller, Hyslop, and Nicol Smith (from a free kick) one each. Clyde were even more easily defeated by 6–2, and Robertson here began his scoring pranks with the best goal of the match. When the Hearts came to Ibrox, they first of all seemed to be falling as easy prey as the others, but finished by almost drawing. Campbell scored twice in the first half and Hamilton once, to which Baird replied with one for the Hearts. Hamilton got a fourth goal for Rangers immediately on turning round, but then the Hearts forwards came away in fine style and Michael and Taylor brought the total to three. They were threatening to equalise when the whistle went. It was a close call for The Record going by the board, and the escape was almost as narrow at Kilmarnock in the succeeding match, for the Rugby Park team twice led in the scoring, and Rangers were handicapped by an injury to Miller. Johnstone gave Kilmarnock their first goal, and after Gibson had equalised, Howie (late Middlesbrough's manager) again beat Dickie. Leading at half-time by 2–1, Kilmarnock seemed to possess a glorious chance to make history, but a brilliant goal by Alec Smith and another by M'Pherson, who slipped through after having been shadowed throughout the game, kept The Record safe.

Thus, 22 successive victories had been obtained in the League, but the next adventure was to see the great sequence broken. On travelling through to Tynecastle to meet the Hearts in the return game, the Rangers found the Ibrox form confirmed up to the hilt. They could only draw (1–1) with a strong, dashing, clever Hearts team which now possessed a grand line of attack composed of Taylor, Walker, Michael, Livingstone, and Baird. These five had developed a strong, effective combination, and when the job in hand was more than normally important they were always capable of finding a little bit extra. Although the Tynecastle draw put an end to Rangers' string of wins, they had still something valuable to preserve, and that was the avoidance of defeat. The task became more and more difficult, because some of the players got in among a good deal of bad luck in the matter of injuries. In one week Nicol Smith, Campbell, Hamilton, and Hyslop were all under treatment.

It became necessary to reinforce the available talent for the forward line, and so John Graham, of Alva, was signed in time to take part in the Glasgow Cup replay with Third Lanark, on 23rd September, of which more anon. Graham was a youngster when he came to Ibrox, but he soon settled down at outside right and played in the majority of the League matches. Something of a sprinter, he was fond of cutting in for a shot. He had played a little for King's Park, for whom an elder brother had done yeoman service as a back, and he had the refusal of an offer from Newcastle United and other English and Scottish clubs. He was only a month in the Rangers when he won a Glasgow Cup badge, and in his first season gained a League championship medal, so that his experience approximated to that of " Tommy " Low in 1896-97 when this Parkhead youngster gained the three cup badges in his first season at Ibrox.

Following hard upon the Rangers' visit to Tynecastle, the Hearts went to Parkhead and defeated Celtic by 2–0, this being Celtic's first League reverse of the season. It gave the race for the Championship a definite turn in Rangers' favour, and when the Light Blues visited the East End to play the Celtic in what was really Rangers' home fixture, there was a full realisation in both camps of what was at stake. Lord Emly was present to kick off, and he was escorted to the centre by Dan Doyle, smiling as usual. Nicol Smith, Campbell, and Hyslop were absent, injured, but the Celtic were also under strength, though, as events proved, they were less seriously affected by the changes than were Rangers. Until a minute or so from the end Celtic led by 3–2, and hundreds had left the ground believing that the Light Blues had at last been defeated in the League. A great finishing rally, however, in which the lad Graham was conspicuous, brought the equaliser, and so Rangers had played 28 League matches with the loss of only two points in draws.

Clyde, at Ibrox, gave no trouble at all, but the match was interesting from the fact that Peter Somers, who became a great Celtic forward, after a short period with Blackburn Rovers, was in the Clyde team, on loan from Parkhead. Andrew Sharp made his League debut for the season in the Rangers ranks, and formed a fine right wing with Graham. The score was 7–0—29 *League matches, now, without a defeat.* One of the most thrilling games ever witnessed in Edinburgh was provided by the visit of the Rangers to Easter Road. Hibernian's young players were steadily developing. Lads like Callaghan, M'Cartney, and Harrower had given the team a nice balance which, in the very near future, was to prove the dominant quality in winning the Scottish Cup for the second time in the club's career. But in this League game steadiness, which came from experience, pulled the Rangers through. Dickie's wonderful goalkeeping, which included the saving of a penalty kick, was crowned near the end by two brilliant goals, following fast on each other, from Alec Smith's deadly left foot—30 *League matches without a defeat.* Dundee's cleverest forward in their match at Ibrox was the old Ranger, " Tommy " Low, but all his efforts were in vain. Alec Smith, who was at the very height of his powers during this period, brought the Rangers forwards along in overpowering fashion, and six goals were scored against Stewart, the Dundee custodian, who, be it noted, made some marvellous saves—31 *League matches without a defeat.*

While Rangers were defeating Dundee, the Hearts were, for the second time within two months, taking points from the Celtic, and the championship began to seem a very good thing for Ibrox. Before the next League engagement was entered the Glasgow Cup had been recovered. Celtic were beaten in the Final after two gruelling battles, and possibly the effects were telling when St. Bernards were encountered at Ibrox. In any case, Rangers got a scare, for after leading by 3–1 at the interval, they lost two goals in quick succession. D. Cameron, the St. Bernards centre, who, a season later, joined the Rangers, scored both in the same smart, quick way in which he got goals for the Ibrox team during the short time he was with them. The end was in sight and a point seemed doomed when " Jacky " Robertson drove home one of his " cannon balls " and won the match— 32 *played and not a defeat.* Hamilton scored all three goals against St. Mirren, at Paisley, after the Saints had crossed over a goal up, Ronald Orr, a great little forward, who went to Newcastle United and played twice against England—in 1902 and 1904—beating Dickie from a penalty kick—33 *League matches played and still undefeated.*

A sentimental and historic interest was attached to the thirteenth League match of the season. It was the last played on First Ibrox, the ground which, twelve years before, had been opened by Preston North-End under not very happy auspices. Times had changed. Rangers during their tenure of First, or Old Ibrox, had won the Scottish Cup three times, the Glasgow Cup five times, the Scottish League twice, and the Glasgow League also twice. Twice since masterful Preston North-End had charmed and discomfited the loyal Light Blue followers on that memorable Twentieth of August, 1887, had the Old Ibrox been enlarged, but now the club, like a lusty, vigorous boy, had outgrown its old garments. It was to be New Ibrox henceforth, the same Ibrox, more or less, that we see to-day. Not so dolorous as the prologue was the final act of the twelve-year drama. Kilmarnock, then newly promoted to the First Division, possessed several clever young players, notably James Howie and Robert Findlay (later of Celtic), but they lacked experience. Rangers won by 6 goals to 1—34 *League matches without a defeat.* In the next match, with St. Mirren, played at Meadowside by courtesy of Partick Thistle, the Saints did not play nearly so well as at Paisley, although they scored first. Rangers were frequently behind in the scoring in this season. They were inclined, sometimes, to become a little sleepy, but a goal for the other side was like the touch of a spur, and then away they would go at the gallop. Alec Smith whipped on the equaliser, Neil beat Patrick the second time, Hamilton got a third, and Neil a fourth from a penalty kick—35 *matches and still strangers to defeat.* Rangers were to see the year out with their long League sequence unimpaired by reverse. Everything comes to an end, however, and the first day of the New Year ended this grand record. Following the match with St. Mirren, the team went to Edinburgh and defeated St. Bernards by 1–0, but the League ordered a replay and St. Bernards later on closed the Rangers' campaign. New Ibrox was opened on 30th December, 1899, with an Inter-City League match against the Hearts. Chairman Henderson handed Captain Robert C. Hamilton a brand new ball, the first kick on the new turf was administered, and then the Light Blues proceeded to hansel Greatest Ibrox with a 3–1 victory. And to John Wilkie fell the distinction of scoring all three goals. A gold watch was offered by an ardent follower of the club to the player who scored the first goal on New Ibrox, but as this put the goalkeeper and the backs at a disadvantage, it was unanimously agreed that whoever won the watch would hand it to James Wilson, the trainer.

Two days later, in their seventh match within ten days, the Rangers' record was broken. They went to Parkhead already assured of the Championship, but keen, nevertheless, to win against their doughty rivals, the Celtic. True to tradition, the Celts, who had been four times defeated in the League and had been playing not too well, rose to the occasion. Marshall, who had been out of the team, injured, was at centre-half again. He could always bring out his best for the great duels with the crusaders from

Ibrox, and in this game there is no doubt he exercised a powerful influence. Bell scored the first goal of the New Year, and although Alec Smith promptly equalised, Divers, another Celt who specialised against Rangers, got two more before the interval. A smartly-taken goal by Wilkie in the second half brought a draw within sight, but the strong defence of Davidson and Tom Turnbull (whose first game against the Rangers this was), baulked the keen Ibrox forwards. On the day's showing the better team won.

From 12th February, 1898, until this 1st January, 1900, Rangers had not suffered a single defeat in the League. They had played 35 matches (19 at home and 16 away), winning 31 and drawing 4. Sixty-six points were gained of a possible 70, and 145 goals were scored for the loss of 39. It was a record worthy of a great team and its managers, and is worth setting down, as shown on opposite page.

Following the Hearts to New Ibrox came Hibernian to be defeated by 3–0 in an Inter-City League match on the day after the Rangers' Scottish League record had been smirched. On the third day of the year, however, Everton walked into the new ground and became the first conquerors of the Rangers there. But that was merely an incident of no special value. These holiday matches and tours were enjoyable in their way, but they did not assist a team to keep up to the high-water mark of form. There is no doubt at all that the effects of the Rangers' Christmas tour contributed greatly to the New Year's day reverse at Parkhead. The " day-after " feeling is not a good companion with which to fight to preserve a great record. In the Scottish League, the Light Blues had still three games to play and they won the lot, so that they could now claim to have gone through two seasons

FIFTY YEARS OF FOOTBALL——1899-1900.

Date.	Opponents.				Goals.	Points.
1898.						
March 19	St. Bernards, -	-	Home,		8—1	2
April 9	Third Lanark,	-	Home,		0—0	1
,, 11	Celtic, - -	-	Away,		0—0	1
Aug. 20	Partick Thistle,	-	Home,		6—2	2
,, 27	St. Mirren,	-	Away,		3—1	2
Sept. 3	Hearts, - -	-	Away,		3—2	2
,, 10	Third Lanark,	-	Home,		4—1	2
,, 19	St. Bernards,	-	Away,		2—0	2
,, 24	Celtic, - · -	-	Away,		4—0	2
,, 26	Third Lanark,	-	Away,		3—2	2
Oct. 1	Hearts, - -	-	Home,		3—1	2
,, 8	Dundee, -	-	Away,		2—1	2
Nov. 5	Partick Thistle,	-	Away,		5—0	2
,, 19	Hibernian,	-	Away,		4—3	2
,, 26	Clyde, - -	-	Home,		8—0	2
Dec. 3	St. Bernards, -	-	Home,		5—2	2
,, 17	Dundee, -	-	Home,		7—0	2
,, 24	Hibernian,	-	Home,		10—0	2
,, 31	St. Mirren,	-	Home,		3—2	2
1899.						
Jan. 2	Celtic, - -	-	Home,		4—1	2
,, 7	Clyde, - -	-	Away,		3—0	2
Aug. 19	Third Lanark,	-	Away,		5—1	2
,, 26	Clyde, - -	-	Away,		6—2	2
Sept. 2	Hearts, - -	-	Home,		4—3	2
,, 9	Kilmarnock, -	-	Away,		4—2	2
,, 18	Hearts, - -	-	Away,		1—1	1
,, 25	Hibernian,	-	Home,		3—2	2
Oct. 8	Celtic, - -	-	Home,		3—3	1
,, 14	Clyde, - -	-	Home,		7—0	2
,, 21	Hibernian,	-	Away,		2—0	2
Nov. 4	Dundee, -	-	Home,		6—0	2
,, 25	St. Bernards,	-	Home,		4—3	2
Dec. 2	St. Mirren,	-	Away,		3—1	2
,, 9	Kilmarnock, -	-	Home,		6—1	2
,, 16	St. Mirren,	-	Home,		4—1	2
					145—39	66

In 1899-1900, both matches with Celtic were played at Parkhead, and
both matches with St. Bernards at Ibrox. Rangers' Home match with
St. Mirren was played at Meadowside Park.

151

of the League with only one defeat against them. Here
are the figures :—

		Played.	Won.	Lost.	Drn.	Goals. For.	Agst.	Points.
1898–99,	-	18	18	0	0	79	18	36
1899–1900,	-	18	15	1	2	69	27	32
		36	33	1	2	148	45	68

On the day that the club's last League match of the
season was played against St. Bernards, seven Rangers
players were assisting Scotland to defeat Wales, at
Aberdeen. One of the seven was Dickie. He had played
in every other League match during the season and
absolutely every League match of the previous season,
while in 1900-1 he was never absent during the
club's third successive and successful fight for the
Championship. That is to say, Dickie, during three
successive seasons, played in 55 League matches, the
highest possible being 56. He was dependable to the
minute.

In this season of **1899-1900**, the cup achievements of the
team were at once gratifying and disappointing. To
defeat the Celtic in the final ties of the Glasgow and Charity
cups, with a score for the two matches of 6–1, was all that
could be desired, but the balance was thrown on the wrong
side when Celtic, in the fourth round of the Scottish Cup,
won a replay at Parkhead by 4–0. The curious feature of
this disaster—it was regarded as such at the time, of
course—was the fact that in the first game at Ibrox, the
Light Blues should have had the issue safe by the interval.
The forwards played grand football in the open, but could
not finish. Five minutes after turning round, Alec Smith
romped away on one of his tearing runs and beat Dan
M'Arthur. From that point it was a game worth going

WILLIAM MACANDREW.

Honorary Secretary, 1892-93 and 1893-94. Honorary Treasurer, 1895-96, 1896-97, 1897-98, and 1898-99.

See page 52.

LEAGUE RECORD CHAMPIONS, 1898–1899.

Played 18 : Won 18 : Lost 0 : Drawn 0.

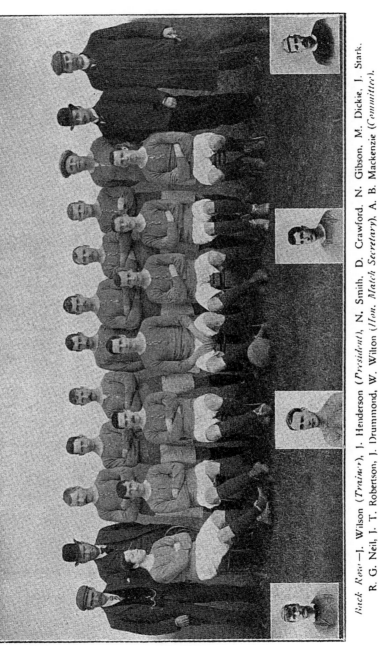

Back Row—J. Wilson (*Trainer*), J. Henderson (*President*), N. Smith, D. Crawford, N. Gibson, M. Dickie, J. Stark. R. G. Neil, J. T. Robertson, J. Drummond, W. Wilton (*Hon. Match Secretary*), A. B. Mackenzie (*Committee*).

Sitting—J. Campbell, J. Graham, J. MacPherson, R. C. Hamilton (*Captain*), F. Speedie, And. Sharp, A. Smith.

Insets—J. Miller, D. Mitchell, J. Wilkie, T. Hyslop.

See page 170.

miles to see. Campbell equalised for Celtic from a penalty kick and Bell gave them the lead. From having seemed likely winners, Rangers found themselves fighting to draw, but they were accustomed to be a goal down. It was their boast, that though sometimes defeated, they, like Napoleon's Old Guard, never surrendered. So, just to illustrate the point, John M'Pherson scored in the last minute. Everybody was happy—for one short week. Celtic's forwards in the replay struck a game of a lifetime. Their opponents also struck the game of a lifetime in the opposite sense. Hodge, who had a wicked way of scintillating against the Light Blues, scored the first goal, M'Mahon got the second, and after the interval Divers and Russell brought the Celtic total to four. I give the teams on that fateful day because the Rangers team was the same that defeated a slightly different Celtic in the Glasgow Cup final by 1–0 :—

> **Celtic.**—M'Arthur ; Davidson and Battles ; Russell, Marshall and Orr ; Hodge, Campbell, Divers, M'Mahon and Bell.

> **Rangers.** — Dickie ; N. Smith and Drummond ; Gibson, Neil and Robertson ; Graham, Wilkie, Hamilton, M'Pherson and A. Smith.

In the Glasgow Cup final, the Celtic backs were Turnbull and Storrier ; Battles was at right half and Russell at centre half, while Gilhooly was at inside right. Celtic went on to win the Scottish Cup with a 4–3 victory over Queen's Park in the Final. The tables were turned completely in the Charity Cup. In the Final, the Rangers' forwards played with dazzling effect. The Celtic defence had to give up five goals.

Thus, the Rangers finished the season champions of the League and holders of the Glasgow and Charity Cups.

just as in this year of their Jubilee, 1923. The team and individual honours, summarised, were :—

Scottish Cup		Glasgow Cup		Charity Cup	
Morton (H),	4–2	Third Lanark (A), 0–0		Third Lanark 2–0	
Maybole (H),	12–0	Third Lanark (H), 5–0		(Hampden)	
Partick Thistle (A),	6–1	Queen's Park (H), 7–3		Celtic	5–1
Celtic (H),	2–2	Celtic (Cathkin), 1–1		(Hampden)	
Celtic (A),	0–4	Celtic (Cathkin), 1–0			
	24–9		14–4		7–1

v. England	v. Wales	v. Ireland	v. English League
N. Smith.	M. Dickie.	N. Smith.	N. Smith.
J. Drummond.	N. Smith.	N. Gibson.	N. Gibson.
N. Gibson.	D. Crawford.	A. Smith.	J. T. Robertson.
J. T. Robertson.	R. G. Neil.		A. Smith.
A. Smith.	J. T. Robertson.		
	R. C. Hamilton.		
	A. Smith.		

1900—1901.

Two Notables—James Stark's Debut—Finlay
Speedie's Entry—One Match, One Medal—
A Cup and the League—Thriller with Celtic—
24 Caps.

PREPARATORY to the opening of season **1900-1901**,
there was a short period of hustle, a going to and
fro in search of a few new players and the
transferring of one or two from the Ibrox staff. James
Stark, a young half-back of Glasgow Perthshire, was
signed in May, 1900, and made his debut before the month
was out, the occasion being a match on behalf of the widow
and children of an old Vale of Leven stalwart, James
Wilson. Stark gave the club seven years' good service,
tried his fortunes with Chelsea for a season, returned to
Ibrox, and then joined the ranks of Greenock Morton.
Playing in a quiet, easy going manner, as if to say, " Why
worry about it ? we'll get there without any great fuss,"
Stark was none the less effective. He economised effort
by keeping his eye on the ball, and by anticipating its
flight, was usually in a position to embarrass the opponent
for whom a pass was intended. When James Quinn was
at the height of his powers as a scorer in the Celtic team,
no one was a greater hindrance to him than Stark. There
is a story told of Quinn going into a sports emporium to
purchase a ball for presentation purposes, and being asked
by the polite shopman, " Would he just take it with
him ? " " Oh, no," Quinn replied, with some alarm,
" If I met Jamie Stark, he would be sure to take it from
me." Stark became captain of the team, and he led a
Scottish eleven against England at the Crystal Palace in

1909, when, by the way, Quinn was in front of him once more but playing in the same direction.

A new forward named D. S. Cameron was secured from St. Bernards. It is curious that at this time George Livingstone might have become a Ranger. He had been developing rapidly in the Hearts' forward line, and negotiations were opened with the object of giving him as a partner to Alec Smith. But the terms stood in the way and he went to Sunderland instead, there to become a colleague of James Miller, who had come from Sunderland to Ibrox and found it easy to go back again since the people of Wearside held a very high opinion of his ability. Livingstone stayed a season with Sunderland, returned north to play for Celtic, and eventually, in January, 1907, did actually pull a light blue jersey over his head. "Elgin" Miller was transferred to Middlesbrough, Hyslop to Partick Thistle, and Graham to the Hearts, but only for a short period. The season had commenced before there came to Ibrox a forward who was afterwards to take a prominent part in shaping the fortunes of the club. This was Finlay Speedie, then a shining light in the ranks of Clydebank Juniors. He was signed in October, 1900, and his first cup-tie for Rangers was in the Final of the Glasgow Cup, against Partick Thistle, which the Light Blues won by 3–1. Speedie, therefore, had the possibly unique experience of winning a Glasgow Cup medal after playing in only one tie. In his first season, also, he gained a League championship award. From Ibrox he went to Newcastle United in 1907, and it is needless to say that his departure was regretted by followers of the club. Speedie and Smith were a magnificent left wing. From the day they first came together, which was against Dundee, at Ibrox, on 20th October, 1900, they took to each other like sweethearts. Speedie's low, accurate passes, given at the right angle for the Darvel man to pick up in his stride, gave to the wing play a beautiful rhythm which had been lacking since James Miller departed. Half the former burden was lifted from the shoulders of Smith, and the effect was seen in the rapid way he reached shooting distance and got goals. In the International against England in 1903, at Sheffield, the pair gave one of the finest exhibitions of wing combination ever witnessed in a representative match. The English outfield defence was completely mastered, and only superhuman goalkeeping by T. Baddeley, of Wolverhampton Wanderers, saved the Saxons from a very heavy defeat. As it was, the Scots won by 2 goals to 1.

This season of **1900-1** was notable for the admission to the League of Queen's Park. A question affecting the management of the First and Second Divisions threatened a serious rupture as between Rangers, Partick Thistle, and the Hearts on the one hand, and the remaining clubs on the other hand, but the breech was healed and all became good friends again. Rangers started off in great style in the League, but in their third game, against Kilmarnock, at Ibrox Park, Neil was severely injured and did not play again for three months. By a strange fatality, he made his re-appearance in the return match with Kilmarnock, at Rugby Park, and after 25 minutes, sustained a cut above the eye and could take no further part in the game. Stark thus secured his opportunity and he made excellent use of it. After playing four matches and winning them all, the Rangers had a gruelling Glasgow Cup-tie with Celtic, at Parkhead, which was drawn 3–3. Two days later, on the Edinburgh autumn holiday, they went through to Easter Road without Drummond and Neil to meet Hibernian. Up till then Hibernian had only once defeated the Rangers in the League, and few expected that they would improve their account that afternoon. What happened gave rise to a wonderful scene of enthusiasm among their followers. The younger members of the team played with extraordinary dash, and, as sometimes happens, every kick seemed to possess a telling value. Raisbeck, a brother of the International half-back, scored early in the game, and though Campbell equalised before the interval, it was all the Rangers could do to hold their own. The sensational act occurred in the second half, for Handling, Raisbeck, and Atherton scored in succession, and Rangers had to accept one of the heaviest defeats (4–1) ever sustained in the League. It was one of those incidents which come as a reminder that no team is invincible against the most modest of rivals. Even the winners were amazed at the success which crowned their efforts. But there was talent in that Hibernian team, and it came to full maturity in the following season when they conquered Rangers in the semi-final of the Scottish Cup and went on to win the trophy by a victory over Celtic in the Final. The Easter Road defeat threw the Light Blues two points behind Celtic, who were undefeated in six engagements. Before the great rivals met, at Parkhead, Celtic had surrendered two points in drawn games and they faced up level. Parkhead had seldom been a valley of delight for Rangers, although of late years they have been much happier in their results there. Their fault that day was the failure of Campbell and Smith on the wings. Divers scored for Celtic in the first half, and after Cameron had equalised, Celtic's Campbell got the winning goal. Hibernian, who were also making a strong bid for honours, suffered their first defeat on the same day, Morton beating them by 3–1 at Greenock. Celtic again took a two points lead over Rangers, but from that time onward, the Light Blues fought a winning fight and their ultimate triumph was attributable as directly to a fine spirit of determination as to actual cleverness. It was a good fighting team that wore the colours. They continued to revel in creating difficulties so that they should prove their ability to surmount them. In several of their matches they were behind at the interval, yet from the day they were defeated at Parkhead they never suffered a reverse in the League. Celtic, on the other hand, had to surrender to Kilmarnock, at Rugby Park : to the Hearts, at Parkhead : and to Dundee, at Parkhead. Before Rangers and Celtic met on New Year's day, at Ibrox, in the return fixture, the Light Blues had taken the lead in the race for the first time during the season. Almost everything depended upon the result here. Unfortunately, neither team was at full strength, but the reserves were capable and the match was regarded as a genuine test. As they lined up the sides were :—

> **Celtic.**—Donnelly ; Davidson and Storrier ; Russell, Lonie, and Orr ; M'Oustra, Divers, Campbell, M'Mahon, and Findlay.

> **Rangers.**—Dickie ; N. Smith and Drummond ; Gibson, Neil, and Robertson ; Graham, M'Pherson, Hamilton, Speedie, and Campbell.

Alec Smith was the absentee from the Rangers team and Celtic were without M'Arthur and Battles. This was William Lonie's first season with Celtic. He had played for them against Dundee a few weeks previously and a writer, lacking, evidently, the gift of insight, described him as " not class enough for League play." Findlay, the outside left, was the ex-Kilmarnock player, an exceptionally clever winger. Although Rangers were slightly the better team in the first half, they could not break through the stubborn defence of Davidson and Storrier, and there was no scoring up to the interval. In the second half, some magnificent forcing play by Robertson, the best player on the field that day, enabled Speedie to get into shooting position and the young one whipped on the first goal that meant, perhaps, a championship. Fifteen minutes later, M'Pherson, still gliding and wriggling through as blithely as ever, put on a second goal. The match thereupon was won, for although M'Mahon beat Dickie, after a corner kick, Rangers never were in danger. They now required only one point to make the championship their own for the third season in succession, and they got it, and another to keep it company in the next match with St. Mirren, at Paisley, where they won by 4–1.

In three successive seasons of the League, Rangers played a total of 56 matches, of which 50 were won, 3 lost, and 3 drawn. They scored 199 goals and lost 70. In this latest season of 1900-1, Dickie and Robertson did not miss one of the 20 matches of the campaign. Hamilton, Gibson, and M'Pherson played in 19. N. Smith, Campbell, and Drummond played in 18, and Alec Smith in 17. Stark, who was regarded as a reserve, took part in 12, and Speedie, who only came into the League team after nine matches had been played, never missed one afterwards, his appearances numbering 11.

It was not in the League, however, that Rangers had their most thrilling experience. This was reserved for the first round of the Glasgow Cup, with Celtic at Parkhead. The game had a sensational finish such as is seen only once in a lifetime. M'Mahon scored the only goal of the first half with one of his puzzling " headers," which always seemed so easy to save, from the spectators' standpoint, but were so utterly baffling to the goalkeeper. The second half had not long started when Storrier placed a free kick, and as he did so, M'Mahon ran between Smith and Crawford and was in front of Dickie when the ball came through so that he had an easy task scoring a second goal. In desperation, the Rangers half-backs and forwards made a massed attack and secured a goal, but with only eleven minutes to play they were still behind and seemed doomed. Then occurred a rapid series of incidents that staggered the huge crowd. A great roar signalled the equalising goal by Robertson who cut through his own forwards to clear the way for the shot. The echo of the cheers had scarcely died down when another great roar went up, for Hamilton had raced away and put Rangers in the lead for the first time. Here was a transformation. With two swift, dramatic strokes Rangers had turned certain defeat into as certain victory. So it seemed. But the drama was not over yet. Twenty seconds from the end, with the intense excitement gnawing at the hearts of the onlookers, Hodge ran past Crawford, and with practically the last kick of the match, laid the ball into the net. It was a case of won, lost, drawn for Celtic, and for Rangers, lost, won, drawn. Hamilton played inside left in this match with Cameron at centre, but in the replay, at Ibrox, the positions were reversed with good results. It is doubtful if the forwards gave a finer exhibition all season. Cameron sent Rangers on the lead after twenty minutes, and though Campbell scored twice for Celtic before the interval, the Rangers' front line was moving so confidently that there was no alarm among the club's followers. This optimism was completely justified. Scarcely had the second half begun when Hamilton headed the equaliser from Campbell's centre. A third goal, also by Hamilton, followed quickly, and when Campbell came along with a fourth, the issue was as good as settled, although with events of the previous Saturday in mind, everybody discreetly withheld conclusions. In a last effort to rally the Celts, Battles went to centre forward, and just to show the uncertainty of things, Findlay beat Dickie with only a minute or two to go. So, Rangers just ran home with a score of 4-3, and when they beat Third Lanark in the semi-final by 2-1, they were favourites to win the Cup, especially as the Cathkin team had been growing stronger and stronger. John Cross was at centre half, and he held such a good grip of Cameron, who began the game at centre for Rangers, that Hamilton had again to take over his favourite position. This was the difficulty with the team at this time, for neither Cameron nor Hamilton was suited to inside left. But the problem was solved by the coming of Finlay Speedie, and in the Final against Partick Thistle, at Parkhead, the formation was as shown in the teams appended :—

> **Rangers.**—Dickie ; N. Smith and Drummond ; Gibson, Stark, and Robertson ; Campbell, M'Pherson, Hamilton, Speedie, and A. Smith.

> **Partick Thistle.**—Wilkie ; Kay and Haggart ; Harvey, Proudfoot, and Goudie ; Atherton, M'Nicol, Campbell, Hyslop, and Muirhead.

The Thistle were weakened by the absence of Freebairn and Gibbons. Campbell, who played centre, was a back. Goudie, the left half, was a Rangers reserve transferred, and Hyslop was the same Tom who had helped to win the Cup for the club he was now trying to keep from winning it. He scored the Thistle's only goal after M'Pherson, Robertson and Hamilton had given Rangers a lead of three. This was the Thistle's second appearance in the Final of the Glasgow Cup, which they have never won.

For their defeat in the Glasgow Cup, Celtic were fully compensated by a victory over Rangers in the first round of the Scottish Cup, at Parkhead. M'Pherson having turned ill, could not play, and Andrew Sharp had to be brought back from Morton, to whom he had been transferred. The Celtic had Quinn available, but he was regarded as too inexperienced to be played in a match of such great importance. He could not have done any worse than any of the ten forwards who did play. The certain consequences of defeat seemed to weigh heavily upon the two teams, and a match that had aroused great expectations fell absolutely flat. The goal that decided it was in keeping with the setting. Twenty-two minutes after the start, Findlay took a corner kick for Celtic, and Drummond, in trying to clear, put the ball past Dickie. In the last half hour, Rangers threw themselves into a forlorn effort to save the tie. M'Arthur, in making one of his daring saves, was injured, and Divers went into goal. Even then Rangers could not beat down the defence. Their light forwards were foiled by the stalwarts opposed to them. Battles, Davidson, Russell, and Orr were all big men, and Lonie was not a mite. Celtic went right through to the Final and were defeated by the Hearts in a memorable match at Ibrox by 4-3.

Before the Charity Cup ties came on, Rangers and Celtic met in two Inter-City League matches, each winning at home, Rangers by 4–2 and Celtic by 1–0. I think it is correct to say that, in the Ibrox match, Quinn made his first appearance at centre. He scored the first goal, but despite that, when the teams met in the first round of the Charity Cup, at the Exhibition grounds, at Gilmorehill, he was on the wing again. Neither side could score, so they came at each other on the following evening when neither M'Pherson nor Alec Smith was able to play. George Livingstone made his debut for Celtic and partnered Quinn on the left wing. Again the Rangers forwards were beaten for physique, but Nick Smith and Drummond, and also Dickie put up a grand defence, and the only goal lost was snapped by Hodge ten minutes after the cross-over. Thus, over the season, the two great rivals had provided their adherents with a mixed dish. Each won a Scottish League and an Inter-City League duel, Celtic beat Rangers in the Scottish and Charity Cup, and Rangers won the Glasgow Cup-tie. But while the Rangers could win the League Championship and Glasgow Cup, their redoubtable rivals were left barren of trophies. The Hearts had literally swept the Scottish Cup from their grasp, and in the Final of the Charity Cup, Third Lanark were victorious over them by 3–0.

The Rangers Cup record for the season of 1900-1 is summarised so :—

Scottish Cup.		Glasgow Cup.		Charity Cup.	
Celtic (A),	0–1	Celtic (A),	3–3	Celtic,	0–0
		Celtic (H),	4–3	(Exhibition)	
		Third Lanark (H),	2–1	Celtic,	0–1
		Partick Thistle		(Exhibition)	
		(Celtic Park),	3–1		
	0–1		12–8		0–1

Of individual honours the team received a generous share, but not, you may be certain, without justification based upon merit, for Scotland did not lose a single International match. Here is the list :—

v. England.	v. Ireland.	v. Wales.	v. English Leag	v. Irish League.
J. Drummond.	N. Smith.	N. Smith.	N. Smith.	N. Smith.
J.T.Robertson.	J.T.Robertson.	J.T.Robertson.	J. Drummond.	N. Gibson.
R.C.Hamilton.	R.C.Hamilton.	N. Gibson.	J.T.Robertson.	J. M'Pherson.
A. Smith.	A. Smith.	A. Smith.	N. Gibson.	A. Smith.
	J. Campbell.		R. G. Neil.	
			R.C.Hamilton.	
			A. Smith.	

Robertson captained the Scottish team against England, which drew 2–2, at the Crystal Palace. Hamilton scored one of Scotland's goals. Neil was captain of the League team against the English League, at Ibrox, which won by 6–2 after a perfectly brilliant exhibition of forward play.

The forward line was R. Walker, J. Campbell (Celtic), R. S. M'Coll, R. C. Hamilton, and A. Smith. Hamilton scored three goals and Smith one. Scotland defeated Ireland, at Celtic Park, by 11–0. Hamilton scored four goals and Campbell two. Scotland drew with Wales 1–1, at Wrexham, and Robertson scored the goal. The Scottish League defeated the Irish League, at Belfast, by 2–1, and the two goals were scored by Alec Smith and Nicol Smith. Gibson was chosen to play against England but withdrew. Hamilton was chosen to play against the Irish League but withdrew. Against the Anglo-Scots, in the trial game, which was then a serious test for caps, the Home team was practically a Rangers composition. N. Smith, Drummond, Gibson, Neil, Robertson, Campbell, Hamilton, and A. Smith all played. The Home Scots made a draw of 0–0 with a powerful Anglo-Scots eleven. Pretty much a case of Rangers versus England, Wales, and Ireland, you might say.

1901—1902.

The Disaster—Hazardous Campaign—The Exhibition
Cup—Won and Lost—Greatest League Struggle—
Championship Gained—New Players.—John Walker
—Wm. Lennie.

FROM the standpoint of those most closely associated
with the club, including, of course, the more ardent
followers who had no other investment than their
enthusiasm, the season of **1901-1902** was both poignant
and cheerful, to an extent not exceeded since the Rangers
strode on to the stage.   With practically the same team
that had retained the League Championship and the Glasgow
Cup in the previous season, a brilliant start was made with
the winning of the Glasgow Exhibition Cup, one of the
most beautiful trophies ever offered for competition.
Such value did the club place upon it that it was insured
for £100, though the risk of losing it by accident was
entirely their own, for they won it outright.   The Glasgow
Cup was held for a third successive year, although, in this
case, it has to be pointed out that the Final with Celtic
was not decisive.   After a drawn match, played at Ibrox,
Celtic declined to replay there, and the Glasgow F.A.
awarded the Cup to the Rangers, the only thing they
possibly could do.   Reaching the semi-final of the Scottish
Cup, the Light Blues succumbed at Ibrox to a clever
Hibernian team, and then went on to win the League
championship for the fourth consecutive season.   There
was something in these achievements which was entirely
satisfying, but everything was clouded over by the
catastrophe of 5th April, 1902, when, during the International match between England and Scotland, a portion
of the west terracing on Ibrox Park gave way, causing the

166

death of over a score of people and injury to several hundreds. The exact figures were, 25 killed, 24 dangerously injured, 168 seriously injured, 153 injured, and 172 slightly injured. This was the saddest day in the whole history of the Rangers club. The officials had done everything that was humanly possible to obtain guarantees that the new structures, upon which they had lavished great expense, were safe for the spectators. It was a terrible price to pay for the lesson which all clubs catering for huge crowds learned from the disaster. Nothing except solid earth could be trusted to withstand the sway of a great mass of spectators. Splendid and noble were the services rendered by football and athletic organisations throughout the kingdom to provide financial assistance to those who had suffered. It is impossible to do justice in mere words to the spontaneous generosity shown not only by Scottish clubs, but by the Football Association and the Football League of England, and by individual clubs south of the Border. From far off South Africa, Scottish " exiles " who had loved the game when at home, and loved it still, sent contributions. During the remainder of the season, the energy of the Rangers executive was devoted more to organising relief than to winning matches. It was decided to offer the Exhibition Cup for competition. No conditions were laid down. In the altered circumstances, the risk of losing possession of a trophy more prized, perhaps, than any honour yet gained, was considerable, but it was not a time to dwell upon a detail of that kind. The Exhibition Cup became the British League Cup. Sunderland and Everton, as champions and runners-up, respectively, of the English League, and Rangers and Celtic, as holders of similar positions in the Scottish League, entered the lists. Celtic defeated Sunderland and Rangers defeated Everton, and so, once again, the two old Glasgow rivals found themselves in the arena. This time Celtic won by 3–2, after two hours of strenuous contest.

When the cup was presented by the Exhibition authorities, the competition was put in charge of members of the Scottish League Committee. On the motion of the Celtic representative, it was agreed that it become the property of the club that won it, with the option of handing it over to the League for annual competition. Rangers had scarcely had time to study the elegant design of their guerdon, when suggestions were made in certain public prints that they would shortly give it over to the League. Very likely they would have done so after a reasonable and courteous interval. The disaster created a new and unexpected means of bringing the trophy into competition, but it did not necessarily destroy the excellent proposal of the Celtic representative that it might be offered to the League. To swell the funds in the Glasgow Charity Cup-ties, clubs outside of the city were invited to take part, and in the first round Rangers were defeated by Hibernian, by 1–0. Such, in brief outline, is the story of 1901–2.

John Wilkie came back from Middlesbrough, where he had tarried a while ; David M'Dougall, an Irvine Meadow XI. product, who had once had a brief spell with Bristol, was brought back from Partick Thistle ; new players were Noble M'Pherson, a St. Johnstone goalkeeper ; J. R. Hamilton, a forward, and brother of " R. C." ; Hugh Morton, a half-back, from Darvel ; Hugh May, a forward from Wishaw United, and brother of John May ; and George Young, a back, from Beith. None of the new men managed to supplant any of the old ones. M'Dougall was a clever outside right, and he did excellent work in the earlier games before Campbell took charge of that position.

The Exhibition Cup, the ties in which were all played at Gilmorehill, was brought on in August. It evoked very great interest, and the matches were all watched by big crowds. The ground was neutral all the way through, thus fulfilling an ideal condition for cup-ties. A fair field and no favour was the order, and, with the pick of Scottish clubs accepting the invitation to bid for the prize, the honour of winning it was rightly regarded as equal to a triumph in the Scottish Cup. As there is no record of the ties easily available, the results should be of wide interest :—

First Round.

Third Lanark,	-	- 3	Morton,	-	-	- 1
Rangers,	- -	- 8	St. Mirren,	-	-	1
Celtic,	- -	- 1	Hibernian,	-	-	0
Hearts,	- -	- 2	Queen's Park, -		-	1

Semi-Final.

Rangers,	- -	- 4	Third Lanark,		-	1
Celtic,	- -	- 2	Hearts,	-	-	- 1

Final.

Rangers,	- -	- 3	Celtic,	-	-	- 1

Those who witnessed the Final with Celtic will remember the hum of excitement that ran through the game. The pace on a hardened pitch was tremendously fast. The play was worthy of two great teams. It fell to Campbell, the brilliant Celtic forward, to score the first goal after one of his long, puzzling dribbling runs for which he was equally famous in England and Scotland. The whole Celtic team seemed inspired by this fine individual feat, and for a short spell Speedie had to fall back to assist in stemming the attack. Drummond and Neil were glorious defenders. In time, the Rangers' forwards began

M   169

to get the ball again. Some quick combination on the wings and a low pass through the centre gave Hamilton one of his favourite opportunities. Away he raced for goal and M'Farlane was powerless to save the long swinging shot. From that point, the Light Blues never looked back. Fifteen minutes after crossing over, Neil crashed on a second goal in the thick of a storming onslaught, and seven minutes from the end, Hamilton made victory—a great and deserved victory—secure with a third goal. The teams which took part in this memorable contest, creditable alike to vanquished and victor, were :—

> **Rangers.**—Dickie ; Smith and Drummond ; Stark, Neil, and Gibson ; M'Dougall, Wilkie, Hamilton, Speedie, and Smith.
>
> **Celtic.**—M'Farlane; Davidson and Battles ; Moir, Marshall, and Hynds ; Hodge, Livingstone, Campbell, Drummond, and Quinn.

" Jacky " Robertson had got a splinter in his eye while at work and he did not play until the Glasgow Cup Final, also against Celtic, when he took the place of M'Dougall at outside right, the latter having been injured in the match at Gilmorehill. The deplorable dispute to which the Glasgow Cup Final gave rise was regretted by the Rangers as keenly as by others. It was not of their making, however. The Glasgow F.A. Committee selected Ibrox Park for the match by 4 votes to 3, and when a draw resulted, the Committee, by a similar vote, decided that the replay should also take place there. Celtic, however, took the view that Rangers should, voluntarily, have agreed to replay at Parkhead. Rangers were unwilling, but offered to play on neutral ground. Celtic declined to replay anywhere except at Parkhead. They scratched, and the Cup went to the Rangers for the third year in succession. It is not the function of this historical sketch to apportion blame but merely to state the facts. Had the Glasgow F.A. Committee ordered the replay at Parkhead, Rangers would have gone there. No Final was played on the ground of a competing club from that year until 1916-17, when Celtic and Clyde agreed to decide the issue at Parkhead. In the following season Rangers and Partick Thistle decided the Final on Ibrox. We are not in Paradise yet. These little discordant notes merely emphasise the harmony which, on the whole, prevails amongst members of the great football fraternity.

With the Exhibition Cup and the Glasgow Cup in custody, Rangers set out to hold the League championship. They had already created a record by winning it three years in succession, and to embellish the record seemed well within their powers. That was the popular belief when they went to Kilmarnock for their opening engagement. But popular belief got a rude surprise, for Kilmarnock, in the height of a storm, rattled on three goals in the first fifteen minutes against the wind and won by 4–2, giving rise to a demonstration of joy such as had never been witnessed on dear old Rugby Park. It was the first victory in history of Kilmarnock over Rangers in a match of any importance, and on that account the men who worked the awful havoc deserve to have their names inscribed. They were :—

Craig ; Busby and Agnew ; M'Pherson, Anderson, and Mitchell ; Reid, Wylie, Graham, Howie, and Norwood.

It is a fair assumption that in the victorious team there would be no happier man than M'Pherson, a David who was a slayer of the Goliaths. He was an old Rangers warrior, glad of the chance to show that he had still a kick in him. This was not the only staggering blow the Rangers were to receive in the League. They won their next five games easily, but in their seventh match, Hibernian brought them up with a jerk, at Ibrox. Gibson and Robertson were both out of commission, but Hibernian were a grand young team, rendered splendidly confident by the lockfast security of Harry Rennie, in goal. There was no finer custodian in Britain at that time, and no team that could play a more virile, dashing game. They were the severest antagonists the Rangers encountered during the season. They beat the Light Blues in the semi-final of the Scottish Cup, again at Ibrox, and in the first round of the Charity Cup, and all Rangers had to put against that catalogue was a 3–2 win in the League at Easter Road. When the Rangers lost a point in a drawn game with Third Lanark, at Cathkin Park, in the next match, their chance of winning another flag seemed next to hopeless. Hugh Wilson, once a member of the greatest Sunderland team, and Wm. Maxwell, who played against England in 1898, were in the Third Lanark ranks. This drawn game put the Rangers four points behind Celtic, who had played eight matches and lost only one point. As it happened, Celtic were due at Ibrox on the following Saturday. A great deal depended upon the result. Nothing but a win seemed to be of any use to the Rangers, and as they could only draw, many of their followers stopped thinking of the championship. The Rangers team, with the exception of Campbell for M'Dougall, was the same that had won the Exhibition Cup. Celtic had Watson for Davidson at back, Orr for Hynds (transferred to Manchester City) at half-back, and Crawford and M'Mahon in place of Hodge and Drummond forward. Stark accidentally put the ball past Dickie early in the game and gave the Celtic the lead, but before the interval Neil equalised. Thirty-five minutes after the change of goals, Speedie put Rangers ahead, and until two minutes from the end victory appeared secure. Then Livingstone—the same George—bolted through the Ibrox defence and gave Quinn an opening to equalise. If some of the pessimistic followers thereupon threw up the sponge, the team didn't. They were not the old invincible confederacy, but they could fight. Against all the odds they went through to Edinburgh, following the match with Celtic, and beat Hibernian, who led by 2-1 until a few minutes from the finish. Stark put another ball past Dickie—poor Dickie!—but Wilkie equalised, and after the Hibs. had again taken the lead, Alec Smith came away in a great burst of brilliance and paved the way for two rapid goals by Neil, the first of these from a penalty kick. Hundreds of people had left the ground under the impression that the Rangers were a beaten team. A few things occurred within a day or so of this event which, though not bearing directly upon the Rangers' history, had a certain interest for them. R. S. M'Coll who, later, became a wearer of the Light Blue, left Queen's Park to join Newcastle United, and played his first match for the Tyneside team on 9th November, 1901. He was not in the Hampden team which opposed Rangers five days previously, which fact was deplored by the amateurs, who lost by only 2-1. Celtic transferred David Storrier to Dundee and got Thomas M'Dermott, a good forward, in exchange. R. Findlay returned to Kilmarnock from Celtic. By this time Celtic's lead had been reduced to three points, but a third serious blow to the Rangers restored to the Parkhead club their five points superiority. Third Lanark went to Ibrox and won by 4-1. There was some excuse for this crushing reverse even if the merits of the winners were freely admitted. Speedie and Hamilton were absent, Drummond broke down near the interval, and Robertson, who was playing at inside left, was injured towards the close. These things told in the second half when Third Lanark got three of their goals, scored by Maxwell (2) and Maconnachie. James Brownlie kept goal and performed some wonderful saving. Sloan, M'Cue, and Hugh Wilson were a half-back trio who had both height and skill at command.

Even the Mark Tapleys at Ibrox now began to push aside the idea of championship. Five points behind Celtic and only four matches to play! It seemed a sure job for the undertaker. But suddenly, as in the twinkling of an eye almost, the struggle took on a new phase. In successive matches Celtic were defeated by the Hearts, at Parkhead (2–1), and Queen's Park, at Hampden (3–2). Rangers, meantime, had defeated Morton, at Ibrox, and so from being five points in arrears, they were now only one behind the Parkhead rival. Would they reach the winning post in front, after all? Celtic, in their sixteenth engagement, could only draw with Hibernian at Parkhead, and thus, in three successive games, had surrendered the five points' advantage held three weeks previously. The situation was painfully exciting. It was rendered more so when Celtic, in their last match but one, beat Kilmarnock, and stood 26 points with only Rangers to meet at Parkhead on New Year's day. Rangers had now 20 points for 14 matches. A victory for Celtic on New Year's day would give the flag to Parkhead. That Ne'erday match will not readily be forgotten by those who had the doubtful privilege of seeing it. Here were the teams :—

Celtic.—M'Farlane ; Watson and Battles ; Lonie, Marshall, and Orr ; Hodge, Livingstone, Campbell, M'Mahon, and M'Oustra.

Rangers.—Dickie ; N. Smith and Drummond ; Gibson, Neil, and Robertson ; Campbell, Wilkie, Hamilton, Speedie, and A. Smith.

The referee was Mr. Nisbet of Cowdenbeath, which fact is an essential point in the story, as will be learned directly. From the outset it was apparent that the players were on edge. The spectators added fuel to the furnace by cheering every kick. The championship was at stake, and everybody knew, and felt, it. Early in the game, Battles placed a free kick and M'Mahon headed the ball past Dickie. Not long afterwards Nicol Smith had his turn of taking a free kick. He sent the ball towards M'Farlane, and there was a dash for it by a crowd of players. Then it was seen in the net, but the Celtic vigorously protested that it had not touched anyone on the way. Referee Nisbet thought otherwise and awarded a goal which occasioned a storm of protest. At half-time the score was unaltered. Five minutes after the interval Hamilton pushed the ball out to Campbell who went in to score. Celtic claimed that Campbell had handled, but the referee differed again. Immediately he was surrounded by expostulating Celts, and under the impression that M'Mahon had attempted to trip him, he ordered the famous Celt off the field. It seemed for a moment or two as if some of the Parkhead team would leave the field in a body, but John Campbell, the centre forward, took the ball to the spot and prepared to kick off. His lead was followed, and shortly afterwards, Robertson scored a fine goal following a corner kick. Twenty minutes from the end, Marshall scored for Celtic who were playing desperately to equalise when Hamilton got the ball sent up to him, and, racing right up the field, scored a fourth goal. Celtic disputed this goal also, on the ground of offside. The match finished amidst a great clamour among the crowd, but the last was not yet heard of it. Celtic protested against short time having been played, but when the matter came before the League, Mr. J. H. M'Laughlin, on behalf of the Celtic, explained that the protest had only been lodged in order to bring before the League certain statements which Mr. Nisbet was alleged to have made to an Edinburgh and a Glasgow newspaper. Mr. Nisbet refused to answer questions put to him by the Committee and he was struck off the roll of referees.

So now the Rangers, with three games to play, could win the championship by acquiring five more points. Their three matches were with Queen's Park, at Hampden, and St. Mirren and Dundee at Ibrox. Queen's Park were beaten by 1–0, Robertson, playing outside right, scoring the goal. Three points were yet necessary. Against St. Mirren, the situation was desperately bad. Neil, Crawford, and Drummond were all injured. No sooner had the defence been patched up when word arrived that Dickie was down with influenza. In their dilemma, the officials turned once again to the old campaigner, John M'Pherson. He stepped between the posts. He lost two goals which nobody could have saved, but Speedie scored two beauties, and another ball struck a St. Mirren back and went into the net, the Rangers winning by 3–2. Now they were level with Celtic at 26 points, and had only to draw with Dundee to become champions. Rangers had not forgotten that a defeat from Dundee in 1898 had then given Celtic the championship, but now only Longair was left of the brave Dundonian band. But though Rangers had still eight members of the old team left, Dickie, Neil, Wilkie, and Campbell were injured and could not serve. Noble, M'Pherson, Graham, and J. R. Hamilton were drafted in, and so well did the team play that three goals were scored in the first half, " R. C.," " J. R.," and Speedie getting them. Turnbull scored for Dundee, but Rangers were always winning ; and so, for the fourth year in succession, the Championship came to Ibrox. In all their career the club never gained such a splendid uphill triumph.

In the four successive years in which the championship was won the record was :—

	Played	Won	Lost	Drawn	Goals For	Goals Against	Points
1898-99, -	18	18	0	0	79	18	36
1899-1900,	18	15	1	2	69	27	32
1900-1, -	20	17	2	1	60	25	35
1901-2, -	18	13	3	2	43	29	28
	74	63	6	5	251	99	131

One of the most remarkable features of this combined success was the fact that ten players were with the club in the four campaigns. Of the grand total of 74 matches played, Matthew Dickie took part in 70. The number of games played by the ten who shared in the four championships were as follows :—

	1898-99	1899-1900	1900-1	1901-2	Total
M. Dickie, -	18	17	20	15	70
R. C. Hamilton,	18	16	19	16	69
A. Smith, -	18	16	17	18	69
N. Gibson, -	18	16	19	13	66
R. G. Neil, -	18	15	9	16	58
N. Smith, -	13	10	18	15	56
J. Campbell, -	16	8	18	12	54
J. Drummond,	6	16	18	12	52
J. M'Pherson,	15	13	19	5	52
D. Crawford, -	17	8	4	8	37

The Scottish Cup story of this season of 1901-2 centres in the semi-final tie with Hibernian, at Ibrox. Johnstone, Inverness Caledonian, and Kilmarnock were defeated in turn. Hibernian had been showing consistent form of a high standard since their last meeting with the Light Blues and they came full of confidence. The Rangers half-backs failed to cope adequately with the nimble Easter Road forwards, but Smith and Drummond were putting up a resolute defence when Divers, whom the Hibs. had secured from Celtic, scored near the interval from a position which many impartial onlookers regarded as offside. Early in the second half M'Pherson had to retire for good with an injury sustained previous to half-time. M'Geachan scored a fine second goal for Hibernian and made the victory legitimate and thoroughly deserved. Near the close, M'Cartney got his right leg broken, and playing a man short, the Hibernian triumph was the more meritorious. They met and defeated Celtic in the Final by 1–0 at Parkhead, and supplemented this achievement by winning the Glasgow Charity Cup, again defeating Celtic in the final by 6–2. In that season the Hibs. also won the Rosebery Cup and the M'Crae Cup.

This was John M'Pherson's last match for Rangers. He could have wished to signalise his farewell to the game in more auspicious circumstances, but he could look back on a magnificent record of personal achievement. He had played goal, back, half-back and forward for the team, had won three Scottish Cup medals, had played in 15 of the 18 League matches in 1898-99, when not a single point was lost, and had gained 13 International honours. Fortunate the club to possess such a man and a player !

By the time the Charity ties were commenced, Rangers had signed William Lennie, of Queen's Park, an outside right, who had graduated from the Maryhill junior team ; John Walker, of Liverpool, an all-round forward, who had

been with the Hearts before going South ; and Alec Mackie,
of Raith Rovers. These players took part in the first
round tie against Hibernian, who won by a goal from a
shot by Callaghan that went into the net off Drummond.
Rangers did not mind the Charity Cup defeat, but they
were keen upon holding the Exhibition Cup, now the
British League Cup. The Final with Celtic was played
on 17th June, at Cathkin Park, with the teams as
follows :—

> Celtic.—M'Pherson ; Davidson and Battles ; Lonie,
> Marshall, and Orr ; Crawford, Campbell, Quinn, M'Dermott,
> and Hamilton.

> Rangers.—Dickie ; N. Smith and Crawford ; Gibson,
> Stark, and Robertson ; Lennie, Walker, Hamilton,
> Speedie, and A. Smith.

This was the first season of David Hamilton with Celtic.
Somers was then playing with Blackburn Rovers, but the
two became a great left-wing partnership in the Parkhead
team in later years when Quinn was centre and Bennett and
M'Menemy were the right wing. In this Final, Quinn
scored all three Celtic goals. He got the first after seven
minutes from a centre by Hamilton. Fifteen minutes
later he scored a second goal, but before the interval
Speedie twice registered. There was no scoring in the
second half and the extra half-hour was over all but 30
seconds when Lonie ran up the wing and secured a corner
from which Quinn scored the winning goal and took the
Cup to Parkhead. Thus ended a long and hazardous
season. As is well known, the International match at
Ibrox was declared unofficial, and was replayed at
Birmingham some weeks later as the official fixture, the
result in each case being a draw—1–1 and 2–2. N. Smith,
Drummond, Robertson, and A. Smith played in both

matches. The season's Cup achievements and individual honours gained were :—

Exhibition Cup.		Scottish Cup.		Glasgow Cup.	
St. Mirren,	8–1	Johnstone (H),	6–1	Normal Ath. (H),	5–0
Third Lanark,	4–1	Inverness		A Bye.	
		Caley. (H),	5–1		
Celtic (Final),	3–1	Kilmarnock (H),	2–0	Partick Thistle (H),	4–1
		Hibernian (H),	0–2	Celtic (H),	2–2
	15–3		13–4		11–3

Charity Cup.		British League Cup.	
Hibernian,	0–1	Everton (A),	1–1*
(Cathkin)		Everton (CelticPark),	3–2*
		Celtic (Cathkin),	2–3*
	0–1		6–6

* After Extra Time.

v. England.	v. Ireland.	v. Wales.	v. English L'gue.	v. Irish League.
N. Smith.	N. Smith.	J. Drummond.	N. Smith.	J. Graham.
J. Drummond.	J. Drummond.	J. T. Robertson.	N. Gibson.	J. M'Pherson.
J. T. Robertson.	J. T. Robertson	R. C. Hamilton.	A. Smith.	
A. Smith.	R. C. Hamilton.	A. Smith.		
	A. Smith.			

Hamilton scored three goals against Ireland and Alec Smith one. Robertson and Smith each scored one goal against Wales. Nicol Smith was chosen to play against Wales but withdrew. Hamilton requested that he should not be chosen against the English League owing to his having to sit for an examination. Graham and M'Pherson were on the reserve strength of the club when chosen to play against the Irish League.

1902—1903.

ALL good Rangers people should have a special reverence for the season of 1902-3, It was the season in which the Scottish Cup was last brought to Ibrox, and, strange to say, the Cup was the only honour won. Since then, Rangers have been in five Scottish Cup finals and have been defeated by Celtic, Third Lanark, Partick Thistle, and Morton. In 1908-9 the Cup was withheld after a riot at Hampden Park. The most coveted of trophies is not always won by the best team in the country, despite the fact that it is supposed to stand for absolute supremacy. In 1921 and 1922, when Rangers were in the final and did not win the Cup, they were probably the finest combination in Scotland. In this season of 1902-3, when they defeated the Hearts in the Final, they were probably not the most talented side from John o' Groat's to Berwick. They were defeated five times in the League and Hibernian were defeated only once. The first round of the Glasgow Cup ended their interest in the ties, for Third Lanark beat them by 1–0. A similar adverse score by St. Mirren in the first round of the Charity Cup relieved them of further anxiety in that direction. What happened was that in the Scottish Cup games of 1902-3 the team was fortunate to strike a high level of all-round excellence. They had no dark streaks and they certainly were not favoured by luck. The Cup success was the more remarkable, because, owing to the outlays necessitated by the disaster at Ibrox Park in the previous April, every penny had to be given its full value. No fewer than 22 players were placed on the transfer list simply because there was no money to pay them. Among the 22 were John Wilkie and John Campbell. Before the season was very old, however, it became necessary to reinforce both the defence and attack. Alexander Fraser, of Clydebank Juniors, a clever young athlete, soon made himself a fixture in the back division, for Nicol Smith had to go to Matlock House, Manchester, to have an injured knee treated, and David Crawford was not able to devote as much time as formerly to the game. Angus Macdonald was secured to make good the weakness at outside right, and he made his debut in John Drummond's benefit match in August.

Drummond was now the veteran of the team. He joined in March, 1892, about a year earlier than Nicol Smith. He was in the eleven that first won the Scottish Cup for the Rangers in 1894, and he was likewise a member of the teams that captured the Cup in 1897, 1898, and 1903. He is the only Rangers player who figured in all four Finals won by the Light Blues, as will be seen from the following list of

Rangers' Teams which won the Scottish Cup.

1893-94.	1896-97.	1897-98.	1902-3.
D. Haddow.	M. Dickie.	M. Dickie.	M. Dickie.
N. Smith.	N. Smith.	N. Smith.	A. Fraser.
J. Drummond.	J. Drummond.	J. Drummond.	J. Drummond.
R. Marshall.	N. Gibson.	N. Gibson.	G. Henderson.*
A. M'Creadie.	A. M'Creadie.	R. G. Neil.	J. Stark.
D. Mitchell.	D. Mitchell.	D. Mitchell.	J. Robertson.
J. Steel.	T. Low.	J. Miller.	A. Macdonald.
H. M'Creadie.	J. M'Pherson.	J. M'Pherson.	A. Mackie.*
J. Gray.	J. Miller.	R. C. Hamilton.	R. C. Hamilton.
J. M'Pherson.	T. Hyslop.	T. Hyslop.	F. Speedie.
J. Barker.	A. Smith.	A. Smith.	A. Smith.

* In the 1902-3 Final, the Rangers played three games with the Hearts. In the first two games, N. Gibson and John Walker played. Owing to injuries, their places in the deciding game were taken by George Henderson and Alec Mackie.

Strong and fearless, Drummond was not the kind of player to win sweet compliments from opponents. He could give hard knocks and he could take them. The game of football he looked upon as a virile man's game, and he went about his work with a breezy disregard for the gentle feelings of all and sundry. With sleeves up to the elbow and the inevitable cap drawn well down over his eyes, " Jock " cut a very defiant and very formidable figure. But though he seemed fierce, with a poise of challenge and an aggressively set jaw, there was humour in the eyes. He took risks, at times, in making a swift pounce at the man on the ball, for a miss meant delay in getting round, but he and Nicol Smith had an almost perfect understanding, and Dickie knew exactly what was intended by the various moves that took place in front of him. Smith and Drummond! For years these two names stood for the most powerful sectional defence in the country. Except for occasional periods when Drummond went off his game or Smith was injured, they were comrades-in-arms for well nigh ten and a half seasons. Death severed the partnership in January, 1905, when Nicol Smith was called away. Drummond was twelve years a Ranger, and in his last season, 1903-4, he played in 21 matches and had the felicity of scoring a goal. When at the height of his powers, his manner of clearing his lines was an exhilaration. His favourite method was to take a short, sharp run to meet the ball knee-high in the air, and when the impact came and the missile went screaming down the wind, " Jock " was filmed in the poise of a steeplechaser clearing an obstacle in elegant style, all of him in the air at once. Against England he was capped six times, and he gained 17 caps in all. Well, in the season to which this chapter is devoted, this great Rangers player got his benefit in a match with his old friends the Celtic. The proceeds amounted to £47 12s. Drummond received a cheque for that amount, and it has never been recorded that the eastern winds wafted a grumble from Falkirk to Ibrox. Let modern impresarios blink and think. As captain of the Scottish team against England in 1896, at Celtic Park, Drummond played the best of all his International games. What a sight it was to see him stride in on the advancing English right wing and take the ball away with well-timed intervention. The crowd exulted the more over his breezy style of captaincy since he was leading the Scots to their first victory in seven years.

Well on in November of 1902 there came to Ibrox a talented young half-back named George Henderson. He had played for Queen's Park in 1900-1 and 1901-2, and had transferred to Dundee in January, 1902. Dundee thought highly of him, but as it was necessary for him to reside in Glasgow a natural difficulty arose. There were indications that Rangers would soon require to recruit their half-back strength and so they accepted the chance to sign him. Though Henderson played in only one League match that season he was fortunate enough to win a Scottish Cup badge after being only five months a Ranger. The same good luck attended Alec Fraser, Angus Macdonald, and John Walker in their first season at Ibrox. The Cup record of the team was one of triumphal progress, though in the Final with the Hearts, at Parkhead, three games were played before a decision could be reached. Auchterarder Thistle left seven goals at Ibrox in the first round, and Kilmarnock then came along and surrendered four to John Walker (2), Robertson and Macdonald. When the third round ballot sent the Light Blues to Parkhead, it was felt that the crisis was nigh. Up till this time Rangers and Celtic had met in six Scottish Cup-ties, four times at Celtic Park and twice, in the final, at Hampden.

HIS MAJESTY KING GEORGE V. AT IBROX PARK.

The Guard of Honour.

On 18th September, 1917, His Majesty King George V. visited Ibrox Park and held an Investiture.

See page 275.

WINNERS OF LEAGUE, GLASGOW CUP, AND CHARITY CUP, 1922—1923.

The same players are signed for 1923—1924, with T. Cairns (*Captain*).

Back Row—M. M'Donald. T. Reid, A. Kirkwood, J. Walls. J. Kilpatrick, R. Ireland, J. Rollo, F. Roberts, W. M'Candless.

Middle Row—W. Struth (*Manager*), T. Hamilton, D. Meiklejohn, J. Jamieson, T. Craig, J. Nicholson, G. Henderson, A. Johnston, A. Dixon. H. Lawson, W. Robb, G. T. Livingstone (*Trainer*).

Sitting—A. Archibald. T. Muirhead. T. Cairns, R. Manderson (*Captain*), A. Cunningham, A. L. Morton. C. Hansen.

Charity Cup. Glasgow Cup.

Rangers had won the 1894 Final and Celtic that of 1899. The four preliminary ties at Parkhead had all provided Celtic with victories. Be it noted that not once had the draw given Rangers the privilege of playing at home. Little wonder that there were doubting Thomases in the Ibrox camp when once again the ballot was unkind. Now, however, the spell was to be broken. Deadly finishing by the Rangers forwards, the dashing, inspiring lead set by Alec Smith and Hamilton, designed to make the younger players in the team forget the seriousness of the occasion—these two factors paved the way to a fine victory, achieved in the first half-hour. In four minutes Alec Smith went through with a pass from Walker and scored. Nine minutes later, Walker, keeping the ball to himself, dashed in on M'Pherson and registered a second goal. A third goal by Hamilton, not long afterwards, settled the issue. The Celts played pluckily to improve their position, but Gibson, Stark and Robertson combined gallantly with Fraser and Drummond in enabling Dickie to keep his goal intact. The 3–0 win remains to this day the most decisive Scottish Cup success achieved by Rangers against Celtic, although two seasons later, in the semi-final for the Cup, the Light Blues won on Parkhead by 2–0. The team that gained that first Cup victory of 3-0 at Celtic Park was :—

> **Rangers.**—Dickie ; Fraser and Drummond ; Gibson, Stark, and Robertson ; Macdonald, Speedie, Hamilton, Walker, and Smith.
>
> **Celtic.**—M'Pherson ; Watson and Battles ; Moir, Lonie, and Orr ; Murray, M'Dermott, Campbell, M'Mahon, and Quinn.

For the semi-final tie, Stenhousemuir declined an invitation to play at Ibrox, so Rangers went to the 'Muir, and Hamilton and Robertson divided four goals between them. During the season, " R. C." collected 30 goals and " Jacky " seven.   Lorne scored one for Stenhousemuir, who had Leslie Skene between the posts, and were a capital working combination.   Now came the Final with the Hearts, who, like the Rangers, had already won the Cup three times.   Celtic Park was the venue, and three stirring contests were waged before Rangers walked off the field victors.   In one respect the Light Blues were always playing with a certain advantage arising from the fact that they were a team of round pegs in round holes. Charles Thomson, who was in the Hearts team as a right back, had not then settled the question of whether he was a back, half-back, or centre forward.   He finished the first and third games at centre in an effort to save the tie. Still, the teams proved to be splendidly matched in the first two trials of strength.   In the first match there was no scoring up to the interval, but a few minutes after it, Stark, following close up behind the forwards, sent a low, hard shot past M'Wattie.   Then a fierce storm broke over the ground and play had to be suspended, but the rivals were soon out and at it again, and with the Hearts forces re-arranged and Robert Walker operating in the masterful way he could assume at times, the game swung round in their favour.   Near the end Walker swerved in past Robertson and Drummond and gave Dickie no chance with a nicely-placed scoring shot.   The same elevens faced up in the second match.   Here the Hearts played their best game of the three.   Walker was in dazzling form and he got his colleagues to respond with rare vivacity. But Dickie, Fraser and Drummond defended grandly and not a goal was scored.   When the third, and what was to be the concluding, struggle fell due, both teams were feeling the effects of the two strenuous duels.   Albert Buick had to call off from the Hearts team, in which he had figured at centre half, while Rangers had to rest Neil Gibson, the right half, and John Walker, the inside right. George Henderson and Alec Mackie were brought in and the teams which took part in the deciding game were :—

Hearts.—H. M'Wattie ; C. Thomson and Andrew Orr; George Key, John Anderson, and George Hogg ; Robt. Dalrymple, R. Walker, Wm. Porteous, John Hunter, and David Baird.

Rangers.—M. Dickie ; A. Fraser and J. Drummond ; Geo. Henderson, Jas. Stark, and J. T. Robertson ; Angus Macdonald, A. Mackie, R. C. Hamilton, F. Speedie, and A. Smith.

Rangers won against the run of fortune. Mackie signalised his introduction by scoring a clever goal after fifteen minutes, during which the forwards kept working in with low, clippy passing. Mackie was very smart at shooting a moving ball. He seldom trapped it, and consequently the goalkeeper had little chance to judge how it was likely to come to him. The game was going well for the Light Blues when what looked like a fatal disaster befell them. In turning to tackle " Bobby " Walker, who had swung away from him, Drummond ruptured a thigh muscle and had to retire from the field. This occurred near the interval, and the ten who were left had to brace themselves for a big effort. Speedie fell back into Drummond's place. He had previously played back more than once and was quite at his ease. Thomson came out of the Hearts rear to lead the attack and a furious onslaught was directed upon the Rangers defence. It stood the strain bravely, and then a chance came to Hamilton when Stark slipped a ball through to him. In a twinkling he was striding away towards M'Wattie. There was a flapping of wings among the Hearts half-backs as they got up speed for the chase. But Hamilton could travel fast, and before a pursuer could reach him he had thrust through between the Tynecastle backs and shot a second goal. Thus was the Cup won for the fourth time.

In the League, Rangers took third place after having been four times champions in succession. They were five times defeated, twice by Hibernian, and once by Dundee, the Hearts, and Third Lanark. Hibernian were the champions and Dundee the runners-up. Not since that season has the championship gone out of Glasgow. Third Lanark won it in the following season, and in the nineteen seasons between then and now, either Celtic or Rangers have gained the League crown. Fifteen International honours came the way of Rangers players, Finlay Speedie getting all the Association caps, a remarkable distinction for one so young. He scored a goal against both England and Wales. The list of honours was :—

v. England.	v. Wales.	v. Ireland.	v. English League.
J. Robertson.	J. Robertson.	J. Drummond.	N. Gibson.
R.C. Hamilton.	F. Speedie.	F. Speedie.	J. Robertson.
F. Speedie.	A. Smith.	A. Smith.	R.C. Hamilton
A. Smith.			J. Walker.
			A. Smith.

At the annual general meeting in May, 1903, Mr. William Craig was appointed to a place on the Board of Directors. This was not his introduction to the inner temple. In 1897, before the club was incorporated, Mr. Craig served on the General Committee and he retained his seat in the following year. Thus he assumed his directorship with a full knowledge of what was required to keep the club on a high level of success. In any enterprise in all the world there is no more hazardous task. Mr. Craig would not have retained the confidence and trust of his colleagues had he not possessed qualifications. That he does possess that confidence is shown by the fact that for eleven years he acted as vice-chairman, and as such was the club's ambassador to certain " courts " of rival potentates who required to be convinced that their side of the case under discussion might be subject to reasonable amendment. That, of course, is merely a polite way of putting it. Sometimes, and with certain people, the polite way of stating a case is not the effective way. Very well. Mr. Craig can be as blunt as you like. He doesn't take a sledge hammer to kill a fly, but, likewise, he doesn't play about with a rapier when a heavier weapon is more suitable. Since he undertook the responsibilities of a director, the Rangers club has not been lacking in the attainment of modest success. We shall do no more than justice to Mr. Craig if we attribute part of it to his ability to apply to the administration of the club's affairs a large contribution of commonsense, a rare quality, indeed. His colleagues on the Board paid him a fitting compliment when, in July of this year (1923), they chose him chairman upon the resignation from that position of Sir John Ure Primrose. Vice-chairman since 1919 of the Scottish Football Association, on the Council of which he has sat for fifteen years, Mr. Craig may some day be Premier of that august body.

1903—1904.

Nearly the Cup—John Drummond's Farewell— End of Great Partnership— "Bobby" Neil's Last— Team's Troubles—Fine Charity Cup Win— Clever Freshmen.

IT takes a lot of clubs to make competitive football worth carrying on, and it is a fine thing that the honours should go round. In the season of **1903-4**, Celtic won the Scottish Cup, Third Lanark the Glasgow Cup and the League Championship, and Rangers the Charity Cup. Third Lanark were a splendid combination, and no one could withhold congratulation from them when they achieved their great ambition. They had never won the League championship. They have never won it since. Celtic and Rangers tied for third place in the League with 38 points each for 26 matches, with the Light Blues in possession of the superior goal average. In the Scottish Cup Final, Celtic defeated the Rangers by 3-2. Rangers defeated Celtic in the Charity Cup Final by 5-2. Both League matches between them were drawn. We desire to give the full measure of credit to the teams which triumphed over the Rangers. Justice and fairness, like charity, begin, however, at home. But for a series of accidents, which deprived the club of the services of some of their most reliable players at the crucial period of the season, an even better record would have been established. The Scottish Cup might— without stretching supposition—have been won for a fifth time. We shall see what grounds existed for such surmise.

When the season opened, the new players signed were Duncan Campbell, from Yoker, who could play back or half-back ; James Hartley, a smart right wing forward, reared in Dumbarton, but who had been over the Border playing with Lincoln City ; and Tom Paton, a centre forward out of the same team that gave Neil Gibson to the Rangers. In October, J. G. Watson, an amateur goalkeeper, was added to the staff as reserve to Dickie, and in December another custodian, W. R. Allan, from Falkirk, who stood six feet in his socks, was also signed. The outside right position having proved difficult to fill adequately, Charles Donnachie, a clever young forward, was secured from Cambuslang Hibs. in January, and he took part in the Scottish and Charity Cup-ties. David Crawford returned to St. Mirren after nearly nine years' service at Ibrox, and William Walker was transferred to Clyde, with whom he had a long and distinguished career. Neil did not play very often, and this proved to be his last season. He retired in good company, for Dickie and Drummond, when the campaign closed, also bade farewell to the scene of so many of their gallant deeds.

Robert G. Neil was a great little half-back, comparable with, and not unlike, Holt, of Everton, who for a period was England's greatest centre half. There was nothing florid about Neil's style. He was always cool and thoughtful, and his methods were essentially constructive. His imperturbable nature was never more strikingly shown than in the memorable match against his old club, the Hibernian, at Easter Road, in the season of 1898–99, when, with practically the last kick of the game, he converted the penalty which preserved the Rangers' unequalled League record. It was a moment painful for all concerned in the tenseness of the strain, yet " Bobby " took the kick as if nothing at all depended upon it. He was a demon at converting penalty kicks, and he got good practice, for in the period between 1897–1899, opposing defenders conceded many penalties in trying to stop the implacable Rangers attack.

Matthew Dickie was nine years a Ranger. Those of you who have read the previous chapters of this history know, from stated facts, that the club never possessed a player more dependable. He gave the officials not a moment's anxiety. It was said that you could set your watch by the time he walked into Ibrox or any other rendezvous appointed. Some players have praise lavished upon them who do not deserve it. Dickie deserved more than he was wont to receive. He had none of the theatrical tricks that appeal to certain minds, but he was eminently safe and he could be positively brilliant. In extolling his usefulness to the team, none were more profuse than Nicol Smith and John Drummond, and they were the men best able to judge. Alec Smith's declaration was this : " I never knew Matt Dickie to make a mistake without more than making up for it by his own personal effort."

Well, in this season of **1903-4** the Rangers went sailing gaily into the League tournament. They began by taking two points from Third Lanark, the destined champions, and did not suffer a reverse until they met them in the return game, which was the Rangers' eighth. This latter match Third Lanark won by a goal to nothing, chiefly owing to the strength of their half-backs—Cross, Sloan, and Neilson. It was not until the Light Blues went to Dundee, in their fourteenth fixture, that they were defeated again, and their third loss (5–4) was not sustained until they met St. Mirren, at Paisley, in a very remarkable game, which was the Rangers' twenty-second engagement. Young Donnachie made his League debut here. Of the 66 League matches played between Rangers and St. Mirren up to the end of season, 1922-23, the Saints won eight, and this match at Love Street is the only one in which they have scored five goals against the Light Blues. The team that achieved this outstanding feat was :—

Rae ; Jackson and Cameron ; Greenlees, Robertson, and M'Avoy ; Lindsay, Wilson, Bruce, Reid, and Smith.

Four penalty kicks were awarded in the second half and all were converted, three by Lindsay for St. Mirren and one by Hamilton for Rangers. More than one of them was adroitly exploited, for the referee was so ready to give the extreme award that the Saints forwards took full advantage of his generosity. Only one of the penalties was admitted by the Rangers players to be justified, and it was incurred when Nicol Smith handled. Rangers led at the interval by 2–1, then the penalties all came in quick succession and St. Mirren led by 4–3. Lindsay scored a fifth, and good, goal—his fourth in the match—and Stark registered Rangers' fourth. It was the most extraordinary experience the Light Blues had had in all their League career. Naturally, they were the more pleased when, later in the season, they returned to Love Street and won a Scottish Cup-tie without permitting the breezy Saints to score even once. Up to the day the Rangers met the Hearts, at Tynecastle, in the twenty-fourth match on their card, they were bidding for the championship. They had defeated the Hearts on the previous Saturday in the Scottish Cup, but in the tie, N. Smith, A. Smith, Stark, and Robertson were all more or less injured and could not participate in the League game. The young substitutes gave a good account of themselves, but the Hearts won by 2–1 and so made it impossible for Rangers to overhaul Third Lanark.

In the League match with Celtic, at Ibrox, Alec Bennett

193

played his first match for the Parkhead team against the Rangers. He had been signed near the end of season 1902-3, as a centre forward, and his first big match for Celtic was in the Charity Cup Final of that season against St. Mirren, when he scored three goals. But against the Rangers he was on the right wing, for Gilligan had, in the meantime, been secured by Celtic from Dundee and he was a centre all the time. That was the beginning of Bennett's partnership with M'Menemy which was to prove so profitable to their club. In fact, it was in this season of 1903-4 that the new Celtic team was shaping into the formation which in subsequent years took a string of honours to Parkhead. They had given Dan. M'Arthur, Harry Marshall, and Peter Meechan to Clyde, and "Sandy" M'Mahon to Partick Thistle, who were also joined by John Wilkie, whose old partner "Johnny" Campbell was now playing for Hibernian.

So beset with injuries were the Rangers players at certain times that Gibson had to be played at outside right, where he acquitted himself well; Robertson was all over the forward line; Harry Dinsmore, of Queen's Park and Third Lanark, was secured to take the injured Smith's place at outside left against the Celtic, at Ibrox, and so on. Dinsmore had cause to remember his only appearance in Rangers' colours, for he sustained a broken leg. It seemed as if the club would require an infirmary to themselves. There was not a single member of the recognised League eleven who was not in Blanket Bay at one time or other, and sometimes half a dozen were ailing together. Under the circumstances, it was marvellous that such a splendid attempt was made to hold the Scottish Cup, and that the Charity Cup was won in such rollicking style as wiped out the sting of previous failures.

FIFTY YEARS OF FOOTBALL——1903-1904.

It was a curious feature of the draw that in the first round of the Scottish Cup there should be brought together the two clubs which had fought that desperate three-game Final of the previous season. Both Rangers and the Hearts had three changes to show, Dickie, Drummond, and Macdonald being the missing ones from the Light Blues' ranks, while the Hearts had successors to Anderson, Buick, and Dalrymple. The sides proved to be as evenly matched as in the 1903 Final, and with a little luck the Hearts would have drawn. Hamilton scored the only goal of the first half for Rangers, but Robert Walker, soon after the interval, ran in to pick up the ball which Robertson passed back, and his shot equalised the score. Rangers got the lead again from as dashing an individual effort as had been seen on Ibrox for years. John Walker, himself an old Hearts raider, went through with the ball at his feet and his shot sent it tearing into the net at great speed. That was John Walker's favourite method of getting his goals. He would suddenly cause a break in the combination by thrusting out by himself and the defence was frequently taken by surprise, having set themselves to counter a passing movement. He scored 15 goals during this season, which was a good performance for one who never knew in which position he was to be played. Rangers' third goal was also scored by Walker, and then the Hearts rallied. Mark Bell registered a second goal for them, and until the end the tie throbbed with excitement. If ever a club had to struggle for a place in the Final it was the Rangers this season. Their next two ties were with the Hibernian, at Easter Road, and St. Mirren, at Paisley. It would have been no discredit to have lost on either ground. By only a margin of a goal they won on both. They were all over Hibernian in the first half but could not get goals commensurate with their outfield play. The Hibs. came away strongly in the second half, but some grand defence pulled the Light Blues through with a 2–1 victory. Remembering what had happened to them in the League game at Paisley, Rangers went to Love Street completely on their guard, and they had now their full Cup team available. The Saints' forwards were changed a little, and now the line was Lindsay, Swan, Reid, Wilson, and Smith. Every inch of ground was contested, the Saints making a courageous bid at least to save the tie. But four minutes from the interval Hamilton tried one of his old-time swoops, and before Jackson and Cameron could close in on him, he was in on Rae and had swept the ball high into the net. It was the only goal scored. Now into the semi-final, the Rangers were fortunate to get the luck of the draw. Morton, for whom Tom Sinclair was in goal, were beaten at Ibrox by 3–0, Walker scoring twice and Hamilton once.

Had the Final with Celtic been played at once, it would have been a real test. Unfortunately, the match between the Scottish and English Leagues intervened, and Hamilton, the scorer of 36 goals during the season for his club, was injured and played very little afterwards, which illustrates again that honours bestowed are often a mixed blessing to club and player. Fraser was injured in a League game and he also had to stand out of the Final, thus allowing Drummond to come alongside of his old partner Nicol Smith for the last time in a Scottish Cup-tie. They had been partners in the Final of 1894 when Rangers defeated the Celtic and won the Cup for the first time. Celtic on the way to the Final had disposed of St. Bernards, 4–0 ; Dundee, 5–0, after two drawn games of 0–0 and 1–1 ; and Third Lanark, 2–1. They would have played Bennett, but he was down with influenza, and so the teams which lined up on New Hampden before 64,323 spectators, the largest crowd in the history of the game in Scotland, were :—

> **Celtic.**—D. Adams·; D. M'Leod and W. Orr ; J. Young, W. Lonie, and J. Hay ; R. Muir, J. M'Menemy, J. Quinn, P. Somers, and D. Hamilton.

> **Rangers.**—J. G. Watson ; N.Smith and J.Drummond ; G. Henderson, J. Stark, and J. Robertson ; J. Walker, A. Mackie, F. Speedie, C. Donnachie, and A. Smith.

This was the first big match played on present Hampden, and it was regarded as a test of its capacity to accommodate an International, which test proved entirely satisfactory. It was a glorious spring day and the teams rose to the occasion. They gave an exhibition of football such as had not been witnessed in a Final for years, and which has not been excelled since. Rangers, feeling that they were playing under a severe handicap, opened with magnificent dash, and inside of twelve minutes Speedie twice beat Adams. Celtic's young, strong forwards, however, came more and more into the game and before the interval, Quinn, in centre by the seeming unfortunate chance of Bennett's absence, scored two fine goals. Crossing over on level terms, the rivals put skill against skill, nerve against nerve, and there looked to be every likelihood of an indecisive battle when, seven minutes from the end, Quinn caught Smith and Drummond wide apart, and with a terrific drive, shot the winning goal. As events proved, the absence of Fraser and Hamilton was disastrous for the Rangers, while, on the other hand, the accident which caused Quinn's transference to centre went far to win the Cup for the Celtic. In addition, John Walker should not have played. He was ailing at the start and very sick at the interval. Drummond, who was in his twelfth season, played heroically, but he could not command the old quickness of intervention. He had, besides, never fully shaken off the effects of the rupture sustained in the previous season's Final against the Hearts. The match was his farewell, and though no one could foresee it, this was also Nicol Smith's last Scottish Cup-tie though, in his case, it was the grim Commander Death that decided.

For this defeat the Rangers found solatium in a sweeping Charity Cup success. After defeating Third Lanark by a goal scored by Speedie, they went to Hampden again to renew the Scottish Cup rivalry with Celtic. The only change in the Celtic team was Bennett for Muir on the right wing, for now it was realised that Quinn's place was in the centre. The Rangers team showed several changes and was :—

> Watson ; N. Smith and Fraser ; Henderson, Stark, and Campbell ; Donnachie, Mackie, Speedie, Robertson, and A. Smith.

Frankly, the eleven did not inspire hope, but what an awakening the players caused among the crowd ! They seemed to know that they were lightly thought of and they played to confute the critics. The Celtic defence surrendered only one goal, to Mackie, in the first half, but when first Robertson, and then Donnachie added goals early in the second half, enthusiasm among the club's followers swelled to a great pitch. Celtic tried all the manœuvres which had served them well in the Scottish Cup Final, but they were now tackled and harried before they could develop a movement. In a scrimmage, Hamilton got the ball past Watson, but two more goals, in quick succession, by Robertson and Speedie (from a penalty), put the issue far beyond doubt. Few victories have brought greater credit to the winners. During the

season the team's cup record and the honours gained
were :—

Scottish Cup.		Glasgow Cup.	Charity Cup.	
Hearts (H),	3-2	Third Lanark (H), 0-2	Third Lanark	
Hibernian (A),	2-1		(Hampden),	1-0
St. Mirren (A),	1-0		Celtic	
Morton (H),	3-0		(Hampden),	5-2
Celtic				
(Hampden),	2-3			
	11-6	0-2		6-2

v. England.	v. Wales.	v. Ireland.	v. English L'gue.	v. Irish L'gue.
J.T.Robertson.	J.T.Robertson.	G. Henderson.	J.T.Robertson.	N. Smith.
	J. Walker.	J.T.Robertson.	J. Walker.	J.T.Robertson.
		J. Walker.	R.C. Hamilton.	J. Walker.
		R.C.Hamilton.		R.C.Hamilton.
		A. Smith.		

Hamilton was chosen to play against England, but the
injury sustained against the English League caused him to
withdraw. He was generally regarded as Scotland's best
centre forward, and had he been able to play, Scotland
would probably not have been defeated by 1-0. Bloomer
scored in the match played at Celtic Park on a pitch
churned into slush after a snowstorm. Hamilton scored
two goals against the Irish League and one against
Ireland. Robertson, who was captain of the Scots against
England, and who played in every representative match,
scored the only goal against the English League. Nicol
Smith was captain against the Irish League.

1904—1905.

Two Cup Finals—A League Decider—Tom Sinclair— Alec Craig—His Ordeal—An Abandoned Tie— More Injuries.

FOR the break-up of what we might call the old champion team, the club's officials and followers were quite prepared. A great confederation of players, like great empires and everything else human, must come to an end some time. The officials were prepared. But they were not fortune tellers. They could not foresee that the apparently adequate arrangements made to meet the inevitable changes would prove far from equal to the inroads made on their resources by the demon of injury. It was the highest tribute possible to the initiative of Manager Wilton and his directors that the club, in face of an ever-increasing list of incapacitated players, reached the Final of the Scottish and Glasgow Cups and tied with Celtic for the League Championship. That not a single honour was won may be taken not as an indication of failure to meet the needs of the situation, but simply as proof that there is a breaking point to all effort at fighting misfortune.

When the season opened, the new players available were Andrew Easton, a big, powerful back from Millwall Athletic : George Gilchrist, another back, from Clyde : John May, a half-back from Derby County, who had given a brilliant display in the Anglo-Scots trial match of the previous season, and who was a brother of Hugh May, a former Rangers forward : James Turnbull, a centre forward from Falkirk : Adam Gourlay, a half-back from Renfrew Victoria : and Archie Kyle, a

BOARD OF DIRECTORS, 1923—1924.

Back Row.—John MacPherson, William Struth (*Manager*), George Small, and W. Rogers Simpson (*Secretary*).

Front Row.—Ex-Bailie Joseph Buchanan, J.P., William Craig, J.P. (*Chairman*), Sir John Ure Primrose, Bart., LL.D.,
and Ex-Bailie Duncan Graham, J.P., O.B.E.

forward from the junior Parkhead. May and Kyle remained longest with the club. Of the old brigade, John Drummond went to Falkirk, then members of the Second Division of the League : Matthew Dickie took over the guardianship of the Clyde team's goal ; and Neil Gibson joined Partick Thistle, being still good enough to get his cap against Ireland this season. Before the season was very old, more changes occurred, " to " as well as " from." Early in September, R. S. M'Coll, then launching out in the business of confectioner in Glasgow, was transferred from Newcastle United to Ibrox, just in time to play against his old club, Queen's Park. He was partner to Alec Smith and had R. C. Hamilton, once his colleague at Hampden, at his right elbow. In October, Tom Sinclair, the Morton custodian, was signed, and he played his first game as a Ranger against Dundee, at Ibrox Park, on 29th October. In this match the forwards were Walker, Mackie, M'Coll, Kyle, and Smith, and they played so cleverly together that an English club manager declared he had seen nothing so good all season, and that they were worth £5,000 to any club over the Border. Injuries had so weakened the defence by the month of December, that Tom M'Ewan, an old St. Bernards stalwart, was brought up from Bury to partner Nicol Smith. He did not have that pleasure, however. Nicol had taken ill some days previously and he never recovered. To take the great Darvel back's place, Robert Campbell was secured in January, from Partick Thistle. He is not to be confused with R. G. Campbell, who was still playing for Queen's Park. Robert Campbell belonged to Lugar. The defensive problem, however, was not yet solved, and so, early in March, 1905, Alec Craig, of Rutherglen Glencairn, was enlisted, and he made his debut in a Glasgow League match against Partick Thistle on 4th March. By this time, Rangers had reached the semi-final of the Scottish Cup, and Craig, then just a mere lad, and only a few days a senior, found himself facing Celtic, at Parkhead, in what was to prove, for him, the most trying ordeal of his career. Celtic had already defeated the Rangers in the Glasgow Cup Final by 2-1. On New Year's day, the League game at Ibrox had to be abandoned through the crowd breaking in, and when it was replayed in February, Celtic won by 4-1. For the " Scottish " tie with Celtic, Rangers were in dire straits for a forward line. Hamilton had had his knee operated upon and part of the cartilage removed, and it was feared he would not play again. M'Coll and Walker were also injured. Donnachie, now a reserve, was placed at outside right and Jacky Robertson installed at centre. To partner Craig at back, Alec Fraser was also brought from the reserves. There seemed nothing for it but to go out of the ties in the most graceful manner possible. Nobody had much doubt about Celtic winning when the teams lined up :—

> **Celtic.**—Adams ; M'Leod and Orr ; Young, Lonie, and Hay ; Bennett, M'Menemy, Quinn, Somers, and Hamilton.

> **Rangers.**—Sinclair ; Fraser and Craig ; Henderson, Stark, and May ; Donnachie, Speedie, Robertson, Kyle, and Smith.

To the surprise of everyone, the Rangers defence refused to accept the prevalent estimate of their hopeless inferiority to a Celtic forward line of established fame. No one was more disdainful of the common valuation than the boyish-looking Craig. He did not wait for the attack to come to him but went through his half-backs to meet it and foil it. In a first half of revelations there was no scoring. Near the interval Donald M'Leod ruptured a thigh muscle and had to retire. When twenty minutes of the second half had gone, Speedie added to the day's surprises by scoring, and, fifteen minutes later, Robertson made the crowd blink by registering a second goal from Alec Smith's centre. There was enough of sensation in this for one afternoon, but more was to come. Ten minutes from the end, Referee Tom Robertson ordered Quinn to the pavilion under the belief that he had broken the laws of the game towards Craig. Some rowdies broke into the field and all the players were forced to seek the shelter of the pavilion. When the tumult had quietened down, the referee asked the teams to resume, but this was the second time they had been compelled to quit, and though Rangers were prepared to go out, the Celtic players had had enough. Mr. J. H. M'Laughlin, on behalf of the Celtic, formally intimated that his club withdrew from the tie. It was a dismal ending to a fine contest between the old rivals, and the sympathy of all fair-minded people was with the Celtic officials. One of the misfortunes attached to clubs of eminence is that they cannot decide the character of those who shall give them what is called support. Rangers know this to their cost. But no one can presume to cast a stone with a moral platitude strung to it. There came a time when the Rangers club, suffering from just such an infliction as stung the Celtic that day, looked for sympathy and received only veiled insult. That, also, perhaps, is the penalty of eminence.

For the third successive year, Rangers went into the Final, and for the second time in succession, they were to fail to inscribe their name on the Cup. Third Lanark were formidable opponents. They had defeated Leith Athletic 4-1, Motherwell 1-0, Aberdeen 4-1, and Airdrieonians 2-1, and had not lost a match since the first week in December. They had their full forces available, but Rangers had permanently lost Mackie, for business reasons, and Hamilton, though on his legs again, was timorous of his knee giving way. May, injured also, could not play in the Final, and so a draw, without scoring, was regarded as a performance of merit on the part of the Light Blues. For the replay, Tommy Low, who since his former association with the Rangers, had done service with Dundee, Woolwich Arsenal, and now Abercorn, was recalled to fill his old position of outside right. The teams that played in the second and decisive game were :—

> **Third Lanark.**—Raeside ; Barr and M'Intosh ; Comrie, Sloan, and Neilson ; Johnstone, Kidd, M'Kenzie, Wilson, and Munro.

> **Rangers.**—Sinclair ; Fraser and Craig ; Henderson, Stark and Robertson ; Low, Speedie, M'Coll, Kyle, and Smith.

Rangers' defence was only half as good as in the first game. Third Lanark's forwards were fifty per cent. improved. Hugh Wilson, a great old warrior, was the life and soul of the Cathkin team's attack. He scored the only goal of the first half, and in the second half, he put on a third after Johnstone had notched a second. Near the end, Smith beat Raeside from one of Low's corner kicks. The better, and, shall we say, the more representative team won? Not since then have Third Lanark been able to take the Cup to Cathkin. The trophy was accepted by Mr. J. B. Livingstone, then the only remaining link with the office-bearers of the club of sixteen years before when it was won for the first time by Third Lanark. At the presentation, one of the guests was Andrew Thomson, a member of the victorious Cup team of 1889.

It was still possible for Rangers to bring the League championship to Ibrox, for with 41 points, they came equal with Celtic by winning the last match on their card.

Rangers had the better goal average, 83 scored against 28 lost, compared with Celtic's 68–31. A deciding game had to be played. It took place at Hampden Park, and again the Rangers had to face a vital issue under strength. They were the club of forlorn hopes. Here were the teams :

> **Celtic.**—Adams ; Watson and Orr ; M'Nair, Lonie, and Hay ; Bennett, M'Menemy, Quinn, Somers, and Hamilton.

> **Rangers.**—Sinclair ; Fraser and Craig ; Gourlay, Stark, and May ; Robertson, Speedie, M'Coll, Donnachie, and Smith.

Mr. Kirkham was brought from Preston to act as referee, and he was entertained to a fast, exciting match, unmarred by any untoward incident. There was no scoring in the first half, but twenty minutes after the interval, M'Menemy gave Celtic the lead and Hamilton, almost immediately, scored a second goal. Five minutes later, Robertson registered for Rangers, who made a bold effort to equalise but failed, and thus the Parkhead team began a series of six championship triumphs which the League recognised by the presentation to them of a shield. This was an odd proceeding, for when the Rangers established their unequalled record of winning every League match in the season of 1898-99, and again when, from 1899 to 1902, they won four successive championships, the League did not so much as present a barren compliment. It is not the fact of recognising a club's magnificent achievement that is odd. It is the celebration of one performance and the ignoring of another, even more remarkable, that impels surprise among people who do not pretend to grasp the more subtle distinctions upon which the League decide these things.

There remained only the Charity Cup-ties, and in the first round Partick Thistle, making their debut in the competition, defeated the Rangers by 5–0. By that time the Light Blues were stale and indifferent, but the Thistle were a splendid side and went into the Final to be beaten, in turn, by Celtic by 2–0.

Before the season ended, Jacky Robertson joined Chelsea as manager. James Croal was signed as a back, but as everybody knows, he later became a great forward with Falkirk, and played for Scotland against England in 1914. R. Dalrymple, once prominent with the Hearts, was secured from Plymouth as an outside right. J. Gray was a good half-back from Aston Villa. John Walker had played a little for Morton, but he sustained a leg injury which practically ended his playing career.

Of International honours, Rangers players in **1904-5** received fewer than for many years. Robertson, Speedie, and Smith played against the English League, and Robertson and Smith against Wales. That was all. The club's Cup record was :—

Scottish Cup.		Glasgow Cup.	Charity Cup.	
Ayr Parkhouse (H),	2–1	A Bye.	Partick	
Morton (A),	6–0	Third	Thistle (A),	0–5
Beith (H),	5–1	Lanark (H), 3–0		
Celtic (A),	2–0	Celtic		
Third Lanark		(Hampden), 1–2		
(Hampden),	0–0			
Third Lanark				
(Hampden),	1–3			
	16–5	4–2		0–5

1905—1906.

CLUBS which set for themselves a high standard must submit to be judged by that standard. Though Rangers in 1905-6 reached the Final of the Glasgow Cup and won the Charity Cup, the season was one of the least successful since their great revival in 1890. They were defeated in the third round of the Scottish Cup by Port-Glasgow Athletic, at Clune Park, though they could win the League match there by 4-1. They finished fourth in the League for only the second time in sixteen years. Eight matches were lost of the 30 played, which was two more than were lost over the four seasons from 1899 to 1902. Well, it is good to be philosophical. The material which wins matches with monotonous regularity was not at command. But the experience was not lost upon the officials. It has its reflection in the position of the club to-day. The Cup reverse at Port-Glasgow amounted to a sort of tragedy, because on the run of the play the tie might have been won by a fair margin. On a pitch that was a composition of mud, glue, and water, the forwards played much too close. True, they shot hard and often, but the Port-Glasgow goalkeeper, Ward, was in an inspired mood, both before and after his team got their only goal. He was not a big fellow, but on this afternoon he seemed to borrow some extra inches and he was cat-like for quickness. This was the only time Port-Glasgow Athletic ever met the Rangers in a Scottish Cup-tie, and the significance of their victory is best conveyed by the fact that in the sixteen League engagements played between the clubs, the Rangers were winners 13 times and were only once defeated.

James Galt had signed for Rangers in January, 1906, and he played fairly regularly until the end of the season. Another John Walker, a back, was secured from Beith, but he was not eligible for the ties, being committed with the Ayrshire club. It was this same John Walker who, later, gained celebrity with Swindon Town, and was capped against England, Wales, and Ireland in 1911, 1912, and 1913. R. G. Campbell, who had joined Celtic from Queen's Park, was transferred by the Parkhead club to Ibrox on 18th January, 1906, in order to take the Rangers out of a difficulty, a favour the latter were able to repay in the following season when Tom Sinclair took over the care of the Celtic goal after Adams had come by an injury to his hand. John Rankine, a smart forward from Cowdenbeath, was also signed, and J. M'Fie, another clever, though light forward, played well at either inside right or left. These two and also James Speirs, who joined in August, 1905, were in the eleven that won the Charity Cup. Over all, the team was to the light side. They played pretty football, but the forwards could not hope to win in a match where the opposing defence cared to mix it, as the boxers say.

When the team went to Aberdeen in the second round of the Scottish Cup, R. C. Hamilton had a great distinction conferred upon him. He was singled out by a polite lunatic who presented him on the ground with a closely written document of several pages which sought to convince the amazed Rangers centre that if the lunatic had his rights, he would be worth £15,000,000. " R. C." made a pretence of reading the epistle and then gravely informed the potential millionaire that he would do his best for him. Which entirely satisfied the gentleman.

At the end of the season, " R. C." joined Fulham, and he was there when James Miller, his old comrade of the great Rangers team of 1898-99, died in Chelsea. After a season with Fulham, Hamilton returned to Ibrox, but, of course, he could not command the old dash or the old screaming shots. He never was the same player after the operation to his knee.

James Croal went on loan to Ayr Parkhouse. Speedie, after a long absence, through injury, played a game or two towards the close of the season, but did not take part in the Charity Cup-ties. One who did, however, was an old Ranger, James Jackson. Since his former days at Ibrox, he had played for Newcastle United, Woolwich, Leyton, and West Ham. He returned to Ibrox in time to play against Celtic in the first of the Charity ties. A. Newbigging was signed about the same time for goal. Many thought he was an Englishman, but, on the contrary, he was very much a Scot. His starting point was Lanark, and he had been with Abercorn, Notts Forest, Bristol, and Reading before getting into a light blue jersey. He stood out of the Charity-Cup ties to let Tom Sinclair win the medal. In the tie with Celtic, Jackson played a great spoiling game, and the young forwards fairly ran through the strong Celtic defence, scoring five goals. The Final was against Queen's Park and the Rangers team remained unchanged, the sides being :—

Queen's Park.—J. C. Adam; R. M. Young and J. S. Thomson; J. Riley, G. Higgins, and J. Dick; J. Nicholl, T. T. Fitchie, J. M'Lean, Hugh Logan, and C. Hamilton.

Rangers.—Sinclair; Campbell and Jackson; Gray, May, and Craig; Rankine, M'Fie, Speirs, Kyle, and Smith.

Queen's Park had the nucleus here of a team that was to blossom out in the following season. They ran the

THE STORY OF THE RANGERS.

Light Blues hard for the Cup and were defeated by only
a one-goal margin. Speirs and Kyle led the way in the
scoring, then Dick converted a penalty kick, and before
the interval Speirs scored again. In the second half,
Logan got a second goal for Hampden and almost snatched
another. The Rangers Cup record for this season of
1905-6 was :—

Scottish Cup.		Glasgow Cup.		Charity Cup.	
Arthurlie (A),	7–1	Clyde (A),	0–0	A Bye.	
Aberdeen (A),	3–2	Clyde (H),	2–1	Celtic (A),	5–3
Port-Glasgow		Third		Queen's Park	
Athletic (A),	0–1	Lanark (H), 0–0		(Hampden),	3–2
		Third			
		Lanark (A), 1–3			
	10–4		3–4		8–5

Alec Smith was the only Rangers player capped against
England and he also played against Ireland along with
John May, who was the sole representative of the club
against Wales. Against the English League, May and
Kyle were honoured.

1906—1907.

F. Speedie Goes—T. Sinclair with Celtic—"R. G.'s" Scoring Feat—James Gordon's Record—George Law's Debut—Charity Cup Won.

IF the season of **1906-7** did not bring great lustre to the Rangers' record, it was not time wasted. The Glasgow Charity Cup was the only honour won by the First Eleven, but the Reserves made a handsome haul in capturing the Scottish and Glasgow Second Eleven Cups and the Scottish Union Championship. The Celtic were enjoying their period of greatest prosperity then, and when they met the Rangers in the Final of the Charity Cup, they had already won the League Championship, the Scottish Cup, and the Glasgow Cup. In the following season of 1907-8, that fine Parkhead team did actually accomplish the magnificent feat of securing all four prizes open to the first-class clubs of Scotland. An unfortunate incident, with a not unhappy sequel, occurred in the Rangers' opening match, on 16th August, 1906. Celtic came down to Ibrox to play in Finlay Speedie's benefit match. In trying to save a shot, David Adams, the Celtic goalkeeper, lacerated the palm of his hand on a nail which had, inadvertently, been left in one of the posts after the five-a-side football held at a sports meeting. Before the Celtic officials left the ground that evening, the Rangers offered them the services of Tom Sinclair (who was now reserve to Newbigging) until such time as Adams was fit to resume. The offer was gratefully accepted. Sinclair went into the Celtic team and did not lose a goal in the first six League matches nor in the first two Glasgow Cup-ties. Celtic won the Cup and he got a medal. More than that, he won a Scottish Second Eleven Cup medal with the Rangers, was then transferred to Newcastle United, and with them won an English League Championship award— all in one season. It was an experience unique in its peculiar features. The first goal lost by Celtic in the League was in their match immediately following the transfer back to the Rangers of Sinclair. Speedie took part in the first game of the twice-played Glasgow Cup-tie against Queen's Park, but by this time he had got the wanderlust, and to satisfy him the directors transferred him to Newcastle United. He made a name for himself on Tyneside as a centre half and centre forward, travelled a bit over England, and eventually gravitated into the ranks of old Dumbarton, the club of his heart.

It was the studied policy of the officials at Ibrox to cultivate young players, and it was successful enough up to a point. But no team can hope to be successful without a generous blend of experience, however eager and unsparing of themselves the young men may be. David Taylor, of Bannockburn, a strong, fast centre half, played his first match in September, 1906 : so did William Henry, a back of the resolute type. In November, J. Dickie, the most boyish-looking recruit since " Tommy " Low's time, was secured from Strathclyde to fill the outside right position. The defence was in safe hands, but the forwards were too light. To try to solve this difficulty, R. G. Campbell was invited to try his luck at centre in a benefit match against Morton at Ibrox. Before the teams went on to the field, a Morton official said to an Ibrox director, " You're brave, playing a back at centre forward." To which the Ibrox director jokingly replied, " I'll bet you ' R. G.' scores six goals." As a matter of fact, Campbell scored seven and got the credit in the papers next morning, but the referee wrote to say that he had not allowed the seventh because he had blown his whistle for time-up just as the ball went in off the bar. Campbell often played centre forward after that. He got 14 goals during the season of 1906-7, 35 goals in 1907-8, and 17 in 1908-9. It must be remembered, too, that he was not a fixture at centre forward, but was frequently drafted into the defence either as a back or centre-half. He had the curious experience of signing on, nominally, in successive seasons, as a back, forward, and half-back. Heavily built and not at all speedy, he made no pretensions whatever at artistry. As a forward he knew his job was to get goals, and he secured most of them by waiting for a chance and hitting the ball so hard that it was common sense on the part of the custodian to get out of the way. In this season of 1906-7 he scored eight goals in three successive League matches following the game with Morton, and in the Charity Cup-tie he scored the goal that defeated Third Lanark in the semi-final and also the goal by which the Celtic were beaten in the Final.

R. S. M'Coll played only one game this season. He had taken a fancy for his old club, Queen's Park, to whose membership he was readmitted in the following season, and his first match, as a reinstated amateur, was against the Rangers. It may have been sheer imagination, but many considered he played a finer game on this occasion against the Light Blues than he had ever played for them.

Recognising that still more driving force was needed in attack, the transfer of George Livingstone from Manchester City was negotiated. But he was not immediately available, for the English F.A. had previously swept down upon the Manchester City household and, for various technical offences, had imposed very drastic suspensions on officials and players. Livingstone's suspension expired on 31st

THE STORY OF THE RANGERS.

December, 1906, and it was hoped to play him in the New Year's day match with Celtic at Ibrox, but he did not make his debut until the first-round Scottish Cup-tie with Falkirk, at Brockville Park. That Ne'erday game with Celtic was the most meritorious played by the Rangers all season. Celtic were romping away with the championship. They had played nineteen matches and were undefeated. Rangers were in dire difficulty for a team. It was regarded as the mere tossing of the dice to play Galt and Mainds in the half-back line. The only regular first-eleven forwards available were Kyle and Smith. William Kivlichan, a young student, who in the following season played for Celtic, was given the centre forward position, and Albert Cunningham, an ex-Port-Glasgow boy, partnered the diminutive Dickie on the right. The young ones rose grandly to the test before a 50,000 crowd. Campbell played, perhaps, the game of his life at back, and Stark was magnificent in his manner of inspiring the recruits with confidence. Celtic lost Quinn near half-time, he coming under the ban of Referee Kirkham, of Preston, and, needless to say, the herculean task of the Rangers forces was made easier on that account. But the 2–1 victory was, nevertheless, an achievement of great merit, the only ones comparable with it being the Scottish Cup-tie win at Falkirk and the Charity Cup Final success again against the Parkhead rival. The tie against Falkirk was notable for a famous goal—the winning one—scored by M'Fie, who was playing for Kyle, who was ill. Celtic got an early opportunity to avenge the League reverse, for in the third round of the Scottish Cup, they were drawn at Ibrox. A 60,000 crowd, record for a Scottish club match, saw a badly-selected Rangers eleven deservedly beaten.

Before the Charity Cup-ties gave the club a chance to

annex, at least, one trophy, there came to Ibrox two young players who were destined to gain distinction. One was James E. Gordon, the other George Law. As a junior, Gordon was one of the most promising of the clever band who represented the Renfrew Victoria club. He came to the Rangers as a wing half-back, and as such obtained senior International honours. He could, however, play in any position. As a right half and as a left half he was capped against England, while for the club he played several match-winning games as a centre forward. Towards the close of 1908-9 he revealed himself as a scoring centre, and he finished the season with 14 goals to his credit. For thirteen seasons Gordon shared in the adventures of the Light Blues, and it was by his own choice that the long association was broken. The terms offered him for the season of 1920-21 were such as were believed to be due an old and valued servant. Gordon declined them. Well, to decide was his prerogative. He joined Dunfermline Athletic, then members of the Central League, and met good sportsmen there. But to have finished his career with his first senior club would have been, one might suppose, a pleasant reverie in his old age. Strong of limb and broad-chested, as proficient with the right as with the left foot, and deft with both, Gordon belonged to that class of player which the infallible verdict of public opinion designates as first quality. He had the football sense, the natural ability to play the game which can never hide. Except a Scottish Cup medal, which he sought above everything, Gordon secured all the honours the game could offer. In 1912, 1913, 1914, and 1920, he was capped against England and Ireland; in 1913 and 1920, against Wales; in 1913, 1914, 1915, and 1920 against the English League; in 1910, 1913, 1914, and 1920 against the Irish League; and in 1912, 1913, 1914, and 1915

against the Southern League. Possibly the greatest
game he ever played in an International was his last
against England, at Sheffield, where lashing rain had made
the pitch a mud heap. He was at left half that day, and
the conditions called for supreme judgment when
intervening to check the clever English right wing.
Almost as good was his display in the second half for the
Scottish League against the League of England at Burnley,
in 1914. The Scots looked hopelessly beaten at the
interval when two goals down, but a brilliant second-half
recovery by Gordon, M'Menemy, and Croal swung the
game round and the Tam o' Shanter brigade on the grand
stand went half mad over a 3–2 victory, the last, by the
way, the Scottish League have enjoyed except in the
unofficial match of 1919, at Ibrox.

George Law played his first match for the Rangers on
2nd March, 1907. He was a fine cut of a lad, fair and
fresh, and as straight as a tree. He came from Arbroath,
and at first was rather shy of the big city and the great
crowds, but he soon caught the new atmosphere. In
some respects he was not unlike the great Nicol Smith
but smaller made. He and Alec Craig were the best full
back combination since the days of Nicol Smith and John
Drummond, but they did not remain together nearly so
long as did these doughty warriors. Law's last season at
Ibrox was 1911-12, during which he played in only eleven
matches. So rapid had been his progress that in 1910
he was capped against England, Wales, and Ireland.
This was possibly the worst thing that could have happened
to him. Until then, he had been as happy as a bird on
a branch. He loved the colour of a Rangers jersey and he
played as if he did. But those International honours
came to him before he had learned to resist temptation.
They turned the fierce light of fame upon him. There were

those ready to whisper in his ear that he could do better for himself where there were fresh fields to conquer. He departed from Ibrox when he could have stayed and been welcome. More frank than some others, he would say, in after years, that the day he rued most was the day he refused to act on the advice of Manager Wilton. George Law was a bonnie back, crisp in action, a clean tackler, and neat in his volleying. He had, in fact, style. When he joined Leeds City, he was played oftenest at half-back, but he was a back and nothing else. It was a shame to spoil so good a back, but that exactly is what happened.

Another clever player signed in time for the Charity Cup-ties was John Macdonald, a wing forward. He and Gordon took part in the Cup Final against Celtic, but Law was regarded as too inexperienced for such an ordeal. As showing the changes that had occurred, the teams are interesting :—

> **Celtic.**—Adams ; M'Nair and Orr ; Young, Lonie, and Hay ; Bennett, M'Menemy, Quinn, Somers, and Templeton.

> **Rangers.**—Newbigging ; Jackson and Craig ; Gordon, May and Galt ; Macdonald, Livingstone, Campbell, Kyle, and Smith.

This was Templeton's first season with Celtic and Orr's last. The former did not remain long at Parkhead, for in October, 1907, he was transferred to Kilmarnock, the club for whom he had played before crossing the Border. W. F. Kivlichan (now a doctor practising in the east-end of Glasgow) had left Ibrox for Parkhead before the Charity Cup Final was played, but he deferred his debut against his former colleagues until the following season. The results as between the old rivals over the season were wonderfully even, for each won the home League match

P   217

by 2–1, Celtic won the Scottish Cup-tie by 3–0, and
Rangers won the Charity Cup Final by 1–0. The club's
cup record was :—

Scottish Cup.		Glasgow Cup.		Charity Cup.	
Falkirk (A),	2–1	Queen's Park (A),	2–2	Partick Thistle (H),	3–0
Galston (A),	4–0	Queen's Park (H),	0–3	Third Lanark (H),	1–0
Celtic (H),	0–3			Celtic (Cathkin),	1–0
	6–4		2–5		5–0

Stark, May, Livingstone, and Alec Smith were capped
against the English League, and Livingstone and Smith
against Wales. Not much in the way of individual honours,
but the club could not be expected to carry Scotland on
its back right through the ages.

1907—1908.

Record Money—Thrice-played Final—A Freak Goal—
Big Signings — Harry Rennie — Alec Bennett—
Hamilton's Good-bye—A Last Link.

LIGHTNING, it is said, never strikes twice in the same place. If it is true of lightning, it is not true of a football team on the romp. In this season of 1907–8, Celtic struck the Rangers four shrewd blows—one in the second round of the Scottish Cup, another in the Final of the Glasgow Cup, and two in the League. Not one of the three cups did the Light Blues lay hands upon ; their position in the League was third. Yet, over the season, only three teams could make them strike their colours. One was Celtic, the others were Airdrieonians and Queen's Park. Airdrieonians won both League matches, Queen's Park won the Hampden match and also defeated the Light Blues in the second round of the Charity Cup. There is only one other instance on record—1905–6—of Rangers losing both League matches to Airdrieonians. Of the 44 League games played between Rangers and Queen's Park, the latter have won three. So, if the medicine men were not great for numbers in this season, they carried a fair supply of pills which, strange to say, cured some of the Ibrox ills. Besides, results proved that the actual winning of cups and things is not every-thing, for season 1907-8 was the most successful, financially, which Rangers had ever experienced. The gross receipts from matches alone totalled £14,076.

There was only one player on the roll, when the season opened, who had not hitherto worn the club's colours. This was Alec Barrie, a half-back. He had been five seasons with Sunderland, who generously granted him a free transfer although claiming the right to any fee which

THE STORY OF THE RANGERS.

Rangers might eventually secure for him. R. C. Hamilton, after a season with Fulham, was back to the fold. Like the curate in " Charley's Aunt," he didn't like London— not, at anyrate, so well as Elgin where the directors agreed he should reside. Barrie was designed to take the place of James Stark gone to Chelsea, but the change lasted only one season. Stark returned to Ibrox in October, 1908, and Barrie, about the same time, went to Kilmarnock. Hamilton played only eleven matches. He was not committed in the cup-ties, and when Rangers were defeated by Celtic in the second round of the " Scottish," he was transferred to the Hearts for whom he played in various positions in the forward line. Even at Ibrox, it was difficult now to " place " him since the scoring habit developed by R. G. Campbell made the transference of the latter from centre a proceeding open to challenge. In the Glasgow Cup-ties " R. G." was, therefore, played at centre and " R. C." at outside right. Against Clyde, at Shawfield, Campbell scored two of the four goals, and against Third Lanark, at Ibrox, he registered all three credited to the Rangers. The Final with Celtic, at Hampden, was, in some respects, the most arresting tie that had ever been played. Three games were required to decide it, and for the first time in history, Rangers were defeated by Celtic after a draw with them in this competition. All money and attendance records were broken. According to the official figures, 192,000 persons watched the three games and the total drawings, including stands, amounted to £4,972 17s. 8d. At the gates alone, with a sixpenny tariff, the money taken was :—

First game,	-	-	-	-	£1,685 18 3
Second game,	-	-	-	-	1,223 6 4
Third game,	-	-	-	-	1,167 16 1
					£4,077 0 8

Not once did Rangers lead in the scoring, yet in the first two games they finished so strongly that, it was generally admitted, the tiniest bit of luck would have given them the cup. Celtic owed much to the fine tactical defence of M'Nair and Hay, who, after being played at back because M'Leod and Weir were indisposed, made their removal to half-back a matter of such doubtful advantage that they were retained in the defence until the tie had been won. In the second game, Celtic played Semple, of Rutherglen Glencairn, at outside left because Templeton had been transferred to Kilmarnock, but in the third game David M'Lean took up the centre position and Quinn went into his original place on the left touchline. The teams in the match that decided this stubborn, thrice-fought tie were :—

> Celtic.—Adams ; M'Nair and Hay ; Young, Lonie, and Mitchell ; Bennett, M'Menemy, M'Lean, Somers, and Quinn.

> Rangers.—Newbigging ; Jackson and Craig ; Gordon, May, and Galt ; Hamilton, Livingstone, Campbell, Kyle, and Smith.

Celtic scored twice in the first half, but the Rangers forwards made a magnificent rally after the interval and from the moment Kyle got through and beat Adams, they fought grandly to square the scores. It was the stonewall defence of M'Nair and Hay that beat them. There was nothing very much wrong with the team so far, but when Campbell lost his scoring touch and when Alec Smith went down with sciatica and Gordon with pleurisy, the trouble began. Changes had to be made in all divisions, and before the New Year was very old it was as plain as daylight that something would require to be done to strengthen the team. Nothing, however, happened in this direction until after the defeat by Celtic in the Scottish Cup-tie, at Ibrox. This was rather a stupid defeat brought about by a freakish goal scored by Kivlichan, who was playing centre for Celtic, in the absence of Quinn. Kivlichan had possession of the ball and was almost on the by-line some fifteen yards to the right of the goal. May was on the line, but evidently afraid to tackle him in case he should give away a corner which was the best that seemed in the power of the Celt to contrive. When May refused to come in to. him, however, Kivlichan was compelled to do something. So he spun the ball across towards goal, and, to the amazement of everybody, it screwed round after passing Newbigging and entered the net. If he had tried the same thing a thousand times over he possibly couldn't have succeeded again, but once was quite good enough to be going on with. Celtic went ahead to win the Cup, and later, the League championship and the Charity Cup. It was their year.

There was some hustle at Ibrox near the end of April. James Sharp, of Woolwich Arsenal, who had been twice capped against England, was signed just in time to play in the return League match with Celtic. An offer of £500 was made to the Hearts for Charles Thomson, but apparently this was not enough for he went to Sunderland instead, and became captain of the Wearside team. Robert Noble, an outside right, was secured from Broxburn Athletic. J. Douglas, a Dumfries boy, and a right winger also, was signed early in May, and hard after them came Tom Murray, a centre from Aberdeen, who was English born; Thomas Gilchrist, an inside forward from Third Lanark; William M'Pherson, another inside forward from Liverpool, who was a native of Beith, and had played for St. Mirren before going south; Alec Bennett, of Celtic; and Harry Rennie, of Hibernian. When Bennett signed for Rangers, the Celtic demanded from the Scottish F.A. an inquiry, as they alleged that he had been approached before the end of April which, of course, would have been

contrary to law.   The S.F.A. did inquire and found nothing
to substantiate Celtic's charge.   Bennett did not play in
the Charity Cup-ties, but most of the others did, and the
teams in the second-round tie at Ibrox were :—

> **Queen's Park.**—W. C. M'Kenna ; R. A. Young and
> H. Fletcher ; Wm. M'Andrew, A. F. Murray, and J. Bryce ;
> J. M'Lean, J. Sim, W. Leckie, R. S. M'Coll, and A. E.
> Gordon.

> **Rangers.**—Rennie ; Law and Sharp ; Gordon, Taylor,
> and Galt ; Douglas, Gilchrist, Murray, M'Pherson, and
> M'Donald.

A 3–1 victory for Queen's Park, who thoroughly deserved
it, did not show the new Rangers men in a grand light,
but some of them stayed long enough to prove that it was
not all a matter of " far away birds having fine feathers."
R. C. Hamilton, in recognition of a long and faithful
service, was given a free transfer, and he joined Morton
with whom he remained two seasons.   Speirs and Dickie
threw in their lot with the Clyde, Kyle went to Blackburn
Rovers.   With the permanent departure of Hamilton,
there now remained only Alec Smith as a link with the
great team of 1898–99.   It was a link that nothing seemed
capable of snapping.   The team's Cup record and the
individual honours gained in **1907-8** were as follows :—

Scottish Cup.		Glasgow Cup.		Charity Cup.	
Falkirk (A)	2–2	Clyde (A)	4–0	Third Lanark	
Falkirk (H)	4–1	Third Lanark (H)	3–0	(Hampden),	3–1
Celtic (H)	1–2	Celtic Hampd'n,	2–2	Queen's Park (H)	1–3
		Celtic Hampd'n,	0–0		
		Celtic Hampd'n,	1–2		
	7–5		10–4		4–4

v. England.	*v.* Wales.	*v.* Ireland.	*v.* English League.
J. May	J. Galt.	J. May.	J. May.
	J. Speirs.	J. Galt.	A. Kyle.
			A. Smith.

1908—1909.

The Hampden Riot—What Caused It—A Doubtful Goal—Harry Rennie's Story—James Sharp Goes— George Livingstone, Too—Coming of H. Lock and W. Hogg.

THE year of the Hampden Riot will always be an easy and familiar phrase with which to identify an event which had big consequences, in the same way as we talk of the year of the short corn. We can tell what caused the short corn. It is not so easy to solve the riddle of the riot. Everybody concerned thought someone else was to blame. At anyrate, if there was guilt on anyone's mind, that particular person declined to fall under the spell of the adage which has to do with confession being good for the soul. The inquiry which was set up by the Scottish F.A. served one very useful purpose so far as the Rangers were concerned. It proved that they, as a club, and the officials as individuals, were entirely free from association with any possible contributory causes. Giving evidence at the inquiry, Mr. William Maley, secretary of the Celtic, indicated that his club, after the first game of the Scottish Cup Final had resulted in a draw, were desirous of playing the second game to a finish. This fact was reported in a Glasgow paper on the Wednesday following the first match. Unfortunately, as subsequent events proved, the subject of playing to a finish was not referred to again in the Press. It is quite likely, therefore, that many of those who attended the second game were under the belief that, in the event of another draw, extra time would be played. The presumption amounts almost to a certainty. At the inquiry, James Hay, the Celtic captain, and James Stark, the Rangers captain, stated that they had had no instructions from their officials as to playing extra time. We can, of course, speak only for the Rangers, and we know the captain's statement to be correct. The question of extra time had never been discussed by the directors for the simple reason that the rules of the S.F.A. stipulated for extra time only when a third game became necessary. It was a terribly unfortunate thing that, at the finish of the second game, several of the players lingered on the field after the whistle had sounded. A photograph of this incident, reproduced on the Monday following the match, showed six or seven Celtic players and two Rangers men on the field when they should have been in the pavilion. The official inquiry by no means explained satisfactorily why there was this delay in moving, at once, off the pitch. Had the usual alacrity been displayed in making for the pavilion there would probably have been no riot. The hesitancy of those particular players undoubtedly conveyed the impression that extra time was a matter at issue between the competing clubs. A wild, unruly section of the crowd assumed as much. They undertook to become arbiters in the dispute and thus we had written, on that bright afternoon in April, 1909, the blackest page in Scottish football. Barricades were torn down, a bonfire was set agoing on the track, payboxes were set ablaze with burning brands, the police who attempted to check the mad outburst of animal passion were stoned and kicked, hosepipes were cut, the pavilion became like a slaughter house. On the following day, the Celtic and Rangers clubs drew up a joint statement, which was issued to the Press. It was in these terms :—

> Although it was mooted during the week that extra time might be played in the event of a draw, it was found that the Cup Competition rules prevented this. On account

of the regrettable occurrences of Saturday, both clubs agree to petition the Association that the Final tie be abandoned.

> Statement signed by T. Colgan and John M'Killop on behalf of the Celtic, and by A. B. Mackenzie and John M'Pherson on behalf of the Rangers.

When the Association council met to consider the matter of the riot, a proposal was made to replay the match outside of Glasgow, but Mr. T. White, speaking for both Celtic and Rangers, said the clubs would not play the Final over again. One of them would scratch first. Eventually, by 15 votes to 11, there was carried a motion by the President, Mr. John Liddell (Queen's Park), "That to mark the Association's disapproval of the riotous conduct of a section of the spectators at Hampden Park, and to avoid a repetition, the Cup competition for this season be finished and the cup and medals withheld."

This dismal ending to what possessed all the elements of a great Cup Final-tie was specially deplored by followers of the Rangers, thousands of whom believed that the team should never have had to play a second game. They based their belief upon the argument that Celtic's equalising goal in the first match ought not to have been allowed. Mr. J. B. Stark was the referee and he gave his decision quickly when Harry Rennie, with the ball in his hands, following a long centre from Munro, the Celtic outside right, slewed round to avoid the in-rushing Quinn. There is no purpose to be served in dogmatising upon a point of play, but all who knew Rennie are aware that he scarcely ever stood on his line, and if he was not standing on his line when he held Munro's centre, then a goal was not registered. Rennie was not in the habit of shedding tears over football; he was a philosopher in his way;

but in the pavilion at the finish of this match he cried like a boy from sheer vexation that such a mistaken decision, as he thought it, should have robbed his club of the Cup.

His version of the incident, written by his own hand, is well worth reproducing. He was that kind of man who could throw club partizanship to the winds where honesty demanded it. Had the ball been over the goal line, Rennie would have said so. This is what he says :—

I can visualise the incident now just as clearly as if it had happened only this afternoon. It was a thrilling moment, and it is amazing what passes through a man's brain in a few available and critical seconds. At the time it happened I regarded it, and continue to regard it, as one of the most artful and artistic saves in my merry football career.

All the factors necessary to build up a stirring football episode were there—a Rangers–Celtic Scottish Cup Final ; Rangers leading 2–1 ; the last few minutes of the game ebbing ; a lazy ball with a lot of spin, from the Celtic's right wing, bending out of its course and simply drifting, high up, through the Rangers' goal at the corner formed by the goal post on my left hand side, as I face the field of play, and the cross-bar ; the desperate Celtic forwards, led by the great Celtic centre-forward, J. Quinn, rushing in at a greater rate than that at which the ball was travelling ; a goalkeeper with about a score of International caps to his head, faced with the problem of how to save his goal and win and lose the Cup for the Rangers and Celtic respectively; a huge concourse of sixty or eighty thousand intelligent Britishers throbbing with the intensest of intense expectancy.

What a setting !

Let me tell you that I was supremely conscious of what it all meant. I knew that it was the crisis of the game ; that if I saved that ball in the way in which it ought to be saved, the Cup was ours.

It did occur to me simply to palm that ball out, but in a flash I dismissed that idea as panic and crude goalkeeping, unworthy of the standard of play usually associated with the Glasgow Rangers Football Club, unworthy of the importance of that particular match, unworthy of the many distinguished and talented people who honoured the match by their presence and who expected, and had every right to expect, an exhibition of the finer points of the game ; unworthy, even, of my own reputation.

Therefore, I seized the golden opportunity to give a demonstration of the real art of goalkeeping. I did not snatch at that light, spinning ball ; no, to have done so would have been fatal to success. I stretched my long, vigorous arms upwards, sensed the speed and spin of the ball with ten powerful and sensitive finger tips, and with the profoundest concentration of mind, that entirely obliterated everything but the task on hand, I sighted that ball against crossbar and goalpost and bringing hands and ball down together, I simply " nursed " it into subjection.

While my hands and sight were thus respectively dealing with and sighting the ball to see that it did not completely and entirely pass the goalpost, I half bent and half twisted my extremely lithe body from the waist, throwing back the hips, for the double purpose of adjusting my body relative to my arms (I had to adjust my arms relative to the ball, and the ball relative to the goalpost) and to get into the best position for a spring to evade the charging Jimmy Quinn.

I must say here I knew James Quinn would play me fair, because though he has many a time charged me heavily, he never once, in all our matches, made the slightest attempt to incapacitate me ; in fact, I can recall occasions when he restrained his effort, and I feel sure that it was because he thought that the chance of injuring me was greater than his chance of getting the ball.

He rushed in exactly to schedule time as mentally calculated by me, I side-stepped to the left, and with a leap, punted the ball away to midfield thus accomplishing what I thought to be a high-class and effective bit of goalkeeping.

Then up rushed the referee—from where ?—and decided that the Celtic had scored.

It was the throwing back of the hips that deceived some people ; they naturally thought that I had hauled the ball through the goal. They were wrong. That peculiar movement was one of my secret training stunts, and it was hard luck on the Rangers and on myself to have had that difficult and artful bit of work completely nullified by what, in my opinion, was a wrong decision.

Many onlookers thought that because the bali was over an imaginary straight line, drawn from their point of vision to that particular goalpost that the ball was through the goal. They err, because it would be quite possible for the ball to be over that line and yet not over the line drawn from goalpost to goalpost, and which is the line that matters.

The teams in the first game of the Final were :—

> Celtic.—Adams ; M'Nair and Weir ; Young, Dodds, and Hay ; Munro, M'Menemy, Quinn, Somers, and Hamilton.
>
> Rangers.—Rennie ; Law and Craig ; May, Stark, and Galt ; Bennett, Gilchrist, Campbell, M'Pherson, and Smith.

Hard ground and a high wind made the ball difficult to control, but the game was contested with traditional verve and spirit. Quinn scored after 21 minutes and Celtic led until fifteen minutes from the finish. Then a startling change occurred. Gilchrist had gone to outside right, Campbell to inside, and Bennett to centre. A series of open passes gave Gilchrist a chance and he equalised with a slanting shot. Three minutes later, Bennett put Rangers in the lead, and the Cup seemed won, for the defence was grand. When the end was only a few minutes away, there occurred the incident of the disputed goal. All that need be said is that had it meant the disposal of the Cup, the feeling of resentment among Rangers followers would have been greatly intensified.

The match had proved to the Rangers directors that the team was not quite right. Manager Wilton became very busy, and two days before the replay, the transfer of William Reid from Portsmouth was completed and he had the rather unusual experience—though not his only one of the same kind—of making his debut for his new club in a Scottish Cup Final. This was not the only change. Gordon came in at right half in place of May, and Gilchrist and Campbell stood out of the forward line, which was Bennett, Macdonald, Reid, M'Pherson, and Smith. Celtic gave Munro's position to Kivlichan. It was a fine sporting tussle. Never were players strung to a higher pitch, but they fought fair. After twenty-one minutes, Gordon surprised the Celtic defence by keeping the ball and darting in to beat Adams with a powerful slanting shot. By this goal, Rangers led at half-time, but seventeen minutes after the interval, Hay placed a corner kick from which Quinn equalised. Neither team would risk much afterwards by opening out. They feared each other's attack, and were both content to foil while watching for a stray chance to strike a mortal blow. The chance never came, and so the scores remained unaltered, which was a great misfortune, since it were much better for both that either should have got a winning goal than that the prestige of the game should have been disgraced by the scenes that followed.

A feature of the ties leading up to the Final was the success of M'Pherson as a scorer. Against St. Johnstone, in the first round, he failed to register, but in the ties with Dundee, Queen's Park, and Falkirk, who were each defeated by 1–0, he picked up the vital goal in each case. He was not a great manipulator, but had always his wits about him. Not since that season of 1908–9 have Rangers and Queen's Park met in a Scottish Cup-tie, so it may be interesting to give here a résumé of their encounters :—

1878–79.	Sixth Round.	Rangers	1	Queen's Park,	0
1879–80.	First Round.	Rangers	1	Queen's Park,	5
1882–83.	Second Round.	Rangers	2	Queen's Park,	3
1893–94.	Semi-Final.	Rangers	3	Queen's Park,	1
1897–98.	Third Round.	Rangers	3	Queen's Park,	1
1908–9.	Third Round.	Rangers	1	Queen's Park,	0
			11		10

FIFTY YEARS OF FOOTBALL——1908-1909.

Upon the team in general the Cup Final experience had an unsteadying effect. Up till then, there was a chance of the Leage Championship being won, but after the Final, three League games in succession were lost. Reid played in two League matches, and, failing to find the scoring vein which proved rich in goals for him in later years, was omitted from the team which won the Charity Cup. Gordon was played at centre forward, and in the three ties scored seven goals—three against Partick Thistle, two against Third Lanark, and two against Celtic in the Final. This Charity Cup Final victory over Celtic squared the Glasgow Cup defeat earlier in the season.

During the playing term some important changes had occurred. About New Year time, James Sharp asked to be placed on the transfer list as he wished to return to England. Fulham got him for £1,000, and to them he proved worth it, though somehow he had never managed to fill the position at Ibrox which his undoubted talents justified. Life here seemed too dull for him after his former sojourn on the fringe of London gaiety. Shortly after Sharp's departure George Livingstone was allowed to go to Manchester United at the earnest request of the United's officials, who sent a deputation to Glasgow to press their suit. Except for the usual Army football, this was Livingstone's last spell of activity as a player. He became manager of the Dumbarton club, which was appropriate enough since Boghead Park is within easy reach of the spot where he was born. It was as a member of the young Artizan Thistle club, of Dumbarton, that George Livingstone nurtured a liking for the game. He gained junior cup honours with Parkhead F.C. and his senior career is epitomised in his succession of clubs—Hearts, Sunderland, Celtic, Liverpool, Manchester City,

Rangers, Manchester United. Since he became trainer to the Rangers, in 1920, the team has obtained some wonderful successes. As a player he was a club enthusiast and he expects others to be the same. Hard as nails, he loved to get his shoulder on to an opponent as big as—or bigger than—himself. He was one of Scotland's victorious team against England in 1906, at Hampden Park, and, according to his own theory, he was helping to lay the foundation of the victory when, in the first minutes of the game, he rattled into the stalwart Bob Crompton with a hearty shoulder charge. George's theory was that if he didn't get one in early, " Big Bob," would probably give the Scots forwards more than was agreeable. To counterbalance these losses, Rangers signed, in October, 1908, John Smith, a useful centre forward who had been doing well in Ardrossan Winton Rovers; John M'Kenzie, an Elgin City back, who had shoulders like the gable of a house; and William Yuille, an inside forward from Ashgill Rovers (Lanarkshire). Both Smith and Yuille played against Celtic in a League match at Parkhead, which Rangers won by 3–2, and which had, as a sequel, the calling of the referee and linesmen before the League Committee. A paragraph in the Rangers minute book gives an inkling of the sort of match that was :—

> " It was agreed to pay John Macdonald £2 16s. od., being dentist's bill for teeth to replace those knocked out in Celtic League match."

Celtic may also have had a bill to meet. This was Macdonald's last season with Rangers. He joined Liverpool. Tom Murray returned to Aberdeen, while from Lesmahagow came George Waddell, a bustling, audacious half-back.

None of these comings and goings equalled in importance

the signing, in May, 1909, of Herbert Lock, the Southampton goalkeeper, and William Hogg, the Sunderland forward. Hogg cost the Rangers just £100, yet he was one of the finest forwards in England and had represented his country against Scotland, Wales, and Ireland in 1902. He played for Rangers in various positions in the forward line before settling down at outside right which, undoubtedly, was the place in which he excelled. " Billy " had his little weaknesses, like all of us, but he was a great football player and would have been still more successful had he cared to make use of his strength of shoulder. He did not like charging, and when he tried it he did it like one who was deficient in practice. For a man who carried so much weight, he was wonderfully sprightly and could get up a rare turn of speed. In his first season of 1909-10, he scored eight goals ; in 1910-11, his " bag " was 17 ; in 1911-12, it was 19 ; while in 1912-13, which was his last season at Ibrox, he scored seven goals, playing in only 20 matches before being transferred to Dundee. Devil-may-care in most things, " Billy " Hogg gave the impression of a great, big boy bubbling over with animal spirit. It might have been more to his profit had he seen the more serious side of his profession. A man is what he is, however. If he didn't grumble, why should others on his behalf ? He had his pleasures and he never chortled so loudly as when he had scored a goal in an important match. You would have imagined that his last goal was always his first.

Herbert Lock was a signed player for Rangers three weeks before Hogg, and he was, therefore, the first Englishman to be brought from England to wear the Ibrox colours. Tom Murray, who had already worn Light Blue, was English-born, but he joined Rangers from Aberdeen.

THE STORY OF THE RANGERS.

In 1908-9, Lock, while playing for Southampton, was reserve to Sam Hardy for England's goal against Scotland. Fit to play in the most brilliant company, Lock's misfortune was that a goalkeeper of Hardy's supreme qualities should have been in possession as warden of the national citadel during those years when he himself was worthy of honours. Lock played for ten seasons with the Rangers and helped them to win the League Championship five times. In his second season the club became champions for the first time in nine years. This renewed triumph was the first of three successive ones. The Glasgow Cup was won six times and the Charity Cup twice while Lock was custodian. That he contributed very considerably to the success of the team is undoubted. During his association with the club the praise he so richly deserved was freely accorded, and that is better than having to wait for honeyed words in an obituary notice. Every goal-keeper excels in a particular feature. No custodian was ever seen in Scotland who more often than Lock foiled opposing forwards who were in the position described as having the goal at their mercy. His daring amounted to recklessness. The risks he took made injury to himself inevitable, for he would throw himself at the ball when the man behind it had his foot on the swing for the shot. The impulse to prevent the ball going into the net was stronger than the instinct of self-preservation. As the classic example of Lock's marvellous quickness and absolute bravery, his save at Ibrox against Partick Thistle in the Glasgow Cup-tie of 1912-13, in the second game of three, will stand unchallenged. The score was 1-1 when near the end, Callaghan, the Thistle right-winger, raced past all the Rangers outfield defence and cut in almost up to the post. He never lost his wits, but steadied himself for the shot. Rangers followers, in a mental flash, saw the tie lost.   Then through the air, in a sort of diving spring, went the figure of Herbert Lock, and almost before the crowd could realise what had happened, there was a sickening contact of boot, ball, and man.   The goal was saved, but Lock was out of the game for many a day afterwards.   He was not so good in dealing with balls that required to be taken with uplifted hands, yet as a custodian of all-round ability his superiors have been few.   In his last season with the Rangers, which was 1919-20, he played in 35 of the 42 League matches.   The championship was won for Ibrox and the total goals lost numbered only 25, not the best, but certainly one of the best defensive records possessed by the club.   Herbert Lock was a good club man, faithful to duty and proud of the team's successes, though neither demonstrative nor emotional.

Along with Hogg and Lock came William Hunter, M.A., who had been scoring goals for Airdrieonians.   He was a centre forward by choice, but could play on the left wing. In his first and only season at Ibrox, Hunter scored 19 goals.   He was fast and clever on the ball, but the wear and tear of strenuous football was not altogether to his liking.   Hunter was one of four holding the degree of M.A. who have played for the club.   R. C. Hamilton, Tom Gilchrist, and M. B. Houston were entitled, by intellectual attainment, to affix M.A. to their name. Messrs. Hunter, Gilchrist, and Houston (the last-named played as an amateur) were playing members of the club at the same time.

In the season of 1908-9, Bennett was capped against England, Wales, and Ireland and the English League. Stark played against England, Ireland, and the English League, and May against Wales.   Reid, while still a Portsmouth player, was chosen reserve centre to Quinn

for the match with England. The club's Cup tie record
was as follows :

Scottish Cup.		Glasgow Cup.		Charity Cup.	
St. Johnstone (A),	3–0	A Bye.		Partick Thistle (H),	3–1
Dundee (A),	0–0	Celtic (A),	2–2	Third Lanark (A),	3–2
Dundee (H),	1–0	Celtic (H),	0–2	Celtic (A),	4–2
Queen's Park (H),	1–0				
Falkirk (A),	1–0				
Celtic (Hampd'n),	2–2				
Celtic (Hampd'n),	1–1				
	9–3		2–4		10–5

1909—1910.

Cup Failures—Clyde's Hammer Blows—W. Reid's Goals—Wanted by Preston—J. Gordon's Caps—Triple Crown for G. Law—Good Time Coming.

A WATCH is a wonderful piece of machinery when all the wheels and screws are in place. The Rangers team of **1909-1910** would have been an efficient instrument if screws had'nt been loose. The talent was there in luscious abundance. Half of the season, however, was spent in trying to make the ideal combination and the effort was a failure. The difficulty was aggravated by an injury to Craig which broke, for an extended period, his co-partnery with Law at back. For the greater part of the season, John Mackenzie, the stalwart Highlander, was alongside Law, and though eager and willing, he did not possess the football knowledge of Craig. The forwards were moved about as if they were the pieces in a game of chess. Willie Reid did not get goals because the ever-changing wings did not understand him. He had to give way to Hunter who, like Hogg, was played all over the place, as the saying goes. It seemed impossible to decide whether Bennett was now an outside or an inside right or a left winger. Such a fine half-back as David Taylor could not get a place in the team. Harry Rennie was acting as reserve to Lock. The club was in the position of having a gold mine and getting nothing out of it. Before the New Year, six defeats were sustained in the League. The team got through to the Final of the Glasgow Cup to be defeated by Celtic by a goal to nothing, Quinn being the scorer with one of his sensational bursts which often made a beaten

Celtic team into a winning one. With the turn of the year there was a welcome tendency towards stability, and but for the loss of the Scottish Cup-tie with Clyde at Shawfield, where the mud gave neither side a chance to play football, the second half of the season was distinctly cheering. The Cup-tie defeat at Shawfield saw the worst blow of the season, but the Light Blues were meeting as powerful a Clyde as ever wore the Shawfield colours. Going straight ahead to the Final, Clyde should have won the Cup, for in the first of the three games with Dundee, they held what should have been a commanding lead. In the Shawfield tie the teams were :—

> **Clyde.**—M'Turk ; Watson and Blair; Walker, M'Ateer, and Robertson ; Stirling, M'Cartney, Chalmers, Jackson, and Booth.

> **Rangers.**—Lock ; Law and Mackenzie ; May, Stark, and Galt ; Bennett, M'Pherson, Reid, Hunter, and Smith.

Chalmers scored two goals for Clyde in the second half after the Rangers defence had withstood a severe gruelling. The game became a sheer test of stamina in the mud, and the winners proved the stronger. As showing the calibre of the Clyde team, it should be only necessary to mention that they also defeated the Rangers in the League at Shawfield and in the Charity Cup, which they won for the only time in their career, and finished fifth in the League. They were worthy foemen.

After the loss of the Scottish Cup-tie at Shawfield, the position at Ibrox was such that the club came near to parting with both Reid and Hogg. Preston North-End asked for terms of transfer, but, as subsequent events demonstrated, it was fortunate that no bargain was closed. Reid, in 20 matches, harvested only 14 goals during the season, but his scoring ability became evident in the next campaign and also in succeeding years. Leaving out of account his success as a marksman in representative matches, his record bears witness to the loss the club would have sustained had Preston North-End carried through their fell design. His goals for Rangers were :—

1909-10, -	- 14	1913-14, -	- 29
1910-11, -	- 48	1914-15. -	- 32
1911-12, -	- 40	1915-16, -	- 25
1912-13, -	- 27	1919-20, -	- 9
	Total,	- - **224**	

In the season 1910-11, Reid's complete capture was 52 goals made up as follows :—

Scottish League,	39	Greenock Charity,	1
Scottish Cup,	- 3	English League, -	1
Glasgow Cup,	- 2	Irish League, -	1
Charity Cup,	- 4	Ireland, - -	1

Like several other members of the team, Reid went into khaki during the Great War and did not play during three seasons, otherwise his inventory would have been even more praiseworthy. When he returned from Salonika he donned the old light blue again, but played in only nine matches in the season of 1919-20, and had an average of a goal per match. Not what you would call an artist for style, William Reid had the faculty of goal-scoring highly developed. He could take the ball through in a strong, tenacious manner of running, but he was an economist, and if he could get goals without putting work on the ball, he preferred to get them that way. A slight natural in-turn of the foot enabled him, unconsciously, to put a swerve on the ball, and as he could get tremendous power behind the blow, goalkeepers were often helpless even if they had a perfect view of the ball coming at them. Reid was fond of acknowledging the debt he owed his wing colleagues, Hogg and Alec Smith. " When either Billy or Alec got on the ball," he would say, " I knew it was time for me to get off my mark to be up in time for it coming over." He got many of his goals by striding up to the ball as it was sent along to him and hitting it without any preliminary trapping. In this way he neutralised the goalkeeper's instinct for knowing in which direction he was aiming. Reid's junior club was Baillieston Thistle— then Morton, Third Lanark, Motherwell, Portsmouth, Rangers, Albion Rovers. While with Morton he was transferred to Third Lanark to play in the Scottish Cup Final against the Hearts, at Ibrox, in April, 1906. The Hearts won by 1–0. It is a coincidence that he was transferred from Portsmouth to Rangers to play in the Scottish Cup Final replay of 1909—the notorious Hampden Riot day.

It was now eight years since a League championship flag was run up to an Ibrox masthead, although in 1904-5 there was the dead-heat with Celtic and the play-off which gave Parkhead the prize. The wheel had " come full circle " again, however. Rangers were about to enter upon a period of renewed success which has, with slight variations, continued up to the present day. In that season of 1909-10, George Law got the three caps, England, Wales, and Ireland. He was still just a lad and should have had a great International career before him, but he never represented his country again. Bennett played against England, Wales, and the English League. Gordon was capped against the Irish League and thus modestly began counting his honours which, in the end, placed him third to Alec Smith and Neil Gibson among Rangers

players. Third in the League, the club's 1909-10 Cup
record was :—

Scottish Cup.		Glasgow Cup.		Charity Cup.	
Inverness		Partick		A Bye.	
Thistle (h)	3-1	Thistle (h),	2-1	Clyde (h),	0-1
Clyde (a),	0-2	Third Lanark			
		(a),	2-1		
		Celtic (Hamp-			
		den),	0-1		
	3-3		4-3		0-1

It was not anything to boast about, but nobody was
downhearted. Eyes were directed forward, and plans laid
for the coming campaign.

1910—1911.

Old Glories—League and Cups Won—A Captain's Error—George Chapman—Morton's Bombshell—5--1 at Ibrox—The Magical Alec Smith.

THIS season of **1910-1911** opened a new era of prosperity for the club. Never since then, if we except War years, have Rangers played through a season without landing one of the major prizes. But for an unlucky decision by captain George Chapman in the Scottish Cup-tie at Dundee, 1910-11 might easily have been historic. This tie was the only one lost. The Glasgow and Charity Cups were won, so was the League Championship. The Scottish Cup was won by Celtic, whom the Rangers defeated in the Final of both the other Cups. More than that, the Rangers won the League match at Parkhead and drew the return with Celtic at Ibrox. In the League, the team was defeated five times, all before the New Year. Aberdeen, with whom they ran a neck-and-neck race for the championship, obtained two victories over the Light Blues, a feat never before nor since accomplished by them. St. Mirren won the Paisley match, but in a manner which caused an investigation to be held by the League. Dundee, at Ibrox, with the old Ranger, R. C. Hamilton, at centre, triumphed by 2–1 after Crumley, their goalkeeper, had played with almost superhuman brilliance. Morton, with three ex-Rangers men, Jackson, Stark, and May, in their ranks, came to Ibrox and literally made the district rock by winning with a score of 5–1. A Greenock butcher had offered a lamb for every goal scored against the Rangers, and it was said he didn't look the least bit sheepish when informed of the result. These five League defeats and the Scottish Cup loss at Dundee constituted the total of reverse suffered by the Rangers. Their record for all matches was—

Played 53, won 36, lost 6, drew 11, scored 136 goals, lost 54.

From New Year's Day until the end of the season not a single defeat was sustained, except in the Cup-tie at Dundee. A few weeks after this event, Rangers returned to Dens Park for the League match and inflicted upon Dundee their first reverse at home in two years. The 52 points obtained was Rangers' highest aggregate up till then in a 34-club League, but they beat it by one point two seasons later.

Who were the men who shed this fresh lustre on Ibrox, and by their power of individual skill and combined effectiveness, conjured up the ghosts of the past? Let the figures of the matches played by the recognised first team members answer the question :—

Player.	Position.	Matches.	Goals.
H. Lock, - -	Goal, - - - -	43	--
G. Law, - -	Right back, - -	30	—
A. Richmond, -	Left back, - - -	27	—
R. G. Campbell,	Back and half-back, -	28	1
J. E. Gordon, -	Right half-back, -	37	6
G. R. Chapman,	Centre half-back, -	36	3
Joe Hendry, -	Left half-back, - -	37	1
J. Galt, - -	Half-back, - -	25	1
W. Hogg, -	Outside right, - -	39	17
J. Bowie, -	Inside right, - -	24	4
W. Reid, - -	Centre forward, -	42	48
A. Bennett, -	Inside Left, - -	31	10
A. Smith, - -	Outside left, - -	38	5

In addition to these, John (Jacky) L. Goodwin played in 10 League matches and scored 4 goals ; Wm. Yuille and Adam Gibson each played in 6 League matches, Gibson scoring 5 goals and Yuille 1 ; Robert Brown played in 5 League matches, A. Brown in 3, James Paterson in 2, and Robert Parker in 2 ; Alec Craig and David Taylor each played in 1, as did a wandering Irishman named

J. M'Aulay, from Cliftonville, who afterwards took the liberty of signing for Huddersfield although registered for the Rangers.

George Chapman, who was captain of the team; Robert Brown, from Kilwinning Rangers; Robert Parker, from Ashfield; Andrew Richmond, from Queen's Park; and Joe Hendry, from Morton, began the season with Rangers. Hendry had been signed in the previous April and had played against Falkirk in the last League match of the season, which was his first game for Rangers. James Bowie joined out of Queen's Park in December, and his first match was also against Falkirk. James Paterson, now a doctor in practice in London, was signed in September, 1910, and made his debut at outside left against Hibernian at Ibrox on the 25th of that month. He took the place of Alec Smith who had been with the Rangers almost as long as the new boy had been on this planet. It was not until November that A. Brown, of Galston, who had played also for Newcastle United and Kilmarnock, came to Ibrox, almost at the same time as Jacky Goodwin, of Ayr United. Both were forwards. James Stark and John May left to help Morton to become a first-class club; Harry Rennie and Tom Gilchrist went off to Kilmarnock; and David Taylor, without ever having had a full opportunity to prove his real worth, was transferred to Bradford City. Later, he became a magnificent defender in the Burnley team. Here let us bring to your memory James Croal, who long before this had been signed as a back. Though on the Rangers League registered list, he had been seeing the country with Alloa Athletic and Dunfermline Athletic, and now, in November, 1910, his connection with Ibrox was definitely severed. Falkirk got his transfer for a ten pound note, and, two seasons later, he was the principal instrument in putting Rangers out of the Scottish Cup-ties, on Ibrox Park, in the second round, and in winning the Cup for Falkirk after a brilliant march to the Final. As a forward, not a back, he climbed the shaky ladder of fame. No wonder people said in jest that to win a Scottish Cup badge all a player had got to do was to leave the Rangers. Croal gained the highest International honours as an inside left.

George Chapman, the captain of 1910-11, came to Ibrox with the reputation of being the finest centre half-back in England. He had been two seasons with Blackburn Rovers, previous to which he had played for Raith Rovers and the Hearts Reserves. He did justice to his reputation as a player during his one season with the Light Blues, but his health was not maintained, and he returned to Blackburn Rovers after playing only two matches in 1911-12. He was very fast, but in straining after speed he appeared to go beyond his strength. A most likeable young fellow of 22 years, he made many friends at Ibrox, for it could not be forgotten that he had led the team to greater triumphs than had been enjoyed for many years. One of the finest games of his career was in the New Year's Day match with Celtic, at Ibrox, when, with Quinn at his best, he completely drew the sting from the famous Celt.

Rangers seemed well set for sweeping the boards when the Scottish Cup-ties came on, and this impression was confirmed when they defeated Morton in hollow fashion in the second round, thus taking the revenge that is sweet for the early season League sensation. No great alarm was felt when the draw sent the team to Dundee, although the records could show that Dens Park had been no Happy Valley for the Light Blues. The team had settled down and was playing with a confidence and dash that would not brook despair. In nine League and Cup-tie matches since the New Year they had scored 29 goals and lost only 7. There was real hope but—Captain Chapman, on winning the toss, made what proved to be a disastrous decision. He elected to play uphill and against the wind. It is true Rangers were a great second-half team this season, but against a powerful side such as Dundee the self-imposed task was unreasonably hard. Hogg scored in 15 minutes, and this seemed promising, but soon afterwards Hamilton dealt his old club a shrewd blow by equalising, and before the interval Lee gave Dundee the winning goal. All the courageous efforts of the Rangers forwards in the second half were of no avail against a defence that seemed to grow stronger and stronger as the pressure increased. Herbert Dainty, the Dundee centre-half, never played better in his long and illustrious career than he did that afternoon. The teams were representative of the best in Scottish football :—

> **Dundee.**—Crumley ; Neal and Lindsay ; Comrie, Dainty, and Lee ; Bellamy, Langlands, Hamilton (R. C.), M'Farlane, and Fraser.

> **Rangers.**—Lock ; Law and Campbell ; Gordon, Chapman, and Hendry ; Hogg, Bowie, Reid, Bennett, and Smith.

This stands as Dundee's only Scottish Cup victory over Rangers. Three times have they met with results as follows :—

1896-97.	Third Round.	Rangers	4	Dundee	0
1908-09.	Second Round.	Rangers	1	Dundee	0
1910-11.	Third Round.	Rangers	1	Dundee	2
			6		2

For their Scottish Cup failure the team, of course, derived ample consolation from their Glasgow and Charity Cup victories. The Glasgow Cup was won for the first time in nine years, and there were features attached to the conquest which made it peculiarly gratifying. Against Celtic, in the Final, the team had to battle without Galt (who sprung an ankle tendon) for 53 minutes. Gordon, who played at inside right until Bowie was signed, dropped back to right half, leaving Hogg to get along by himself which he did in his gayest manner. But the feature of the match was the sparkling display by Alec Smith, who, now in his seventeenth season, so charmed James M'Menemy, the Celtic inside right and a great artist, that he picked up the ball at the finish and handed it to the Darvel wonder to keep as a memento. It was one of those graceful little actions which a man remembers as long as he lives. When the rivals met again in the Charity Cup Final, Rangers repeated their success, thanks to a goal, the most audacious ever scored by Reid. Adams, the Celtic goalkeeper, gathered the ball and all the Rangers forwards stood off for him to field it. But Reid did not move more than a yard or so, and when Adams nonchalantly bounced the ball preparatory to kicking it, the Rangers centre nipped in, and stealing the kick, turned the leather into the net. The incident convulsed the crowd and flabbergasted the cheerful Adams. Andrew M'Atee played for Celtic in this Final. It was his first season at Parkhead, and he came in to take the place of William Kivlichan.

So ended a season which brought back some of the old glories. Champions of the League, the team's Cup record in brief was :—

Scottish Cup.		Glasgow Cup.		Charity Cup.	
Kilmarnock (H),	2–1	A Bye.		Clyde (H),	3–2
Morton (H),	3–0	Clyde (A),	1–1	Queen's Park (A),	1–0
Dundee (A),	1–2	Clyde (H),	3–0	Celtic (Hampden),	2–1
		Celtic (Hampden.),	3–1		
	6–3		7–2		6–3

THE STORY OF THE RANGERS.

Thirteen caps were showered upon Rangers players in 1910-11, which began to look like the old days coming back. Alec Smith played his last match against England. In 1906 he was supposed to have definitely finished with England Internationals, yet here he was as virile and as eager as ever, helping to draw the match at Goodison Park, Everton. He beautifully placed the corner kick from which Higgins headed the equalising goal a minute or two from the close. Smith also played against Ireland and against the English League at Ibrox, and, seventeen years after his first match for the Rangers, gave absolutely his best exhibition in a representative game against the Saxon. Alec Bennett played against England, Wales, the English League, and the Southern League ; Wm. Reid against England, Wales, Ireland, the English League, and Irish League ; and Joe Hendry against the Southern League. Nor is it without interest that the outside left in the Scottish team against Wales was R. C. Hamilton, now finishing his career with Dundee. Both of Scotland's goals were scored by this once famous Rangers marksman.

1911—1912.

League Championship—Also the Glasgow Cup— The Shawfield Fiasco—Frenzied Followers—Tie Surrendered—Great Rangers' Year—Law and Craig Depart.

TO obtain an accurate impression of the season of 1911-1912, we must focus upon Shawfield Park. More or less the Clyde team was the arbiter of the fortunes of the Light Blues. As had happened two seasons previously, it was at Shawfield Park that the Rangers ended their Scottish Cup quest. This was the ill-starred day when, with Clyde leading by 3-1 some fifteen minutes from the finish, a section of the crowd invaded the field and caused the game to be abandoned. The question of a replay never required to be discussed, for the Rangers directors unanimously decided to retire from the competition. The directors took the view that the persons who caused the abandonment of the match were followers of the club—it would be a misnomer to call them supporters. It is right to be enthusiastic, but in the name of heaven, how can anyone expect to serve the interests of a club by attempting to take the law out of the hands of those entrusted with its administration? Provocation is no excuse. It is a test, certainly, of a man's fortitude, but pride of club, and especially of a club with the fine traditions of the Rangers, should be a bulwark against a frenzied display of resentment. The incident in the Shawfield tie upon which the intruders sought to excuse their action was a matter entirely for the referee, as all such incidents are. Let us never forget that—

> " The man worth while
> Is the man with a smile
> When everything goes dead wrong."

THE STORY OF THE RANGERS.

Clyde did their best to upset the Rangers' League championship ambitions by winning the Ibrox match a few weeks before the Cup-tie, and, later on, they defeated the Light Blues in the Final of the Charity Cup. All this took place in the second half of the season which period formed an amazing contrast with that preceding the New Year. In their first nineteen matches, the Rangers were never defeated. In the Glasgow Cup, they beat Queen's Park (6–1), Clyde (1–0), and Partick Thistle (1–0) in the Final. They could even conquer Clyde in the League at Shawfield by 2–0 and beat Celtic (the ultimate Scottish Cup winners) in the League at Ibrox by 3–1. If we embrace the second half of the previous season, the Rangers results showed that they had played 46 matches and had suffered only one reverse—in the Scottish Cup-tie at Dundee, on 25th February, 1911. In this season of 1911-12, the first defeat was sustained at Cappielow Park, and it was the only one up to the New Year, which meant that the Light Blues in the year 1911 played 51 matches and had been only twice beaten. It was, perhaps, unreasonable to expect that the pace could be maintained. The commanding lead secured in the League was, however, sufficient to keep the championship at Ibrox for the seventh time, and as the Glasgow Cup was also retained, the season was not without its compensations for the Scottish Cup disappointment. The 24 wins in the League was the highest number of victories the club had ever compiled in the competition, although, of course, such a performance was possible during only the preceding eight seasons owing to the gradual increase in the membership of the First Division. Not a single club could claim home and away League victories over the Rangers, and only Hibernian and Celtic held an advantage in the scoring over the two matches.

FIFTY YEARS OF FOOTBALL——1911-1912.

One or two features of the season stand out prominently. In the Glasgow Cup Final with Partick Thistle, at Celtic Park, Hogg scored the only goal of the match after a run and shot which constituted perhaps his most brilliant combined effort as a Rangers player. Partick Thistle were a very fine team this season and they were greatly fancied to win the Cup, a pleasure they have never experienced. Their right back, M'Kenzie, was off the field with a strained muscle when the goal was scored, but this fact could not diminish the brilliance of Hogg's achievement, since, on his side of the field, the Thistle defence was intact. The two League games with the Celtic were among the best ever played between the old antagonists. At Ibrox, the Light Blues played like champions and their 3-1 victory held out the promise of great things. Celtic did not have the assistance of Quinn in that match, but in the New Year's Day game, at Parkhead, he was at centre, while Rangers were handicapped by the absence of Galt. Waddell played centre half, but broke down, and Quinn took full advantage of his opportunity and scored three goals. In the Scottish Cup-tie with Clyde, the extraordinary feature was the scoring success of Morrison, then a veteran and a back, who, at the last moment, was placed at centre forward owing to Cameron, the regular centre, having fallen a victim to influenza. There was a wave of smiles when he took up his position on the field, but when he beat Lock after three minutes, and again twelve minutes later, the laugh was with him. Carmichael gave Clyde a third goal after half-an-hour, and Hendry scored for Rangers three minutes after the restart. Rangers were attacking with great vigour when M'Andrew charged down Bennett on the stand side of the field, and a number of spectators who had overflowed on to the track here, immediately rushed over the line. The sequel we know. The teams that day were:—

    Clyde.—Grant ; Gilligan and Blair ; Walker, M'Andrew, and Collins ; Hamilton, Jackson, Morrison, Carmichael, and Steven.

    Rangers.—Lock ; Campbell and Richmond ; Gordon, Galt, and Hendry ; Hogg, Bowie, Reid, Bennett, and Smith.

When the rivals met again in the Charity Cup Final, in May, Rangers found themselves at a disadvantage. Lock had gone home to Southampton, and T. Farrington, the young reserve goalkeeper, was so ill that he should not have played. He pluckily went out, but ten minutes from the interval had to retire, and Campbell, for the remainder of the game, stood guard between the posts and was not once beaten, Clyde's two goals (one from a penalty) having been scored before he became the guardian. George Ormond, of Arbroath, who was signed during the season, and James Riddell, also a newcomer, played for Rangers in the Charity Cup-ties, at back and half-back respectively. Another back signed late in the season was John Robertson, who played on the left. He came from Southampton, like his famous namesake " Jacky," and had previously served with Bolton Wanderers. A successful career with the Light Blues seemed opened out for him, but in the following season, an accident sustained in the Glasgow Cup Final with Celtic ended his playing days.

With an income for the season of £13,032, and the club's trophies comprising the Glasgow Cup, League Championship, Scottish Second Eleven Cup and Glasgow Second Eleven Cup, the curtain was rung down on 1911-12. Alec Craig was now playing for Morton with whom he remained until May, 1914, when he returned to Ibrox.

George Law was with Leeds City.   Changes always.   The Rangers' cup record for 1911-12 was :—

Scottish Cup.		Glasgow Cup.		Charity Cup.	
Stenhouse-		Queen's Park (A),6–1		Third Lanark	
muir (H),	3–1	Clyde (H),	1–0	(P'khead),	1–0
Clyde (A),	1–3	Partick Thistle		Clyde (H'dn.),	1–2
		(Parkhead),	1–0		
	4–4		8–1		2–2

Shortly before the annual meeting in May, 1912, the club suffered a severe loss by the death of Bailie James Henderson who had presided over the administrative affairs for the record period of fourteen years, as president during Rangers' last season as a private club, and then as first Chairman of Directors.   On the motion of Mr. William Craig, it was unanimously agreed by the Board to invite Sir John Ure Primrose, Bart., to become chairman.   Sir John accepted on the understanding that the appointment be interim, a stipulation that acquires a sense of quaintness when regarded from the standpoint of his eleven years' occupancy of the position.   He resigned in July, 1923, and was succeeded by Mr. William Craig. A member of the Rangers club since August, 1887, the month in which First Ibrox Park was opened by Preston North-End, Sir John (then Councillor) was elected Honorary President at the annual meeting in May, 1888, and he vacated that office to become Chairman of Directors. A man of many interests, and possessing that wide and generous outlook which is the foe of bigotry and crusted sectionalism, Sir John brought into football an influence that was cleansing and elevating.   The word sportsman was to him the most precious in all the language.   In his mind, it stood for all that was worth striving for even by one who could attain to the highest civic dignities.   A man was nothing if he could not " play the game," show modesty in the hour of victory, and smile through defeat. In his very young days he played a little for a club long since defunct, and for a period of well over fifty years he remained in the most intimate association with the game. The pre-occupations of business and the time devoted to Glasgow's civic advancement, seemed only to sharpen his interest in his favourite sport. He joined the Town Council in 1886, became a magistrate ten years later, was Lord Provost from 1902 to 1905, and received his Baronetcy in 1903. Glasgow Univeristy, in 1903, conferred upon him the honorary degree of LL.D. These were honours bestowed in recognition of valuable public service, and it can truthfully be said that Sir John prized them not alone for their personal meaning, but also for whatever influence they might enable him to exert towards the uplifting of the sport of which he was so passionately fond. For many years he associated himself closely with the Glasgow Charity Cup Committee, and he was proud of the fact that this competition had given over £70,000 to the most deserving of institutions in Glasgow and the West of Scotland.

The Rangers were conscious of their good fortune in having a man of the culture and high ideals of Sir John Ure Primrose to assist in carrying on the traditions of the club. But it was not only the Rangers who were indebted to him for lending his moral support to their ambitions. Throughout his life, Sir John was constantly ready to answer the call of the most lowly of clubs. Regardless of creed or colour, he was ever happy to preside at their little gatherings. He had wit, wisdom, and fine social qualities. The easy elegance of his manner, his amiability, his almost wizard faculty for saying the right thing at the right time, his diplomacy and tact—all these gifts but served to enrich the sporting atmosphere of the circles in which he moved. He was seventy-six years of age when he presided at the Jubilee dinner of the Rangers club, on 9th April, 1923, yet in all the assembled company, none possessed a younger heart or a more vivacious spirit.

1912—1913.

WITH practically the same staff of players that had won the League Championship and the Glasgow Cup in 1911-12, the club's outlook for **1912-1913** was well coloured with glowing tints. Already the one absorbing question was, " Can the team win the Scottish Cup ? " The League and other cups were regarded as of little account compared with the national trophy, which, since 1903, had regularly eluded the grasp of the club. What happened was, as nearly as possible, a repetition of events of the previous season. In the third round of the Scottish Cup, Falkirk came to Ibrox and surprised themselves and everybody else by defeating the Light Blues by 3-1. No one had a bigger share in the result than James Croal, the player whose transfer Falkirk had secured from the Rangers for a ten pound note. At that time the result seemed to be entirely out of harmony with the supposed merits of the teams, for Rangers were winning the League Championship " hand over fist." It was one of those days when everything comes off for one team and nothing for the other. Falkirk got their goals like picking cherries off a plate. There was no great expenditure of effort required. But, undoubtedly, there was a screw loose—two or three perhaps—in the Rangers' defence. John Hempsey, who had been in charge of the goal since Lock's injury, sustained in making a daring save in the Glasgow Cup-tie against Partick Thistle, was a safe custodian in ordinary circumstances. In this tie, which was the most important of his career, he was obviously unstrung, and at the crucial moments he was

256

not encouraged by the easy manner in which Gordon and R. Brown were beaten by Croal and Terris. Falkirk's three goals were scored by the left-wing pair, and Croal was the malevolent force in engineering all of them. The absence of Bowie and Bennett from the Rangers forward line through injury meant everything to them. Bowie was hurt in the second-round tie with Hamilton Academicals, and Parker, who took his place at inside right, was in no way suited to the position. Besides, no forward possessed by the Rangers had the steadying influence of Bowie. All the same, the Light Blues fought the match out with splendid courage, and after Parker had scored in the second half, Stewart, the Falkirk custodian, gave a wonderful display. In ten minutes he had more strenuous work to accomplish than had Hempsey in the whole game. Victory, however, went to a team worthy of success, as Falkirk proved when they went on and won the Cup. In the Final at Parkhead they defeated Raith Rovers by 2–0. The teams in the well-remembered Ibrox tie were :—

> **Falkirk.**—Stewart ; Orrock and Donaldson ; Macdonald, Logan, and M'Millan ; M'Naught, Gibbons, Robertson, Croal, and Terris.
>
> **Rangers.**—Hempsey ; Gordon and Ormond ; Brown, Logan, and Galt ; Paterson, Parker, Reid, Goodwin, and Smith.

This stands as Falkirk's only Scottish Cup victory over Rangers, a summary of their encounters in the competition being :—

1883-4.	Third Round.	Kinning Park.	Rangers	5–2
1906-7.	First Round.	Falkirk.	Rangers	2–1
1907-8.	First Round.	Ibrox Park.	Rangers	4–1
1908-9.	Semi-Final.	Falkirk.	Rangers	1–0
1912-13.	Third Round.	Ibrox Park.	Rangers	1–3
				13–7

THE STORY OF THE RANGERS.

The similarity of events with those of the previous season did not begin or end with the Scottish Cup defeat. In the Glasgow Cup, a desperate second-round tie was waged with Partick Thistle. Three games were required to decide it. The second game, played at Ibrox, was notable as being the first Cup-tie played for the Rangers by James L. Logan, an old Queen's Park centre half-back, who had come to Ibrox from Aston Villa. His debut for the Light Blues was made in a League match against Kilmarnock a week before the Cup-tie replay. In this second game of the tie, also, Lock came by the injury which put him out of the game for the remainder of the season, and caused the club to sign John Hempsey. The latter made a brilliant debut in the third and deciding game of the tie, which Rangers won by 2–0, and he also touched a high level of ability in the Final with Celtic at Hampden Park. By winning the Cup, Rangers inscribed their name upon it for the tenth time and thus took the lead over Celtic who have never since recovered it.

Had Lock's injury been the last, the team must have achieved greater things. In the "Glasgow" Final, however, Robertson, the left back, had his football career ended by a serious smash on the right knee. Celtic were leading by a goal when Robertson was carried off a few minutes after the change of ends, but the Rangers side seemed inspired by their handicap, and playing with almost unexampled dash and brilliance, gained one of the greatest victories in the club's history. Still, the tale of misfortune was not told. In the New Year's Day League game with Celtic, Reid, Bennett, Alec Smith, and Galt had all to stand down, yet the team was unlucky to lose by 1–0. This was the only League reverse sustained in the second half of the season. At one time, Lock, Hempsey, and Farrington, the three goalkeepers on the club's roll, were all in Invalid

Bay. R. G. Campbell, the captain, stepped between the posts and a 3-1 League victory over Clyde was registered. The unsettling effect of these recurring injuries had its repercussion in the Scottish Cup-tie with Falkirk.

We have referred to the similarity of 1911-12 and 1912-13. Glance at the achievements of the club in these periods of campaigning :—

1911-12, League Champions	Glasgow Cup	Scottish 2nd XI. Cup	Glasgow 2nd XI. Cup
1912-13, League Champions	Glasgow Cup	Scottish 2nd XI. Cup	Glasgow 2nd XI. Cup

Rangers' last League match of the season was, curiously enough, against Falkirk at Ibrox. Falkirk came as Scottish Cup holders. Rangers were already Champions of the League. Falkirk's team was identical with that which won the Cup-tie. Rangers had Ormond and H. Muir at back ; Gordon was at right half in place of Brown ; Parker was out of the forward line and Bennett was in. Rangers won by 2 goals to 1. Falkirk in that season won 14 League matches. Rangers won 24. How uncertain is the contest that is a cup-tie

League Champions for a third successive year, the Rangers cup record was as follows :—

Scottish Cup.	Glasgow Cup.	Charity Cup.
A Bye.	A Bye.	A Bye.
Hamilton Acas. (A), 1-1	Partick Thistle (A), 0-0	Partick
Hamilton Acas. (H), 2-0	Partick Thistle (H), 1-1	Thistle
Falkirk (H), 1-3	Partick Thistle (A), 2-0	(H), 3-1
	Celtic (H'den), 3-1	Celtic (A), 2-3
4-4	6-2	5-4

Sixteen International honours were bestowed upon members of the team. Gordon was capped against England, Wales, Ireland, the English League, Irish League, and Southern League. Reid missed only the match against the Irish League. Logan and Smith assisted in a brilliant

THE STORY OF THE RANGERS.

victory over the English League at Hampden Park. This was Alec Smith's last cap—his 34th—which placed him an easy first among Rangers celebrities. The full list of honours were :—

v. England.	v. Wales.	v. Ireland.	v. English League.	v. Irish League.	v. Southern League.
J. Gordon.	J. Gordon.	J. Gordon.	J. Gordon.	J. Gordon.	J. Gordon.
W. Reid.	W. Reid.	W. Reid.	W. Reid.	J. Bowie.	W. Reid.
		A. Bennett.	J. L. Logan.		A. Bennett.
			A. Smith.		

In winning the League Championship for the three successive years, the players who took a prominent part were the following, the figures given showing the number of League games played by each in the respective seasons :—

	1910-11	1911-12	1912-13	Total
H. Lock, goal, - - -	34	33	6	73
Geo. Law, back, - - -	24	11	—	35
R. G. Campbell, - - -	23	32	23	78
A. Richmond, back, - -	20	12	—	32
J. E. Gordon, - - -	28	29	27	84
G. R. Chapman, half-back, -	28	2	—	30
Joe Hendry, half-back, -	31	32	13	76
Wm. Hogg, forward, - -	30	30	16	76
Wm. Reid, forward, - -	33	32	25	90
Alec Bennett, forward, -	23	25	22	70
Alec Smith, forward, - -	29	26	22	77
J. Galt, half-back, - -	18	26	28	72
Jas. Paterson, forward, -	2	4	21	27
Jas. Bowie, forward, - -	—	24	22	46
John Hempsey, goal, - -	—	—	17	17
Thos. Farrington, goal, -	—	—	7	7
John Robertson back, - -	—	—	12	12
Geo. Ormond, back, - -	—	—	24	24
Jas. L. Logan, half-back, -	—	—	24	24
J. L. Goodwin, forward, -	—	—	19	19
Robert Brown, half-back, -	—	—	12	12

1913 — 1914.

A New Right Wing—A. Scott Duncan—Dainty
James Stewart—T. Cairns' Debut—The Right Mould
Wm. Struth as Trainer—Then Manager.

TO anyone who probes the archives, the results of
season **1913-14** will provide quite a nice little
mystery. The team played some very fine football,
better, indeed, than anything shown during the previous
season when they could win the League Championship
and the Glasgow Cup. But the forwards were lacking
the old driving force, largely because Alec Smith was
now nearing the end of his long race, and also because
William Hogg's transference to Dundee left a vacancy on
the right wing which was not adequately filled until near
the end of September when A. Scott Duncan came up
from Newcastle along with James Stewart, a marvellously
skilful inside right, who had played for England against
Scotland in 1907 and 1911. Stewart, in a manner of
speaking, was too clever on the ball. He loved to execute
the most delightful little touches, but when it came to
pushing ahead, the inclination to give his former clubmate the ball was irresistible. Scott Duncan was worthy
of support, but such an exclusively wing game as the pair
played when together was the more easily countered
because the opposition could prepare for it. Stewart
stayed for only a season at Ibrox, yet he was such an
admirable fellow and his qualities as a player were so
apparent, that regret was sincere that he failed to fit
into the scheme of things. The arrival of Scott Duncan
had one important and beneficial effect. It allowed James
Paterson to leave the right wing berth and to become the

natural successor of Alec Smith on the left. It was with this disposition, and with Bowie, Reid, and Bennett as the inside operators, that the Glasgow Cup was won for the fourth year in succession. It is a curious feature of this season that Third Lanark, who were beaten in the Cup Final by 3–0, and who could not get even one point out of the Rangers in the League, were able to hold them in the Charity Cup Final and win by the margin of a corner. Thus the Rangers were in two Cup finals and finished second to Celtic in the League. What of the Scottish Cup! Well, the third-round tie against a tenacious Hibernian team at Easter Road was one of the games in which the forwards played charming football without smash. Yet on this same Easter Road ground, earlier in the season, the Rangers in the League had won pretty much as they liked.

Celtic won both League matches, but not since then have Rangers surrendered four points in any season to the Parkhead rival. One of the most interesting events was the match played for the benefit of Alec Bennett, in which a team of ex-Rangers players took the field composed of :—

> W. Allan (Hibernian) ; J. Mackenzie (Cowdenbeath) and Finlay Speedie (Dumbarton) ; W. Walker (Clyde), J. Stark (Morton), and Geo. Waddell (Kilmarnock) ; W. Hogg (Dundee), T. Gilchrist (Motherwell), R. C. Hamilton (Elgin), J. Croal (Falkirk), and W. Hunter (Cowdenbeath).

Such a foregathering brought back to the minds of old Rangers men memories of great days and mighty deeds. James Brownlie was referee, and he gave an exposition that brought tears of merriment to the eyes of the spectators.

It was in this season also, that a young man of serious

mien and hardy limbs walked into the home team's quarters, and for the first time put a light blue jersey over his shoulders. The young man was Thomas Cairns, born at Merryton. Desperately keen to make his way in the world, he chafed at the lack of opportunity to show how little he cared for the reputation of the great men who defended the ramparts of rival forces. He played his first game on 29th December, 1913, against Hamilton Academicals, and figured in only seven other League matches during the season. It was not until the following campaign that he established his claim to the inside left position, which for nine seasons he held against all comers, being, in the club's Jubilee year of 1923, still animated by the old spirit of ambition. " Tommy " Cairns will be correctly classed among the type of player who never knows when he is beaten. On the field he had one purpose, and he pursued it regardless of fluctuations of fortune. He was not afflicted with that sensitive imagination which makes some players meet reverse half-way. The looker-on is quick to perceive and appraise the fighting qualities of a man, and that, no doubt, is why Cairns was rewarded with a benefit match which, in the matter of cash receipts, excelled any benefit given to a Rangers player. As a testimonial to his consistency, the following figures of matches played and goals scored are expressive :—

		Matches.	Goals.			Matches.	Goals.
1913–14,	-	8	2	1918–19,	-	30	11
1914–15,	-	41	19	1919–20,	-	50	22
1915–16,	-	38	14	1920–21,	-	48	15
1916–17,	-	28	13	1921–22,	-	54	13
1917–18,	-	33	11	1922–23,	-	45	12

Matches, 375.   Goals, 132.

THE STORY OF THE RANGERS.

Although not commonly regarded as artful or cunning, but rather as a plain, straightforward, earnest worker, Cairns had his own way of scheming to attain his end. Because he had set his mind upon a certain design, and because he adhered to it and failed a number of times in the course of a game, many were disposed to criticise him for being deficient in resource. But Cairns, like other criticised players before him, knew that though his plan might fail after five attempts, he was likely to succeed at the sixth, and he was satisfied if it did so. Bruce and the spider worked along the same lines. Even if the sixth attempt did not succeed, that was no condemnation of the purpose or of the plan of attack. There are splendid failures as well as magnificent successes. The definite, clear-cut effort of Cairns to secure an equalising goal in the famous Scottish Cup Final with Morton, at Hampden Park, on 15th April, 1922, stands as an example of the splendid failure. That he *deserved* to succeed is the point that should be put to his credit. Up to the time when these words are penned, Thomas Cairns' International honours numbered seven. He played against England in 1922 and 1923; against Wales in 1920 and 1923; against the English League in 1922 and 1923; and against the Irish League in 1923. In style, Cairns somewhat resembled John M'Pherson of the old Three Cup and League Record teams. He lay well over the ball and rather trailed than dribbled it, and, if within a reasonable distance of goal, it was always doubtful whether he would pass or shoot, which did not make the opposition any happier. In his first season with Rangers, Cairns more than once had the felicity of partnering Alec Smith—the " baby " and the " father " of the team. Now Cairns himself is the so-called veteran of Ibrox. Thus does time work its changes. Both Cairns and Smith played in the Charity

Cup Final of 1914, but Cairns was inside right to Scott Duncan. This match was notable for the return to the Light Blue ranks of Alec Craig after he had been three seasons with Morton.

A few days before the Final was played, the club mourned the loss of James Wilson, who for seventeen years had fulfilled the duties of trainer. A professional runner in his younger days, he knew all the little secrets of getting and keeping a player fit. He was a man of few words and possessed a generous nature. During his occupancy of the position of trainer, Rangers twice won the Scottish Cup, the Glasgow Cup eight times, the Charity Cup six times, and the League Championship seven times. These triumphs had a contributory source in the care and zeal with which James Wilson handled the various human material placed in his hands. No one was prouder, in a quiet and modest way, of the team's successes.

As successor to James Wilson, there came to Ibrox from the Clyde club, William Struth, also a man well versed in the theories of preparing athletes for supreme tests of endurance. He, too, had learned much in the hard school of professional running, but his knowledge was extended by the scientific study of anatomy, which enabled him to lay his finger on the seat of all the manifold troubles which afflict the muscles and bones of those who battle in the arena of physical controversy. With thorough as his watchword, William Struth brought the men under him into such a condition of physical fitness that they were able to begin a new and glorious era in the club's history once the Great War had ended. Previous to that—in 1917-18—the Glasgow Cup and League Championship were won. Then, in the following season, both the Glasgow Cup and Charity Cup were brought to Ibrox. In 1919-20 the team achieved the remarkable feat of playing 42 League matches and being only twice defeated. They compiled 71 points, and, of course, won the Championship. In these years William Struth was an inspiring influence behind the team. For him the players would have wrought themselves to a standstill. So, when the deplored death of Mr. Wilton, on 2nd May, 1920, created a vacancy in the managership, Mr. Struth was accorded a signal proof of the esteem in which the directors held him by his appointment to the manager's chair. In his first season as manager, the team eclipsed all League aggregate records by amassing 76 points out of a possible 84. Only one defeat was sustained in the course of the campaign of 42 matches, and the flag was won by the extraordinary margin of ten points over Celtic, the runners-up. In the following season, the Glasgow Cup and Charity Cup were again captured, while in 1922-23, the team, for the third time in the history of the club, won the Glasgow Cup, Charity Cup, and League Championship in one season If any man could feel dissatisfied with such a shining array of successes, he would be hard to please.

Yet we know there is one thing wanting to have made the manager's heart perfectly glad. His varied experiences in the quest to share in a Scottish Cup triumph must be almost unique. He was trainer with the Clyde club when they defeated the Rangers at Shawfield Park in 1909-10, and also, when they beat the Light Blues, on the same ground, two seasons later. In both these seasons Clyde went into the Final. Their opponents in the 1909-10 Final were Dundee. In the first game of three, Clyde obtained a lead of 2–0 and the Cup seemed won. The trainer was embarrassed with congratulations, but he said " Wait ; it's not over yet." Nor was it. In a strong finish, and profiting by the over-confidence of the Clyde

players, Dundee scored, then scored again. The game
finished 2-2, and after another draw of 0-0, Dundee won
the Cup by 2 goals to 1. That Final was played at Ibrox,
and so, also, was the 1911-12 Final in which Clyde opposed
Celtic. Early in this latter match, a glaring penalty
against M'Nair for handling the ball was allowed to pass.
It was a vital incident, for the ball was going into the net.
Had Clyde scored then, their chance of at last winning
the Cup would have been rosy indeed. The refusal of
the penalty kick and the excitement incidental to the
dispute which arose unsettled the players for a time.
Celtic were quick to take advantage, and they ran out
winners by 2 goals to 0. During this period the Clyde
team was perhaps the best the old club ever possessed,
and for this happy circumstance William Struth was in
no small degree responsible. He was more than a trainer.
To a large extent he was the architect who planned and
constructed, as those behind the scenes were glad to attest.
That is why the Clyde officials of that great epoch and their
old trainer retain a bond of attachment which time cannot
sever. Is it not a romantic coincidence that in his first
two seasons as manager of the Rangers he should have
seen the Light Blues into the Final of the Cup ? Romantic ?
Yes. And tragical, too, for in each case he saw his lads
undeservedly defeated, first by Partick Thistle and then
by Morton. But that's football and the charm of it. As
becomes a manager, Mr. Struth knows a player. In the
work of team construction he has long ago passed the
elementary stage. If he took charge when the team was
sound from the foundation upward, it was with a confidence
born of the knowledge that he had assisted in laying the
foundations. As an athlete, William Struth won many
prizes on the running track. His devotion to athletics
fitted him well for the task of organising the Rangers'

annual sports gala, and the unprecedented success of the Jubilee gathering at Ibrox Park in August, 1923, was a personal triumph, of which he had reason to feel proud.

Second in the League, Rangers' only trophy in the season of 1913-14 was the Glasgow Cup, the summary of hostilities being as follows :—

Scottish Cup.		Glasgow Cup.		Charity Cup.	
A Bye.		A. Bye.		Clyde (P'head),	2–1
Alloa Athletic (H),	5–0	Clyde (A),	1–0	Third Lanark	
Hibernian (A),	1–2	Third Lanark		(H),	*1–1
		(Hampden),	3–0		
	6–2		4–0		3–2

*Third Lanark won on corners, 4–3.

The individual honours bestowed were :—

v. England.	v. Ireland.	v. English League.	v. Irish League.	v. Southern League
J. E. Gordon.	J. E. Gordon.	J. E. Gordon.	J. E. Gordon.	J. E. Gordon.
W. Reid	W. Reid.	W. Reid.		J. Bowie.

1914—1919.

The War Years—Easy Going—New Players—Andrew Cunningham—Consistent Arthur—R. Manderson— Men Who Helped—The Victory Cup—King George at Ibrox Park.

BEFORE the season of **1914-1915** opened, the Great War had commenced. In common with other clubs, and much more than some, the Rangers found their playing strength depleted as the period of world hostilities extended. It soon became a matter simply of making the best of things under the adverse circumstances. Recognising the futility of maintaining the ordinary rigidity of the laws and regulations, the governing bodies in England and Scotland gave players and clubs almost unrestricted freedom. " Choose where you like " was the order, qualified only by the condition that the player had to show good patriotic reason for leaving one town for another. The Scottish Cup competition was suspended for the full duration of the war, much to the astonishment of a good many plain, honest folk who could not see a great deal of difference between Scottish Cup-ties and League matches or Glasgow Cup-ties. Without entering into the question of the extent to which the call of the khaki affected the team's fortunes, it may briefly be recounted that, except for the winning of the League Championship and the Glasgow Cup in 1917–18 and of the Glasgow Cup and Charity Cup in 1918-19, the war period did not add to the list of Rangers' trophies. But no one at Ibrox showed the slightest vexation about that. Manager Wilton's chief preoccupation during a large portion of the war years was his voluntary work at Bellahouston Hospital, to which the wounded soldiers were brought in a constant stream. To this work, he and William Struth, the trainer, devoted themselves heart and soul. The success of the team became purely a secondary consideration. Usually the business of the club was seen to by them in the silent hours of the night. It is not too much to say that both became indispensable to the work of organising, and caring for, the men who returned wounded from the battlefields of Europe. Personal distinction was the last thing sought by William Wilton, but those who knew the volume, and the ungrudging nature, of the services he voluntarily rendered on behalf of his country and the shattered fighting men would have considered him only adequately rewarded had those in authority seen fit to bestow that recognition more easily secured by many others.

Although the team's successes were only moderate, these war years enabled the club to lay some of the foundation of the success achieved in the field after the restoration of world peace. Robert Manderson first played for the Rangers on 27th March, 1915. He made his debut in a League match against Aberdeen at Ibrox. It is not likely that he will have forgotten the occasion, for his partner, Alec Craig, had to leave him during the game and take guard between the posts after Lock had been injured. The coming of Manderson eventually split the partnership between Craig and Harry Muir. The latter was a fine type of back who played many splendid games for the Light Blues. But, at first, Manderson found it no easier to book his place in the team that had such celebrities as Alec Smith, John Drummond, William Reid, and " Tommy " Cairns. The greatest players of all time have been slow and sure, which is better than—as Carlyle said of a rocket genius—striking twelve all at once. Two weeks after Rangers' Ulsterman had made his bow to an Ibrox crowd, Andrew Cunningham stepped on to the same field wearing a light blue jersey to play inside left to Paterson. The opposition was Partick Thistle who won that match by a goal to nothing. But the ex-Kilmarnock forward was a success immediately, and he played in the War Shield Final, some weeks later, against Morton, at Firhill Park, where the Greenock team gave a charming exhibition and won by 2 goals to 1. Before he joined the Rangers, Cunningham was capped against the English League in 1912, and against the Irish League in 1914. His honours since gained are two against England, two against Wales, two against Ireland, three against the English League, and two against the Irish League—thirteen caps in all. In the success achieved by the team in after-war years, Andrew Cunningham's share was no mean one. A dexterous manipulator, he could play bewitching football when the mood was on him and the conditions were suitable. His style of taking the ball on by close control resembled that of Alexander M'Mahon, but though equally favoured by height, he never made such effective use of his head for scoring as did the famous Celt of bygone years. In any of the inside positions, Cunningham was a forward worthy of respect, but he had not the same fondness for centre as for either of the inside wing positions. An epitome of his career as a Ranger may be given thus :—

	Matches.	Goals.		Matches.	Goals.
1914–15,	- 6	3	1919–20,	- 51	31
1915–16,	- 24	19	1920–21,	- 52	29
1916–17,	- On Service.		1921–22,	- 41	17
1917–18,	- 4	4	1922–23,	- 44	16
1918–19,	- 20	4			
Matches	- 242.		Goals,	- 123.	

THE STORY OF THE RANGERS.

Three other players who still wear light blue came to Ibrox during the war period. These are Alexander Archibald and Thomas Muirhead (joined May, 1917), and Arthur Dixon (joined July, 1917). All three took part in the winning of the League Championship in their first season as Rangers players. In the campaign of 1917-18 Archibald played in all of the 34 League matches and he was also in the team that won the Glasgow Cup. He scored eight goals. In the following season, W. J. Aitken was signed out of Queen's Park, and as he was, like Archibald, an outside right, the latter did not get the same opportunity. Aitken, however, remained only one season at Ibrox, and was then transferred to Newcastle United. There were some, no doubt, who questioned Archibald's ability to stay the course, but how well he has succeeded is shown in his record, appended :—

	Matches.	Goals.		Matches.	Goals.
1917–18,	- 39	8	1920–21,	- 49	19
1918–19,	- 20	7	1921–22,	- 55	15
1919–20,	- 53	9	1922–23,	- 43	4
Matches, - 259.			Goals, - 62.		

Dixon missed only one League match in his first season and he played in all the Glasgow Cup-ties. Over his six seasons he has been one of the most consistent in attendance. In competition matches alone, his appearances were as follows :—

1917–18,	-	-	38	1920–21,	-	-	52
1918–19,	-	-	41	1921–22,	-	-	56
1919–20,	-	-	41	1922–23,	-	-	44
	Total,	-	-	-	272		

Manderson could also claim a fine record of regularity, and it will not be denied that, during the years he was playing at his best, there were few superiors to him in his position. No player could have remained in a team from which so much was expected, and which achieved such great distinction, had he not possessed qualities of a high order. Since he came to Ibrox, his appearances in League and Cup-tie matches have been as follows :—

1914–15,	- - 1		1919–20,	-	- 53
1915–16,	- - 35		1920–21,	-	- 52
1916–17,	- - 41		1921–22,	-	- 52
1917–18,	- - 34		1922–23,	-	- 36
1918–19,	- - 38				
	Total,	-	-	342.	

During the five war seasons, Rangers had the assistance from time to time of many notable footballers. Peter Pursell, who was a registered player in August, 1914, remained at Ibrox until the close of 1918-19, when he declined terms and joined Burslem Port Vale. David M'Lean played centre forward during most of 1918-19 and scored 29 goals in 24 matches. J. Donnachie, of Oldham Athletic, in that same season, played in seven games. In 1913 and 1914 he had represented Scotland against England as an outside left, and it was hoped he would find his native air agreeable, but he didn't. David Brown succeeded David M'Lean in the centre, and he and Donnachie took part in the Victory Cup-tie with Airdrieonians at Broomfield Park, on 29th March, 1919. Like all the competing clubs, Rangers were keen on winning a trophy so unique, but though on the run of the play they might have done so, a preventable goal by John Rankin, the Airdrie outside right, ended their interest in the ties. St. Mirren, who defeated Celtic on the same day, went into the Final to win the Cup. with a fine victory over the Hearts at Parkhead. The teams which played at Broomfield Park are interesting as showing how the whirligig of time brings changes :—

> **Airdrieonians.**—Bernard ; Macdonald and Watson ; Knox, Summers, and Miller ; Rankin, A. Reid, J. Reid, Hart, and Gray.

> **Rangers.**—Lock ; Manderson and M'Queen ; Gordon, Dixon, and Walls ; Archibald, Bowie, Brown, Cunningham, and Donnachie.

George M'Queen, who was some three-and-a-half seasons with Rangers, is now one of Airdrieonians' clever young team which in 1922-23 finished second to Rangers in the League. Only Manderson, Dixon, Archibald, and Cunningham are still first-team players at Ibrox. Walls is on the reserve list.

During the War years, there came on to the Board of Directors two very old members of the club, whose success in business life and useful public service, no less than their long association with the game, rendered their active participation in the management of the club extremely welcome. Ex-Bailie Joseph Buchanan, who joined the Board in 1915, was admitted to membership in 1894, the year in which the Rangers first won the Scottish Cup. He was a staunch friend of the Abercorn before fate laid a cold and heavy hand on that good old club who were members of the League at the origin of the competition. His knowledge of play and players was wide and varied, and, with a mind capable of quick perception and well-balanced judgment, he soon became a valuable helper in the counsels of the Rangers.

In 1917 Ex-Bailie (then Bailie) Duncan Graham, O.B.E., became a director. His advent on the Board was hailed with the warmest satisfaction by his colleagues, because it was recognised that men of his type, who had done civic service and had earned the confidence of the public, raised the prestige of organised football by coming into close association with it. That, indeed, has been proved over and over again. In many directions, the influence of Ex-Bailie Graham has been exerted in a benign way since he linked himself with the Rangers' destinies. It is good to know that while with him, as with others, the motto is "club first," his outlook embraces a wider radius, and that at all times the guiding principle is the welfare of our great national game.

Another incident, memorable in the annals of the Rangers, occurred during the War years. On 18th September, 1917, His Majesty King George visited Ibrox Park for the purpose of holding an Investiture on the field, and presented decorations and medals to a number of officers, non-commissioned officers, and men, and to the next-of-kin of soldiers who had fallen in the fight. At the conclusion of the Investiture, Sir John Ure Primrose, as chairman of the club, and Mr. Wm. Wilton, as secretary, had the honour of being presented to the King by Lord Provost Dunlop. The proceedings bore the official hall-mark, and the Rangers club and Ibrox Park had the pleasant distinction of having their names recorded in the Court Circular. There hangs in the pavilion a framed copy of the Court Circular which chronicles the proceedings, and also the original letter (of which a reproduction is given on page 276) sent on the following day by Lord Provost Dunlop to Mr. Wilton.

William Wilton, Esq.,
        Secretary,
                Rangers Football Club,
                        Ibrox Park.

City Chambers, Glasgow,
19th September, 1917.

Dear Mr. Wilton,

        I desire to write you at once to say how much we were
indebted to you and the Directors of the Rangers Football
Club, not only for giving the use of the Ibrox Park for the
Investiture by His Majesty yesterday, but for all the
excellent arrangements you made to cope with the enormous
crowd assembled and the invited guests.   Everything passed
off most successfully and the King expressed himself as
highly pleased with all the arrangements

        As head of the city I greatly appreciate the co-operation
of your Club on this important occasion and beg that you will
personally accept my cordial thanks for all your trouble.

        With kind regards,

                I am,

                        Yours very truly,

                        Thomas Dunlop

                        LORD PROVOST.

1919—1920.

WE have arrived at a stage in the long history of the
Rangers club when it is necessary to exercise a
nice discrimination in order that full justice may
be done to the wonderful achievements of the team in its
new epoch. With the war ended, a surging reaction
occurred in all forms of sport. Though many fine lads
who had played the game of football now, alas! lay dead
on the battlefields of Europe, there were liberal reinforce-
ments from out of the countless numbers who had
developed a love of play while serving in the Army. It
might be said that every soldier was now a sportsman.
In the first season following the Armistice, enthusiasm for
football reached an unprecedented height. It com-
municated itself to the teams and their supporters. Keen-
ness to win the laurels in open competition · became a
passion. Under these conditions, the Rangers team
accomplished something which will stand comparison with
the most notable exploits of the great old combinations of
1894 or 1897 or 1899. In this season of **1919-1920,** in a
League increased for the first time to 22 clubs, the
Championship was won with an aggregate of 71 points.
The possible maximum was 84. In the 42 matches played,
106 goals were scored and only 25 lost. Only two defeats
were sustained, and both of these might easily have been
avoided. In the ninth match of the series, against
Motherwell at Fir Park, a penalty kick was awarded

against Bowie, who contended at the time, and still contends, that he drew his arm away to avoid the ball which struck it. Motherwell converted the penalty and that remained the only reverse until the club's thirty-fourth engagement in which Clydebank caught the team stale and in a whirlpool of trouble from injuries and strain connected with the memorable thrice-played Scottish Cuptie with Albion Rovers. The two undecided ties with the Rovers had just been carried through, and two days after the match with Clydebank, the third and last encounter took place at Parkhead where a tired and over-anxious and rearranged Rangers team went under to opponents who were as virile and confident as the Light Blues were fatigued and pessimistic. But whatever may have been the regrets arising from the Scottish Cup defeat, nothing could detract from the merit of the League performance. It seemed, in its combined features, one that might remain unequalled for years, yet in the very next season, the Rangers themselves had the distinction of excelling it. There is no doubt, however, that it was in the Scottish Cup-ties that excitement reached an intensity never before, nor since, experienced in Scottish football. When the Rangers met the Celtic in the fourth round, immediately preceding the semi-final tie with Albion Rovers, Ibrox Park held 83,000 spectators, the greatest attendance recorded up till then for a club match in Scotland and only excelled up to the present by the 95,000 at the Final of the same season between Kilmarnock and Albion Rovers, at Hampden. In the long line of epic duels between the old rivals, who had played their first Scottish Cup-tie 29 years before, none had so thrilled the people. The contest was worthy of the occasion. If the Rangers won they were free to say they were glad when the end came, for Celtic, even with Gallagher not too well, fought

out the tie to the bitter end.   In that great test the teams
were :—

> **Celtic.**—Shaw ;   M'Nair   and   Dodds ;   M'Stay,
> Cringan, and M'Master ;   M'Atee, M'Menemy, Gallagher,
> Cassidy, and M'Lean.

> **Rangers.**—Lock ;   Manderson and Gordon ;   Bowie,
> Dixon, and Walls ; Archibald, Muirhead, Cunningham,
> Cairns, and Paterson.

The only goal was scored by Muirhead from Dr. Paterson's
low pass five minutes after the second half had commenced.
Here let us append a register of the Scottish Cup matches
between these doughty opponents.   Eight victories can
Celtic claim against the Rangers' four :—

1890-91	First Round.	Celtic Park.	Rangers 0	Celtic 1
1891-92	Fourth Round	Celtic Park.	Rangers 3	Celtic 5
1893-94	Final.	Hampden Park	Rangers 3	Celtic 1
1898-99	Final.	Hampden Park	Rangers 0	Celtic 2
1899-00†	Semi-Final	Celtic Park	Rangers 0	Celtic 4
1900-01	First Round	Celtic Park	Rangers 0	Celtic 1
1902-03	Third Round	Celtic Park	Rangers 3	Celtic 0
1903-04	Final	Hampden Park	Rangers 2	Celtic 3
1904-05	Semi-Final	Celtic Park	Rangers 2	Celtic 0
1906-07	Third Round	Ibrox Park	Rangers 0	Celtic 3
1907-08	Second Round	Ibrox Park	Rangers 1	Celtic 2
1908-09*	Final	Hampden Park	Rangers 1	Celtic 1
1919-20	Fourth Round	Ibrox Park	Rangers 1	Celtic 0
			16	23

† After a draw 2-2 at Ibrox.   * After a draw 2-2.   Cup withheld.

Had the Rangers players been afforded time for rest
and refreshment all might have gone well.   Within the
space of twelve days, however, they were called upon to
play the three Cup games with Albion Rovers and two
strenuous League matches.   Some of the men bent under
the exactions of strain and injury.   The changing formation

of the teams that grappled with the Rovers tells a story in cameo :—

First Game.	Second Game.	Third Game.
Lock.	Lock.	Lock.
Manderson.	Manderson.	Manderson.
Ritchie.	Ritchie.	Gordon.
Bowie.	Bowie.	Bowie.
Dixon.	Dixon.	Meiklejohn.
Walls.	Walls.	Walls.
Archibald.	Archibald.	Henderson.
Muirhead.	Muirhead.	Muirhead.
Gordon.	Henderson.	Cunningham.
Cairns.	Cairns.	Cairns.
Paterson.	Paterson.	Paterson.

Even the League Championship seemed, for the moment, in danger, but bracing themselves for a last effort, the team ran through the last eight engagements with a loss of only three points in drawn games. The club's cup record for the season was :—

Scottish Cup.		Glasgow Cup.	Charity Cup.	
Dumbarton (H),	0–0	Celtic (A), 0–1	Partick Thistle (H),	4–0
Dumbarton (H),	1–0		Celtic (H),	1–2
Arbroath (H),	5–0			
Broxburn United				
(H),	3–0			
Celtic (H),	1–0			
Albion Rovers				
(Celtic Park),	1–1			
Albion Rovers				
(Celtic Park),	0–0			
Albion Rovers				
(Celtic Park),	0–2			
	11–3	0–1		5–2

The team's last match of the season was on behalf of the Scottish War Memorial funds and was played against Kilmarnock, proud holders of the Scottish Cup. Both teams were keen to win because of the prestige involved.

By 5 goals to o Rangers were victorious. In League matches and cup ties, 129 goals were scored and 31 lost, a tribute alike to defence and forwards.

The individual honours were :—

v. England.	*v.* Wales.	*v.* Ireland.	*v.* English L'gue.	*v.* Irish League.
J. Bowie.	T. Cairns.	J. Bowie.	A. Cunningham.	A. Cunningham.
J. E. Gordon.	J. E. Gordon.	A. Cunningham.	J. E. Gordon.	J. E. Gordon.
		J. E. Gordon.		

The club's income for the season shattered all existing Scottish records. It amounted to £50,946 1s. 1d. Some of the attendances at Rangers matches were amazing. The average at Ibrox Park was about 30,000. There were 75,000 spectators at the League match, at Ibrox, on the occasion of Celtic's visit, and 83,000 when Celtic returned to play the Scottish Cup-tie. At Celtic Park, on New Year's day, 76,000 watched the League match, while on the same ground the Glasgow Cup-tie between the two clubs attracted 63,000 persons. Thus, these four engagements between Rangers and Celtic were witnessed by an aggregate of 297,000 individuals! And the 8,000 at the Scottish Cup Final of 1876-77 was called *colossal*!

1920—1921.

Another Championship—Greatest Aggregate—
Forty-two Matches—One Defeat—Men of Mettle—
Scottish Cup Final—Bowie's Absence—A Fatal
Moment.

ON the subject of the relative merits of the more
notable achievements of any team, it is necessary
to exercise prudence. Conditions are not always
the same. The actual value of one performance might be
higher than another which could claim the more imposing
array of figures. What, for instance, would have been the
possibilities of the 1898-99 Rangers team in 1920-21 ?
That masterful combination won every League match
played. No other team on earth was ever able to make an
exactly similar claim. More than that, the 1898-99 team
played in the final ties of the three cups, and though they
lost them all, it must be remembered that the nervous
tension involved in the making of the League record was
such as to render a reaction inevitable. If we put, side
by side, the League performances of the 1898-99 and
1920-21 teams, one salient contrast will be at once
apparent :—

		Played.	Won.	Lost.	Drawn.	Goals For	Agst.	Points.
1898–99,	-	18	18	0	0	79	- 18	36
1920–21,	-	42	35	1	6	91	- 24	76

Thus, the 1920-21 team had to stay a course more than
double the length of that run by its famous predecessor,

and it sustained only a single defeat. That defeat was
inflicted by Celtic on New Year's day, 1921, when the
Rangers were weakened by injuries. There is no finality
to comparisons between the old and the modern, yet one
thing is certain. From whatever standpoint the achievement of the 1920-21 team is regarded, it must take its
place as one of the most brilliant in the history of the
game. Combined with the League record of the
previous season, which was almost as good, and which
was accomplished by the same team with only one
or two variations, it stands as a monument to the
inflexible courage, skill, and consistency of the players.
From 27th September, 1919, to 31st December, 1920,
the League matches played numbered 56, and of
these the only one lost was the one with Clydebank,
at Ibrox Park, on 5th April, 1920. Let us now put
together the product of these two successive seasons
in order to expose the true value of the championships
won :—

	Played	Won	Lost	Drawn	Goals For	Goals Agst.	Points Won	Points Possible
1919–20, -	42	31	2	9	106	25	71	84
1920–21, -	42	35	1	6	91	24	76	84
	84	66	3	15	197	49	147	168

The 76 points gained in 1920-21 is the highest aggregate
ever obtained by any club. Celtic were runners-up, 10
points behind, and the Hearts, who were third, made 26
points fewer than the Rangers. In addition, the Light
Blues contested the Scottish Cup and Charity Cup Final
ties. Who were the men who helped to write this bright
page in the story of the old club ? Here, at a glance, are

their names with the number of League matches and cup
ties played in each of the two seasons and the goals scored
in both :—

	1919-20.	1920-21.	Goals.
H. Lock, - - - -	46	—	—
W. Robb, goal, - -	10	53	—
R. Manderson, back, -	53	52	—
A. Ritchie, back, - -	27	—	—
J. Gordon, back, etc., -	45	—	11
J. Bowie, half-back, etc.,	53	29	17
A. Dixon, half-back, -	41	52	4
J. Walls, half-back, - -	54	25	4
A. Archibald, forward, -	53	49	28
T. Muirhead, half-back, etc.,	46	23	23
A. Cunningham, forward,	51	52	60
T. Cairns, forward, - -	50	48	37
Dr. J. Paterson, forward, -	48	—	16
D. Meiklejohn, half-back,	14	46	7
Geo. Henderson, forward,	8	35	29
W. M'Candless, back, -	—	36	—
A. L. Morton, forward, -	—	50	9

1919-20.—W. Reid, 9 games, 9 goals ; J. Smith, 8
games ; T. M'Donald, 3 ; A. Johnstone, 2 ; J. Wilkinson,
A. Laird, J. Low, and J. Houghton, 1 each. **1920-21.**—
J. Smith, 20 ; G. M'Queen and H. M'Kenna, 4 ; A.
Johnstone and J. Low, 3 ; T. Reid, H. Lawson, J. Morton,
and R. M'Dermid, 2 ; T. M'Donald, 1.

It needed only a victory in the Scottish Cup Final of
1920-21 to crown a glorious season's play. But Partick

Thistle, ancient and respected opponents, would not have it so. When Rangers played Clyde, on Christmas Day, 1920, James Walls, the recognised and trusted left half-back, sustained a broken leg and did not play again that season. Bowie stepped into the breach when the Cup Final was staged at Celtic Park. Midway through the first half he had to leave the field for a moment for the mere purpose of adjusting his jersey. In that moment, Blair, the Partick Thistle outside right, scored the only goal and won the Cup. There we see a succession of events working inexorably against the Cup aspirations of a club that could win everything else. To forgive is divine. The Thistle, themselves weakened by the absence of J. M'Mullan and W. Hamilton, played heroically. Rangers could not bear them malice. To complete the story we give the teams that played before the smallest Cup Final attendance of modern times :—

> Partick Thistle.—K. Campbell ; T. Crichton and W. Bulloch ; J. Harris, M. Wilson, and W. Borthwick ; J. Blair, J. Kinloch, D. Johnston, J. M'Menemy, and W. Salisbury.

> Rangers.—W. Robb ; R. Manderson and W. M'Candless ; D. Meiklejohn, A. Dixon, and J. Bowie ; A. Archibald, A. Cunningham, G. Henderson, T. Cairns, and A. L. Morto n.

Here, also, is a compendium of the Scottish Cup encounters of the two friends and rivals :—

1880-1.	Third Round.	Kinning Park.	Rangers 3	Partick Thistle 0
1887-8.	Second Round.	Inchview Park.	Rangers 1	Partick Thistle 2
1888-9.	First Round.	Ibrox Park.	Rangers 4	Partick Thistle 2
1896-7.	First Round.	Inchview Park.	Rangers 4	Partick Thistle 2
1899-1900	Third Round.	Meadowside.	Rangers 6	Partick Thistle 1
1920-1.	Final.	Celtic Park.	Rangers 0	Partick Thistle 1
1921-2.	Semi-Final.	Ibrox Park.	Rangers 2	Partick Thistle 0
			20	8

THE STORY OF THE RANGERS.

Rangers' Cup record for 1920-21 and the individual honours gained are appended :—

Scottish Cup.		Glasgow Cup.		Charity Cup.	
A Bye.		Queen's Park (A), 2–1		Queen's Park (H),	5–0
Morton (H),	2–0	Celtic (A), 1–2		Clyde	
Alloa (H),	0–0			(Hampden),	2–0
Alloa (H),	4–1			Celtic (Hampden),	0–2
Dumbarton (A),	3–0				
Albion Rovers					
(Parkhead),	4–1				
Partick Thistle					
(Parkhead),	0–1				
	13–3		3–3		7–2

v. England.	v. Wales.	v. Ireland.	v. English L'gue.	v. Irish League.
A. Cunningham.	A. Cunningham.	A. L. Morton.	A. Cunningham.	W. Robb.
A. L. Morton.	A. Archibald.		A. Archibald.	A. Archibald.
			A. L. Morton.	

1921—1922.

Two Prizes—Nearly Four—League Lost by
a Point—Scottish Cup Lost by a Goal—Final
with Morton—James Gourlay's Puzzler—
International Calls.

RANGERS hold the record for the greatest number of League points secured in any one season. They possess, also, the unequalled distinction of having won every League match played in a season. One feat, however, they have never been able to accomplish. They have never won the four first-class prizes in one season as the Celtic did in 1907-8. We refer, of course, to the League Championship, Scottish Cup, Glasgow Cup, and Charity Cup. On four occasions the Light Blues have fallen short of the complete achievement by one, as witness :—

1896-97.—Won the Scottish Cup, Glasgow Cup, and Charity Cup.

1899-1900.—Won the Glasgow Cup, Charity Cup, and League Championship.

1910-11.—Won the Glasgow Cup, Charity Cup, and League Championship.

1922-23.—Won the Glasgow Cup, Charity Cup, and League Championship.

These examples of the prowess of different generations of players are wonderful as they stand. No one will question that. But in the season of 1921-22, to which we devote this chapter, the Rangers team accomplished something quite as meritorious. They should, as a matter of fact, have come into line with the Celtic by winning all four honours. When we say *should have*, we mean that, with ordinary freedom from accident, which has nothing to do with form, inherent ability or individual lapses, they *would have succeeded* in sweeping the boards. How is this statement to be justified? Well, first of all, the Glasgow Cup was won with a record of 3 goals to 0. The Charity Cup was, likewise, won by a record of 3 goals and 10 corners against 1 goal and 6 corners. In both of these competitions, Celtic were conquered in the Final tie. Now, let us take the League and see where accident intervened. Rangers were winning the Championship comfortably when a series of events occurred which were not entirely beyond control, yet, unquestionably, cost the club premier position. When the team went to Fir Park to meet Motherwell, they had to find substitutes for Meiklejohn, Archibald, and Morton who were called away by the Scottish F.A. to play in the International against Wales. In addition, Cunningham was ill and not available. Rangers were beaten by 2–0 and that defeat was sufficient in itself to deprive them of the championship, for they finished only a single point behind Celtic, the champions. Observe the results of the engagements between Rangers and Celtic during the season :—

League,	-	At Ibrox Park,	-	Rangers	1–1
League,	-	At Celtic Park,	-	Rangers	0–0
Glasgow Cup,		At Hampden Park,		Rangers	1–0
Charity Cup,		At Hampden Park,		Rangers	10–6*
Relief Fund,		At Hampden Park,		Rangers	2–0
		* Corners.			

Figures, we know, do not prove everything. They are significant, however. Rangers were under the necessity of playing Greenock Morton in the League, at Ibrox, when Cunningham, Muirhead, and Alan Morton were away representing Scotland against Ireland, and they had to grapple with Dumbarton at Boghead Park, on the day that Archibald, Cairns, and Morton were playing against England, and Cunningham was again unable to assist through illness. Fortunately, both of these matches were won against heavy odds. Two vital points were lost in the Ibrox match against Raith Rovers. This was the occasion on which William M'Candless played at inside right much to the amazement of the club's sympathetic followers. How he came to be in that position was a source of wide conjecture. The explanation was simple enough. There was no one available at the time, and the willing Ulsterman stepped to the front and volunteered, assured in his own mind that some little experience of playing forward in Ireland when he was a lad, would enable him to fill the bill. Another point was lost in a goalless match against Hamilton Academicals, at Douglas Park, where the conditions were so bad that a modified protest was made to the referee against the players being compelled to risk their limbs. The referee decided that a League match should be played, but it is an iron certainty that the teams became engaged more in saving their necks than in giving an exhibition of football. For a championship to be decided, as it virtually was, under such conditions was, shall we say? ironic. Even with the tide running against them in this way, the Rangers kept the championship issue in doubt until the last day of the season. They drew the concluding match with Clyde, at Shawfield Park. Celtic defeated Morton, at Greenock, by a goal scored when the game was almost ended. The championship was for Parkhead.

Now we come to the Scottish Cup. The incidents of the Final with Morton at Hampden Park, are familiar, probably, to most readers. Twelve minutes after the start, Robb was adjudged to have handled the ball outside his area. Gourlay, from the free kick scored such a goal as possibly neither he nor any other player would repeat in a lifetime. One will not be accused of blind prejudice for stating that Rangers did not, on play, deserve to be a goal down—neither then nor at any other period of one of the strangest Scottish Cup Finals ever played. The goal only winged the team ; it was not a mortal blow. When, however, Cunningham, the captain, had to desert his colleagues suffering from a fractured jaw, the position became critical. For an hour and five minutes the remaining ten Rangers men played with heroic dash and desperate zeal. It was their splendid failure. Morton's good angel smiled upon their courageous defence, and so, for the first time in history, they won a Scottish Cup-tie against the Rangers as the appended record of their battles in the competition will reveal :—

1896–7	Semi-Final.	Greenock.	Rangers 7	Morton 2
1899–1900	First Round	Ibrox Park	Rangers 4	Morton 2
1903–4	Semi-Final	Ibrox Park	Rangers 3	Morton 0
1904–5	Second Round	Greenock.	Rangers 6	Morton 0
1910–1	Second Round	Ibrox Park	Rangers 3	Morton 0
1920–1	Second Round	Ibrox Park	Rangers 2	Morton 0
1921–2	Final	Hampden	Rangers 0	Morton 1
			25	5

Seventy thousand people witnessed the Final in which the combatants were :—

Morton.—Edwards ; M'Intyre and R. Brown ; Gourlay, Wright, and M'Gregor ; M'Nab, M'Kay, Buchanan, A. Brown, and M'Minn.

Rangers.—Robb ; Manderson and M'Candless ; Meiklejohn, Dixon, and Muirhead; Archibald, Cunningham, Henderson, Cairns, and Morton.

Be it noted, in passing, that John M'Intyre and Robert Brown, who played a mighty part in stemming the avalanche of Rangers pressure, had, at a former period, figured in the Ibrox register.

With the Glasgow Cup and the Charity Cup, runners-up

in the Scottish Cup and runners-up in the League—beaten by a goal and a point—Rangers had to be satisfied. One moment. They also won the Lord Provost's Unemployed Fund tournament by defeating Queen's Park (3–1), Partick Thistle (2–0), and in the Final, Celtic (2–0). The team's cup record and International honours were :—

Scottish Cup.		Glasgow Cup.		Charity Cup.	
Clachnacuddin (A),	5–0	A Bye.		Celtic	
Albion Rovers (A),	1–1	Third Lanark (A),	2–0	(Hampden), 10–6*	
Albion Rovers (H),	4–0	Celtic (Ham'den),	1–0	Queen's Park	
Hearts (A),	4–0			(Ham'den),3–1	
St. Mirren (H),	1–1				
St. Mirren (A),	2–0				
Partick Thistle (H),	2–0				
Morton (Ham'den),	0–1				
	19–3		3–0		3–1

* Corners.

v. England.	v. Wales.	v. Ireland.	v. English L'gue.	v. Irish League.
A. Archibald	A. Archibald	T. Muirhead	T. Muirhead	T. Muirhead
T. Cairns	A.L. Morton	A. Cunningham	A. Archibald	A. Archibald
A. L. Morton	D. Meiklejohn	A. L. Morton	T. Cairns	A. Cunningham
			A. Cunningham	A. L. Morton
			A. L. Morton	

Once again, the old club was doing quite well by the old country.

1922—1923.

JUBILEES are celebrated in different ways. Rangers signalised theirs by winning the Scottish League Championship for the twelfth time, the Glasgow Cup for the fifteenth time, and the Charity Cup for the eleventh time. We include the joint success with Dumbarton in the League summation. Directors, manager, and team had an inclination towards adding the Scottish Cup to the little list. It would have been rather nice, of course, but monopolies are distasteful. If the Rangers didn't think so, Ayr United did. The Light Blues got no farther than the second round. Simply rendered, the explanation of the defeat at Somerset Park is that the team did not play well enough to win. The players knew it, and as they were as sensitive to the reverse as others connected with the club, there is nothing to be gained by dwelling upon the subject. This was the only occasion on which Rangers had met Ayr United in a Scottish Cup-tie. In the first round the team gave a specially fine display against their old friends the Clyde, at Shawfield Park. On dear old Kinning Park the clubs played their first Scottish Cup tie forty-three years previously, when Rangers won by 11 goals to 0. There was nothing prophetic in that result for it required a victory at Shawfield in 1923 to enable the Rangers to balance the account incurred during the intervening years. A summary of the

results in the Scottish Cup-ties between the clubs shows
that Clyde must have been " bonnie fighters " even if, in
the aggregate, the scoring is heavily against them :—

1880-81	Fourth Round	Kinning Park	Rangers 11	Clyde 0
1885-86	First Round	Barrowfield Pk	Rangers 0	Clyde 1
1888-89	Second Round	Ibrox Park	Rangers 0	Clyde*3
1893-94	Third Round	Barrowfield Pk	Rangers 5	Clyde 0
1898-99	Third Round	Ibrox Park	Rangers 4	Clyde 0
1909-10	Second Round	Shawfield Park	Rangers 0	Clyde 2
1911-12	Second Round	Shawfield Park	Rangers 1	Clyde 3
1922-23	First Round	Shawfield Park	Rangers 4	Clyde 0
			25	9

* After 2–2 at Barrowfield Park.

In the ties against both Clyde and Ayr United, Wm.
M'Candless played under the disadvantage of an injured
left foot, which, it was feared, might jeopardise his football
career. The fact was not widely known because it was
felt that it would be a mistake to create alarm while there
was the possibility of a complete recovery. Therein lay
the significance of Manager Struth's reassuring statement
at the annual meeting. The capable and popular Ulster
back had stood, splendidly, the test of the games in which
he had played during the summer tour in Switzerland.

Until the tie with Ayr United, the team played on a
high level of consistency. In their first 30 matches—
League, Glasgow Cup, and the " Scottish " tie with Clyde—
they were only twice defeated, Falkirk (2–0), at Brockville
Park, and St. Mirren (1–0), at Paisley, winning the League
engagements. If this standard was not maintained right
through the campaign, the inherent ability of the team
was good enough to win the championship by a margin
of five points over the aspiring and valiant Airdrieonians.
It was good enough, also, to wind up the season with a

THE STORY OF THE RANGERS.

Charity Cup triumph, and so, for the fourth time in the career of the club, three of the four great prizes were brought to Ibrox in one season. Thus, in the last five seasons, the Rangers have, by actual results, shown themselves capable of emulating many of the great old teams that wore the light blue. Let us look at the achievements of that inclusive period :—

1918-19—Won the Glasgow Cup and Charity Cup. Runners-up in the League one point behind the champions.

1919-20—Won the League. Qualified for Scottish Cup semi-final.

1920-21—Won the League. Qualified for Scottish Cup Final and Charity Cup Final.

1921-22—Won the Glasgow Cup and Charity Cup. Qualified for Scottish Cup Final. Runners-up in the League one point behind the champions.

1922-23—Won the League, Glasgow Cup and Charity Cup.

In this Jubilee year a pretty compliment was paid the team by the bestowal of fifteen International honours. Tom Cairns, in his tenth year as a Ranger, was capped against England, Wales, the English League, and the Irish League. In his third season at Ibrox, A. L. Morton played against England, Wales, Ireland, and the English League. Morton's installation at outside left perpetuates a feature of the team that is rather remarkable. No position has been more stabilised over a long period. During the past thirty years and more, the club might be said to have had only four players who became the recognised tenants of the outside left position—John Barker, Alec Smith, Dr. James Paterson, and Alan Morton. Each, in his time, comported himself like a gallant cavalier. John Barker was a member of the team that first won the Scottish Cup ; Alec Smith gained honours galore ; Dr. Paterson could charm the onlookers by the artistry of his footwork ; and Alan Morton had it said of him by *Tityrus*, the editor of the *Athletic News*, that " no Englishman has yet learned to play Morton," a tribute as striking as any player need covet.

League champions once again, the club's cup record and individual honours gained were as appended :—

Scottish Cup.		Glasgow Cup.		Charity Cup.	
Clyde (A),	4–0	Partick Thistle (H),	3–1	Celtic (A),	1–0
Ayr United (A),	0–2	Third Lanark (A),	2–2	Queen's Park	
		Third Lanark (H),	2–1	(H),	4–0
		Clyde (Parkhead),	0–0		
		Clyde (Parkhead),	1–0		
	4–2		8–4		5–0

v. England.	*v.* Wales.	*v.* Ireland.	*v.* English League	*v.* Irish League.
T. Muirhead.	A. Cunningham.	A. Archibald.	D. Meiklejohn.	T. Muirhead.
A. Cunningham.	T. Cairns.	A. L. Morton.	T. Muirhead.	T. Cairns.
T. Cairns.	A. L. Morton.		T. Cairns.	
A. L. Morton.			A. L. Morton.	

On Monday, 9th April, 1923, a Jubilee celebration dinner was held in Ferguson & Forrester's, Glasgow, at which Sir John Ure Primrose, Bart., LL.D., presided. Mr. William Craig was croupier. Among the guests were Sir John T. Cargill, Bart., D.L., an honorary president, who proposed the toast of the club ; Mr. Alexander Walker, City Assessor ; ex-Provost Smellie, Hamilton ; Bailie Hamilton Brown (Clyde F.C.) ; Bailie Crerar (Third Lanark) ; Mr. Thomas Nisbet, Master of Works ; Police-Judge Forsyth, Airdrie ; Mr. A. Leitch, London ; Mr. Thomas White, Mr. J. K. M'Dowall, and Mr. Thomas Steen, chairman, secretary, and treasurer, respectively, of the Scottish Football Association ; Mr. William Maley, Chairman of the Scottish Football League ; and representatives from the various League clubs.

Past officials and players were represented by, among others, Mr. Thomas Vallance, one of the original members ;

THE STORY OF THE RANGERS.

Messrs. William MacAndrew, John R. Gow, Archie Steel, James M'Intyre, John Cameron, David Mitchell, John Drummond, David Haddow, Alec Smith, Thomas Hyslop, Alec Bennett, William Reid, and James Bowie. With the exception of Mr. George Small, who was indisposed, all the members of the Board of Directors and the signed players were present.

That is the Story of the Rangers. They have had good times and bad times, critical times and times of exultation. No club with the same modest origin can claim so distinguished a record of achievement. They were not born in the lap of luxury. They have been the architects of their own fortune, and, simply because of that, they have become equipped with the moral resistive force to grapple with adversity, which is better than being coddled in the cradle and whining when the winds blow cold. May all who look upon the old club with a friendly eye stand prepared, by precept and example, to protect its interests and its good name!

RANGERS' VICTORY YEARS.

Scottish Cup	Glasgow Cup.	Charity Cup.	Scottish League.	Scottish 2nd XI. Cup.	Glasgow 2nd XI. Cup.
—	—	1878-79	—	—	—
—	—	—	—	1889-90	—
—	—	—	1890-91*	—	—
—	1892-93	—	—	—	—
1893-94	1893-94	—	—	—	—
—	—	—	—	—	1894-95
1896-97	1896-97	1896-97	—	—	—
1897-98	1897-98	—	—	1897-98	—
—	—	—	1898-99	1898-99	1898-99
—	1899-00	1899-00	1899-00	—	—
—	1900-01	—	1900-01	—	—
—	1901-02†	—	1901-02	1901-02	—
1902-03	—	—	—	—	—
—	—	1903-04	—	—	—
—	—	1905-06	—	—	1905-06
—	—	1906-07	—	1906-07	—
—	—	1908-09	—	—	—
—	—	—	—	—	1909-10
—	1910-11	1910-11	1910-11	—	1910-11
—	1911-12	—	1911-12	1911-12	1911-12
—	1912-13	—	1912-13	1912-13	1912-13
—	1913-14	—	—	—	—
—	—	—	—	—	1914-15
—	1917-18	—	1917-18	—	—
—	1918-19	1918-19	—	—	—
—	—	—	1919-20	—	—
—	—	—	1920-21	—	—
—	1921-22	1921-22	—	—	—
—	1922-23	1922-23	1922-23	—	—
Four.	Fifteen.	Eleven.	Twelve.	Seven.	Eight.

* Joint Champions with Dumbarton. † Celtic scratched.

RANGERS' SCOTTISH CUP RECORD.

1873-74.

Rangers did not compete.

1874-75.

Round.	Opponents.				Ground.
FIRST ROUND.	2 ; Oxford,	-	-	0	Queen's Park.
SECOND ROUND.	0 ; Dumbarton,	-	-	0	Glasgow Green.
REPLAY.	0 ; Dumbarton,	-	-	1	Dumbarton.

1875-76.

FIRST ROUND.	7 ; 1st L.R.V.,	-	-	0	Burnbank.
SECOND ROUND.	0 ; 3rd Lanark,	-	-	2	Cathkin Park.

1876-77.

FIRST ROUND.	4 ; Queen's Park Juniors,			1	Kinning Park.
SECOND ROUND.	8 ; Towerhill,	-	-	0	Springburn.
THIRD ROUND.	A Bye.				
FOURTH ROUND.	3 ; Mauchline,	-	-	0	Mauchline.
FIFTH ROUND.	3 ; Lennox,	-	-	0	Dumbarton.
SEMI-FINAL.	A Bye.				
FINAL.	0 ; Vale of Leven,	-		0	Hamilton Crescent
REPLAY.	1 ; Vale of Leven,	-		1	Hamilton Crescent
REPLAY.	2 ; Vale of Leven,	-		3	Hampden Park.

1877-78.

FIRST ROUND.	13 ; Possilpark,	-	-	0	Kinning Park.
SECOND ROUND.	8 ; Alexandra Athletic,			0	Kinning Park.
THIRD ROUND.	13 ; Uddingston,	-	-	0	Kinning Park.
FOURTH ROUND.	0 ; Vale of Leven,	-		0	Kinning Park.
REPLAY.	0 ; Vale of Leven,	-		5	Alexandria.

SCOTTISH CUP RECORD.

1878-79.

Round.	Opponents.				Ground.
FIRST ROUND.	3 ; Shaftesbury,	-	-	0	Kinning Park.
SECOND ROUND.	6 ; Whitefield,	-	-	1	Whitefield Park.
THIRD ROUND.	8 ; Parkgrove,	-	-	2	Kinning Park.
FOURTH ROUND.	3 ; Alexandra Athletic,			0	Kinning Park.
FIFTH ROUND.	4 ; Partick,	-	-	0	Kinning Park.
SIXTH ROUND.	1 ; Queen's Park,	-	-	0	Hampden Park.
SEMI-FINAL.	A Bye.				
FINAL.	1 ; Vale of Leven,		-	1	Hampden Park.

A protest by Rangers on the ground that they had scored a second goal was not sustained by the S.F.A., and they declined to replay. Vale of Leven were, therefore, awarded the Cup.

1879-80.

FIRST ROUND.	0 ; Queen's Park,	-	-	0	Kinning Park.
REPLAY.	1 ; Queen's Park,	-	-	5	Hampden Park.

1880-81.

FIRST ROUND.	4 ; Govan,	-	-	1	Kinning Park.
SECOND ROUND.	1 ; Northern,	-	-	0	Springburn.
THIRD ROUND.	3 ; Partick Thistle,		-	0	Kinning Park.
FOURTH ROUND.	11 ; Clyde,	-	-	0	Kinning Park.
FIFTH ROUND.	3 ; Hurlford,		-	0	Hurlford.
SIXTH ROUND.	1 ; Dumbarton,		-	3	Dumbarton.

1881-82.

FIRST ROUND.	2 ; 3rd Lanark,		-	1	Kinning Park.
SECOND ROUND.	W.O. Harmonic. Scratched.				
THIRD ROUND.	3 ; Alexandra Athletic,		1		Kinning Park.
FOURTH ROUND.	2 ; Thornliebank,		-	0	Thornliebank.
FIFTH ROUND.	6 ; South Western,		-	4	Kinning Park.

After a protested game, won by Rangers, 2–1.

SIXTH ROUND.	1 ; Dumbarton,		-	5	Boghead Park.

After a protested game.

1882-83.

FIRST ROUND.	4 ; Jordanhill,		-	0	Anniesland.
SECOND ROUND.	2 ; Queen's Park,	-	-	3	Hampden Park.

1883-84.

Round.	Opponents.				Ground.
FIRST ROUND.	1 ; Northern, -	-	-	0	Springburn.
SECOND ROUND.	14 ; Whitehill, -	-	-	2	Kinning Park.
THIRD ROUND.	5 ; Falkirk, -	-	-	2	Kinning Park.
FOURTH ROUND.	6 ; Dunblane,	-	-	1	Dunblane.
FIFTH ROUND.	3 ; St. Bernard,	-	-	0	Edinburgh.
SIXTH ROUND.	5 ; Cambuslang,	-	-	1	Cambuslang.
SEMI-FINAL.	0 ; Vale of Leven,	-	3		Alexandria.

1884-85.

Round.	Opponents.				Ground.
FIRST ROUND.	11 ; Whitehill,	-	-	0	Kinning Park.
SECOND ROUND.	2 ; 3rd Lanark,	-	-	2	Cathkin Park.
REPLAY.	0 ; 3rd Lanark,	-	-	0	Kinning Park.
THIRD ROUND.	3 ; 3rd Lanark,	-	-	0	Cathkin Park.
FOURTH ROUND.	8 ; Arbroath, -	-	-	1	Arbroath.

After protested game, which Arbroath won by 4—3.

FIFTH ROUND.	A Bye.	
SIXTH ROUND.	3 ; Renton, - - - 5	Renton.

1885-86.

FIRST ROUND.	0 ; Clyde, - - - 1	Barrowfield Park.

1886-87.

Round.	Opponents.			Ground.
FIRST ROUND.	9 ; Govan Athletic,	-	1	Kinning Park.
SECOND ROUND.	5 ; Westbourne,	-	- 2	Kinning Park.
THIRD ROUND.	0 ; Cambuslang,	-	- 2	Kinning Park.

1887-88.

FIRST ROUND.	4 ; Battlefield,	-	- 1	Ibrox Park.
SECOND ROUND.	1 ; Partick Thistle,	-	2	Partick.

1888-89.

FIRST ROUND.	4 ; Partick Thistle,	-	2	Ibrox Park.
SECOND ROUND.	2 ; Clyde, - - - 2			Barrowfield Park.
REPLAY.	0 ; Clyde, - - - 3			Ibrox Park.

1889-90.

FIRST ROUND.	6 ; United Abstainers,	2	Ibrox Park.
SECOND ROUND.	13 ; Kelvinside Athletic,	0	Kelvinside.
THIRD ROUND.	0 ; Vale of Leven,	-	0	Ibrox Park.
REPLAY.	2 ; Vale of Leven,	-	3	Alexandria.

1890-91.

Round.	Opponents.		Ground.
First Round.	0 ; Celtic, - - -	1	Celtic Park.

1891-92.

First Round.	5 ; St. Bernards, -	- 1	Ibrox Park.
Second Round.	0 ; Kilmarnock, -	- 0	Ibrox Park.
Replay.	1 ;. Kilmarnock, -	1	Kilmarnock.
Replay.	3 ; Kilmarnock, -	- 2	Paisley.
Third Round.	2 ; Annbank, -	- 0	Ibrox Park.
Fourth Round.	3 ; Celtic, - -	- 5	Celtic Park.

1892-93.

First Round.	7 ; Annbank, -	- 0	Ibrox Park.
Second Round.	1 ; Dumbarton, -	- 0	Dumbarton.
Third Round.	2 ; St. Bernards, -	- 3	Edinburgh.

1893-94.

First Round.	8 ; Cowlairs, - -	- 0	Ibrox Park.
Second Round.	2 ; Leith Athletic,	- 0	Ibrox Park.
Third Round.	5 ; Clyde, - -	- 0	Barrowfield Park.
Semi-Final.	1 ; Queen's Park,	- 1	Ibrox Park.
Replay.	3 ; Queen's Park, -	- 1	Hampden Park.
Final.	**3 ; Celtic, - -**	**- 1**	**Hampden Park.**

1894-95.

First Round.	1 ; Heart of Midlothian,	2	Ibrox Park.

1895-96.

First Round.	1 ; Dumbarton, -	- 1	Dumbarton.
Replay.	3 ; Dumbarton, -	- 1	Ibrox Park.
Second Round.	5 ; St. Mirren, -	- 0	Ibrox Park.
Third Round.	2 ; Hibernian, -	- 3	Ibrox Park.

1896-97.

First Round.	4 ; Partick Thistle,	- 2	Inchview, Partick.
Second Round.	3 ; Hibernian, -	- 0	Ibrox Park.
Third Round.	4 ; Dundee, - -	- 0	Carolina Park.
Semi-Final.	7 ; Morton, - -	- 2	Cappielow Park.
Final.	**5 ; Dumbarton, -**	**- 1**	**Hampden Park.**

THE STORY OF THE RANGERS.

1897-98.

Round.	Opponents.		Ground.
FIRST ROUND.	8 ; Polton Vale, -	- o	Ibrox Park.
SECOND ROUND.	12 ; Cartvale, - -	- o	Ibrox Park.
THIRD ROUND.	3 ; Queen's Park, -	- 1	Ibrox Park.
SEMI-FINAL.	1 ; Third Lanark,	- 1	Ibrox Park.
REPLAY.	2 ; Third Lanark,	- 2	Cathkin Park.
REPLAY.	2 ; Third Lanark,	- o	Cathkin Park.
Final.	**2 ; Kilmarnock, -**	**- 0**	**Hampden Park.**

1898-99.

FIRST ROUND.	4 ; Heart of Midlothian,	1	Ibrox Park.
SECOND ROUND.	4 ; Ayr Parkhouse,	- 1	Ayr.
THIRD ROUND.	4 ; Clyde, - -	- o	Ibrox Park.
SEMI-FINAL.	2 ; St. Mirren, -	- 1	Paisley.
FINAL.	o ; Celtic, - -	- 2	Hampden Park.

1899-1900.

FIRST ROUND.	4 ; Morton, - -	- 2	Ibrox Park.
SECOND ROUND.	12 ; Maybole, - -	- o	Ibrox Park.
THIRD ROUND.	6 ; Partick Thistle,	- 1	Meadowside.
SEMI-FINAL.	2 ; Celtic, - -	- 2	Ibrox Park.
REPLAY.	o ; Celtic, - -	- 4	Celtic Park.

1900-01.

FIRST ROUND.	o ; Celtic, - -	- 1	Celtic Park.

1901-02.

FIRST ROUND.	6 ; Johnstone, -	- 1	Ibrox Park.
SECOND ROUND.	5 ; Inverness Caledonian,	1	Ibrox Park.
THIRD ROUND.	2 ; Kilmarnock, -	- o	Ibrox Park.
SEMI-FINAL.	o ; Hibernian, -	- 2	Ibrox Park.

1902-03.

FIRST ROUND.	7 ; Auchterarder Thistle,	o	Ibrox Park.
SECOND ROUND.	4 ; Kilmarnock, -	- o	Ibrox Park.
THIRD ROUND.	3 ; Celtic, - -	- o	Celtic Park.
SEMI-FINAL,	4 ; Stenhousemuir,	- 1	Stenhousemuir.
FINAL.	1 ; Heart of Midlothian,	1	Celtic Park.
REPLAY.	o ; Heart of Midlothian,	o	Celtic Park.
Replay.	**2 ; Heart of Midlothian, 0**		**Celtic Park.**

1903-04.

Round.	Opponents.			Ground.
FIRST ROUND.	3 ; Heart of Midlothian,	2		Ibrox Park.
SECOND ROUND.	2 ; Hibernian,	-	- 1	Edinburgh.
THIRD ROUND.	1 ; St. Mirren,	-	- 0	Paisley.
SEMI-FINAL.	3 ; Morton, -	-	- 0	Ibrox Park.
FINAL.	2 ; Celtic, -	-	- 3	Hampden Park.

1904-05.

FIRST ROUND.	2 ; Ayr Parkhouse,	-	1	Ibrox Park.
SECOND ROUND.	6 ; Morton, -	-	- 0	Greenock.
THIRD ROUND.	5 ; Beith, -	-	- 1	Ibrox Park.
SEMI-FINAL.	2 ; Celtic, -	-	- 0	Celtic Park.
FINAL.	0 ; Third Lanark,	-	0	Hampden Park.
REPLAY.	1 ; Third Lanark,	-	3	Hampden Park.

1905-06.

FIRST ROUND.	7 ; Arthurlie, -	-	- 1	Barrhead.
SECOND ROUND.	3 ; Aberdeen,	-	- 2	Aberdeen.
THIRD ROUND.	0 ; Port-Glasgow Ath., -		1	Port-Glasgow.

1906-07.

FIRST ROUND.	2 ; Falkirk, -	-	- 1	Falkirk.
SECOND ROUND.	4 ; Galston, -	-	- 0	Galston.
THIRD ROUND.	0 ; Celtic, -	-	- 3	Ibrox Park.

1907-08.

FIRST ROUND.	2 ; Falkirk, -	-	- 2	Falkirk.
REPLAY.	4 ; Falkirk, -	-	- 1	Ibrox Park.
SECOND ROUND.	1 ; Celtic, -	-	- 2	Ibrox Park.

1908-09.

FIRST ROUND.	3 ; St. Johnstone,	-	0	Perth.
SECOND ROUND.	0 ; Dundee, -	-	- 0	Dundee.
REPLAY.	1 ; Dundee, -	-	- 0	Ibrox Park.
THIRD ROUND.	1 ; Queen's Park, -	-	0	Ibrox Park.
SEMI-FINAL.	1 ; Falkirk, -	-	- 0	Falkirk.
FINAL.	2 ; Celtic, -	-	- 2	Hampden Park.
REPLAY.	1 ; Celtic, -	-	- 1	Hampden Park.

Cup withheld.

303

1909-10.

Round.	Opponents.		Ground.
FIRST ROUND.	3 ; Inverness Thistle, -	1	Ibrox Park.
SECOND ROUND.	0 ; Clyde, - - -	2	Shawfield Park.

1910-11.

FIRST ROUND.	2 ; Kilmarnock, - -	1	Ibrox Park.
SECOND ROUND.	3 ; Morton, - - -	0	Ibrox Park.
THIRD ROUND.	1 ; Dundee, - - -	2	Dundee.

1911-12.

FIRST ROUND.	3 ; Stenhousemuir, -	1	Ibrox Park.
SECOND ROUND.	1 ; Clyde, - - -	3	Shawfield Park.

1912-13.

FIRST ROUND.	A Bye.		
SECOND ROUND.	1 ; Hamilton Academicals,	1	Hamilton.
REPLAY.	2 ; Hamilton Academicals,	0	Ibrox Park.
THIRD ROUND.	1 ; Falkirk, - - -	3	Ibrox Park.

1913-14.

FIRST ROUND.	A Bye.		
SECOND ROUND.	5 ; Alloa Athletic, -	0	Ibrox Park.
THIRD ROUND.	1 ; Hibernian, - -	2	Edinburgh.

1919-20.

FIRST ROUND.	0 ; Dumbarton, - -	0	Ibrox Park.
REPLAY.	1 ; Dumbarton, - -	0	Ibrox Park.
SECOND ROUND.	5 ; Arbroath, - - -	0	Ibrox Park.
THIRD ROUND.	3 ; Broxburn United, -	0	Ibrox Park.
FOURTH ROUND.	1 ; Celtic, - - -	0	Ibrox Park.
SEMI-FINAL.	1 ; Albion Rovers, -	1	Celtic Park.
REPLAY.	0 ; Albion Rovers, -	0	Celtic Park.
REPLAY.	0 ; Albion Rovers, -	2	Celtic Park.

SCOTTISH CUP RECORD.

1920-21.

Round.	Opponents.	Ground.
FIRST ROUND.	A Bye.	
SECOND ROUND.	2 ; Morton, - - - 0	Ibrox Park.
THIRD ROUND.	0 ; Alloa, - - - 0	Ibrox Park.
REPLAY.	4 ; Alloa, - - - 1	Ibrox Park.
FOURTH ROUND.	3 ; Dumbarton, - - 0	Dumbarton.
SEMI-FINAL.	4 ; Albion Rovers, - 1	Celtic Park.
FINAL.	0 ; Partick Thistle, - 1	Celtic Park.

1921-22.

Round.	Opponents.	Ground.
FIRST ROUND.	5 ; Clachnacuddin, - 0	Inverness.
SECOND ROUND.	1 ; Albion Rovers, - 1	Coatbridge.
REPLAY.	4 ; Albion Rovers, - 0	Ibrox Park.
THIRD ROUND.	4 ; Heart of Midlothian, 0	Tynecastle.
FOURTH ROUND.	1 ; St. Mirren, - - 1	Ibrox Park.
REPLAY.	2 ; St. Mirren, - - 0	Paisley.
SEMI-FINAL.	2 ; Partick Thistle, - 0	Ibrox Park.
FINAL.	0 ; Morton, - - - 1	Hampden Park.

1922-23.

Round.	Opponents.	Ground.
FIRST ROUND.	4 ; Clyde, - - - 0	Shawfield Park.
SECOND ROUND.	0 ; Ayr United, - - 2	Ayr.

ANALYSIS OF SCOTTISH CUP RESULTS.

Only the undernoted clubs have defeated Rangers in the competition.

CLUB.	Played.	Won.	Lost.	Goals.	
				For.	Against.
CELTIC, - - -	12	4	8	15	22*
DUMBARTON, - -	8	5	3	15	11
MORTON, - - -	7	6	1	25	5
CLYDE, - - -	8	4	4	25	9
PARTICK THISTLE, -	7	5	2	20	8
QUEEN'S PARK, -	6	4	2	11	10
THIRD LANARK,- -	5	3	2	8	6
HEART OF MIDLOTHIAN,	5	4	1	14	5
HIBERNIAN, - -	5	2	3	8	8
FALKIRK, - - -	5	4	1	13	7
VALE OF LEVEN, -	4	0	4	4	14†
ST. BERNARDS, - -	3	2	1	10	4
DUNDEE, - - -	3	2	1	6	2
ALBION ROVERS, -	3	2	1	8	3
CAMBUSLANG, - -	2	1	1	5	3
RENTON, - - -	1	0	1	3	5
PORT-GLASGOW ATH.,	1	0	1	0	1
AYR UNITED, - -	1	0	1	0	2

* In 1908-09 the Cup was withheld after Rangers and Celtic had played two drawn games in the Final. That Match is not included.

† In 1878-79 the Cup was awarded Vale of Leven after a drawn match in the Final, which Rangers claimed to have won. That result is not included.

GLASGOW CUP RECORD.

1887-88.

Round.	Opponents.		Ground.
First Round.	2 ; Third Lanark, -	2	Cathkin Park.
Replay.	2 ; Third Lanark, -	o	Ibrox Park.
Second Round.	3 ; Pollokshields Ath.,	2	Pollokshields.
Third Round.	5 ; Westbourne, - -	1	Ibrox Park.
Semi-Final.	o ; Cowlairs, - - -	o	Gourlay Park.
Replay.	o ; Cowlairs, - - -	o	Ibrox Park.
Replay.	2 ; Cowlairs, - - -	2	Cathkin Park.
Replay.	2 ; Cowlairs, - - -	1	Barrowfield Park.
Replay (after protest),	3 ; Cowlairs, - -	1	Cathkin Park.
Final.	**1 ; Cambuslang, -**	**3**	**Hampden Park.**

1888-89.

First Round.	10 ; United Abstainers, -	o	Ibrox Park.
Second Round.	7 ; Pollokshields Ath., -	o	Pollokshields.
Third Round.	1 ; Celtic, - - -	6	Ibrox Park.

1889-90.

First Round.	5 ; Pollokshaws, - -	1	Pollokshaws.
Second Round.	6 ; Northern, - -	3	Springburn.
Third Round.	1 ; Third Lanark, - -	1	Cathkin Park.
Replay.	2 ; Third Lanark, -	o	Ibrox Park.
Fourth Round.	o ; Queen's Park, - -	2	Ibrox Park.

1890-91.

First Round.	12 ; Carrington, - -	2	Ibrox Park.
Second Round.	A Bye.		
Third Round.	3 ; Third Lanark, -	3	Cathkin Park.
Replay.	1 ; Third Lanark, -	1	Ibrox Park.
Replay.	3 ; Third Lanark, -	3	Cathkin Park.
Replay.	1 ; Third Lanark, -	3	Ibrox Park.

1891-92.

First Round.	2 ; Third Lanark, -	o	Ibrox Park.
Second Round.	A Bye.		
Third Round.	o ; Queen's Park, · -	3	Ibrox Park.

1892-93.

Round.		Opponents.				Ground.
FIRST ROUND.	6 ;	Northern, -	-	-	2	Ibrox Park.
SECOND ROUND.	3 ;	Linthouse,	-	-	2	Ibrox Park.
THIRD ROUND.	4 ;	Queen's Park, -		-	2	Hampden Park.
SEMI-FINAL.	3 ;	Thistle,	-	-	2	Braehead Park.
Final.	**3 ;**	**Celtić,**	**-**	**-**	**1**	**Cathkin Park.**

1893-94.

FIRST ROUND.	W.O. ;	Whitefield.	Scratched.			
SECOND ROUND.	A Bye.					
THIRD ROUND.	11 ;	Pollokshaws,	-	-	1	Ibrox Park.
SEMI-FINAL.	1 ;	Celtic,	-	-	0	Ibrox Park.
Final.	**1 ;**	**Cowlairs,**	**-**	**-**	**0**	**Cathkin Park.**

1894-95.

FIRST ROUND.	2 ;	Queen's Park, -		-	0	Ibrox Park.
SECOND ROUND.	3 ;	Third Lanark,		-	2	Ibrox Park.
SEMI-FINAL.	0 ;	Partick Thistle,		-	1	Inchview.
REPLAY (after protest).	5 ;	Partick Thistle,		-	3	Inchview.
Final.	**0 ;**	**Celtic,**	**-**	**-**	**2**	**Cathkin Park.**

1895-96.

FIRST ROUND.	2 ;	Queen's Park, -		-	2	Hampden Park.
REPLAY.	2 ;	Queen's Park, -		-	3	Ibrox Park.

1896-97.

FIRST ROUND.	5 ;	Third Lanark,		-	1	Ibrox Park.
SECOND ROUND.	A Bye.					
SEMI-FINAL.	3 ;	Linthouse,	-	-	0	Ibrox Park.
Final.	**1 ;**	**Celtic,**	**-**	**-**	**1**	**Cathkin Park.**
Replay.	**2 ;**	**Celtic,**	**-**	**-**	**1**	**Cathkin Park.**

1897-98.

FIRST ROUND.	6 ;	Partick Thistle,		-	0	Meadowside.
SECOND ROUND.	A Bye.					
SEMI-FINAL.	2 ;	Celtic,	-	-	2	Celtic Park.
REPLAY.	1 ;	Celtic,	-	-	1	Ibrox Park.
REPLAY.	3 ;	Celtic,	-	-	1	Ibrox Park.
Final.	**4 ;**	**Queen's Park,**		**-**	**0**	**Cathkin Park.**

1898-99.

Round.	Opponents		Ground.
FIRST ROUND.	4 ; Cameronians, -	- 0	Alexandra Park.
SEMI-FINAL.	1 ; Celtic, - -	- 1	Ibrox Park.
REPLAY.	2 ; Celtic, - -	- 1	Celtic Park.
Final.	**0 ; Queen's Park,**	**- 1**	**Cathkin Park.**

1899-1900.

FIRST ROUND.	0 ; Third Lanark,	- 0	Cathkin Park.
REPLAY.	5 ; Third Lanark,	- 0	Ibrox Park.
SEMI-FINAL.	7 ; Queen's Park, -	- 3	Ibrox Park.
Final.	**1 ; Celtic, - -**	**- 1**	**Cathkin Park.**
Replay.	**1 ; Celtic, - -**	**- 0**	**Cathkin Park.**

1900-01.

FIRST ROUND.	3 ; Celtic. - -	- 3	Celtic Park.
REPLAY.	4 ; Celtic, - -	- 3	Ibrox Park.
SEMI-FINAL.	2 ; Third Lanark,	- 1	Ibrox Park.
Final.	**3 ; Partick Thistle,**	**- 1**	**Celtic Park.**

1901-02.

FIRST ROUND.	5 ; Normal Athletic,	- 0	Ibrox Park.
SECOND ROUND.	A Bye.		
SEMI-FINAL.	4 ; Partick Thistle,	- 1	Ibrox Park.
Final.	**2 ; Celtic, - -**	**- 2**	**Ibrox Park.**

Rangers awarded Cup, Celtic refusing to replay at Ibrox Park.

1902-03.

FIRST ROUND.	0 ; Third Lanark,	- 1	Cathkin Park.

1903-04.

FIRST ROUND.	0 ; Third Lanark,	- 2	Ibrox Park.

1904-05.

FIRST ROUND.	A Bye.		
SEMI-FINAL.	3 ; Third Lanark,	- 0	Ibrox Park.
Final.	**1 ; Celtic, - -**	**- 2**	**Hampden Park.**

1905-06.

FIRST ROUND.	0 ; Clyde, - -	- 0	Shawfield Park.
REPLAY.	2 ; Clyde, - -	- 1	Ibrox Park.
SECOND ROUND.	0 ; Third Lanark,	- 0	Ibrox Park.
REPLAY.	1 ; Third Lanark,	- 3	Cathkin Park.

THE STORY OF THE RANGERS.

1906-07.

Round.	Opponents		Ground.
FIRST ROUND.	2 ; Queen's Park, -	- 2	Hampden Park.
REPLAY.	0 ; Queen's Park,	- 3	Ibrox Park.

1907-08.

FIRST ROUND.	4 ; Clyde, - -	- 0	Shawfield Park.
SEMI-FINAL.	3 ; Third Lanark,	- 0	Ibrox Park.
Final.	2 ; Celtic, - -	- 2	Hampden Park.
Replay.	0 ; Celtic, - -	- 0	Hampden Park.
Replay.	1 ; Celtic, - -	- 2	Hampden Park.

1908-09.

FIRST ROUND.	A Bye.		
SEMI-FINAL.	2 ; Celtic, - -	- 2	Celtic Park.
REPLAY.	0 ; Celtic, - -	- 2	Ibrox Park.

1909-1910.

FIRST ROUND.	2 ; Partick Thistle,	- 1	Ibrox Park.
SEMI-FINAL.	2 ; Third Lanark,	- 1	Cathkin Park.
Final.	0 ; Celtic, - -	- 1	Hampden Park.

1910-11.

FIRST ROUND.	A Bye.		
SEMI-FINAL.	1 ; Clyde, - -	- 1	Shawfield Park.
REPLAY.	3 ; Clyde, - -	- 0	Ibrox Park.
Final.	3 ; Celtic, - -	- 1	Hampden Park.

1911-12.

FIRST ROUND.	6 ; Queen's Park,	- 1	Hampden Park.
SEMI-FINAL.	1 ; Clyde, - -	- 0	Ibrox Park.
Final.	1 ; Partick Thistle,	- 0	Celtic Park.

1912-13.

FIRST ROUND.	A Bye.		
SEMI-FINAL.	0 ; Partick Thistle,	- 0	Firhill Park.
REPLAY.	1 ; Partick Thistle,	- 1	Ibrox Park.
REPLAY.	2 ; Partick Thistle,	- 0	Firhill Park.
Final.	3 ; Celtic, - -	- 1	Hampden Park.

1913-14.

FIRST ROUND.	A Bye.		
SEMI-FINAL.	1 ; Clyde, - -	- 0	Shawfield Park.
Final.	3 ; Third Lanark,	- 0	Hampden Park.

1914-15.

Round.	Opponents.		Ground.
FIRST ROUND.	A Bye.		
SEMI-FINAL.	0 ; Partick Thistle,	- 2	Ibrox Park.

1915-16.

FIRST ROUND.	4 ; Queen's Park, -	- 1	Hampden Park.
SEMI-FINAL.	7 ; Partick Thistle,	- 2	Ibrox Park.
Final.	**1 ; Celtic, - -**	**- 2**	**Hampden Park.**

1916-17.

FIRST ROUND.	2 ; Partick Thistle,	- 0	Firhill Park.
SEMI-FINAL.	0 ; Celtic, - -	- 3	Celtic Park.

1917-18.

FIRST ROUND.	(corners) 14 ; Clyde (corners)	2	Shawfield Park.
SEMI-FINAL.	3 ; Celtic, - -	- 0	Celtic Park.
Final.	**4 ; Partick Thistle, -**	**1**	**Ibrox Park.**

1918-19.

FIRST ROUND.	A Bye.		
SEMI-FINAL.	3 ; Queen's Park,	- 0	Ibrox Park.
Final.	**2 ; Celtic, - -**	**- 0**	**Hampden Park.**

1919-20.

FIRST ROUND.	0 ; Celtic, - -	- 1	Celtic Park.

1920-21.

FIRST ROUND.	2 ; Queen's Park, -	- 1	Hampden Park.
SEMI-FINAL.	1 ; Celtic, - -	- 2	Celtic Park.

1921-22.

FIRST ROUND.	A Bye.		
SEMI-FINAL.	2 ; Third Lanark,	- 0	Cathkin Park.
Final.	**1 ; Celtic, - -**	**- 0**	**Hampden Park.**

1922-23.

FIRST ROUND.	3 ; Partick Thistle,	- 1	Ibrox Park.
SEMI-FINAL.	2 ; Third Lanark,	- 2	Cathkin Park.
REPLAY.	2 ; Third Lanark,	- 1	Ibrox Park.
Final.	**0 ; Clyde, - -**	**- 0**	**Celtic Park.**
Replay.	**1 ; Clyde, - -**	**- 0**	**Celtic Park.**

GLASGOW CHARITY CUP RECORD.

1876-77.

Round.		Opponents.		
Final.	0 ;	Queen's Park,	-	**4**

1877-78.

First Round.	1 ;	Third Lanark, -	-	2

1878-79.

First Round.	4 ;	Third Lanark, -	-	1
Final.	2 ;	Vale of Leven,	-	1

1879-80.

First Round.	3 ;	Dumbarton,	-	1
Final.	1 ;	Queen's Park,	-	**2**

1880-81.

First Round.	8 ;	Dumbarton,	-	0
Final.	1 ;	Queen's Park,	-	**3**

1881-82.

First Round.	0 ;	Dumbarton,	-	4

1882-83.

First Round.	3 ;	Vale of Leven, -	-	2
Final.	1 ;	Queen's Park,	-	**4**

1883-84.

First Round.	1 ;	Queen's Park, -	-	2

1884-85.

First Round.	0 ;	Dumbarton,	-	2

1885-86.

In a Qualifying Round, Vale of Leven beat
Rangers by 1 goal to 0.

1886-87.

Round.		Opponents.			
FIRST ROUND.	4 ;	Cambuslang,	-	-	2
SECOND ROUND.	1 ;	Renton,	-	-	1
REPLAY.	1 ;	Renton,	-	-	1
REPLAY.	0 ;	Renton,	-	-	1

1887-88.

FIRST ROUND.	3 ;	Vale of Leven,		-	3
REPLAY.	5 ;	Vale of Leven,		-	3
SECOND ROUND.	1 ;	Renton,	-	-	5

In 1888-89 and in 1889-90.
Rangers did not compete.

1890-91.
Rangers, Celtic, and Third Lanark did not compete owing to pressure of League Matches.

1891-92.

FIRST ROUND.	7 ;	Queen's Park,	-	-	1
Final.	**0 ;**	**Celtic,**	-	-	**2**

1892-93.

FIRST ROUND.	3 ;	Third Lanark,	-	-	2
Final.	**0 ;**	**Celtic,**	-	-	**5**

1893-94.

FIRST ROUND.	0 ;	Queen's Park,	-	-	2

1894-95.

FIRST ROUND.	4 ;	Third Lanark,	-	-	0
Final.	**0 ;**	**Celtic,**	-	-	**4**

1895-96.

FIRST ROUND.	1 ;	Celtic,	-	-	6

1896-97.

FIRST ROUND.	4 ;	Celtic,	-	-	1
Final.	**6 ;**	**Third Lanark,**	-	**1**

1897-98.

Round.	Opponents.			
FIRST ROUND.	2 ; Celtic,	-	-	- o
Final.	**0 ; Third Lanark,**		**-**	**1**

1898-99.

FIRST ROUND.	4 ; Third Lanark,	-	-	1
Final.	**0 ; Celtic,**	**-**	**-**	**- 2**

1899-1900.

FIRST ROUND.	2 ; Third Lanark,	-	-	o
Final.	**5 ; Celtic,**	**-**	**-**	**- 1**

1900-01.

FIRST ROUND.	o ; Celtic,	-	-	- o
REPLAY.	o ; Celtic,	-	-	- 1

1901-02.

FIRST ROUND.	o ; Hibernian,	-	- 1

1902-03.

FIRST ROUND.	o ; St. Mirren,	-	- 1

1903-04.

FIRST ROUND.	1 ; Third Lanark,	-	-	o
Final.	**5 ; Celtic,**	**-**	**-**	**- 2**

1904-05.

FIRST ROUND.	o ; Partick Thistle,	-	5

1905-06.

FIRST ROUND.	A Bye.		
SECOND ROUND.	5 ; Celtic,	-	- - 3
Final.	**3 ; Queen's Park,**		**- 2**

1906-07.

FIRST ROUND.	3 ; Partick Thistle,	-	o
SECOND ROUND.	1 ; Third Lanark,	-	- o
Final.	**1 ; Celtic,**	**-**	**- 0**

1907-08.

Round.	Opponents.	
FIRST ROUND.	3 ; Third Lanark, -	- 1
SECOND ROUND.	1 ; Queen's Park, -	- 3

1908-09.

FIRST ROUND.	3 ; Partick Thistle,	- 1
SECOND ROUND.	3 ; Third Lanark, -	- 2
Final.	**4 ; Celtic,** - -	- **2**

1909-10.

FIRST ROUND.	A Bye.	
SECOND ROUND.	0 ; Clyde, - -	- 1

1910-11.

FIRST ROUND.	3 ; Clyde, - -	- 2
SECOND ROUND.	1 ; Queen's Park, -	- 0
Final.	**2 ; Celtic,** - -	- **1**

1911-12.

FIRST ROUND.	1 ; Third Lanark, -	- 0
SECOND ROUND.	1 ; Clyde, - -	- 2

1912-13.

FIRST ROUND.	A Bye.	
SECOND ROUND.	3 ; Partick Thistle,	- 1
Final.	**2 ; Celtic,** - -	- **3**

1913-14.

FIRST ROUND.	2 ; Clyde, - -	- 1
SECOND ROUND.	1 goal 3 corners ;	
	Third Lanark, 4 corners, 1	

1914-15.

FIRST ROUND.	A Bye.	
SECOND ROUND.	3 ; Third Lanark, -	- 0
Final.	**2 ; Celtic,** - -	- **3**

1915-16.

FIRST ROUND.	A Bye.	
SECOND ROUND.	0 ; Celtic, - -	- 3

THE STORY OF THE RANGERS.

1916-17.

Round.	Opponents.	
FIRST ROUND.	A Bye.	
SECOND ROUND.	0 ; Celtic, - - -	2

1917-18.

FIRST ROUND.	0 ; Partick Thistle, -	2

1918-19.

FIRST ROUND.	3 ; Third Lanark, - -	0
SECOND ROUND.	2 ; Celtic, - - -	0
Final.	**2 ; Queen's Park,** -	**1**

1919-20.

FIRST ROUND.	4 ; Partick Thistle, -	0
SECOND ROUND.	1 ; Celtic, - - -	2

1920-21.

FIRST ROUND.	5 ; Queen's Park, - -	0
SECOND ROUND.	2 ; Clyde, - - -	0
Final.	**0 ; Celtic,** - - -	**2**

1921-22.

SEMI-FINAL.	10 corners ; Celtic, corners 6	
Final.	**3 goals ; Queen's Park, 1 goal.**	

1922-23.

SEMI-FINAL.	1 ; Celtic, - - - -	0
Final.	**4 ; Queen's Park,** -	**0**

ANALYSIS OF RANGERS' LEAGUE RESULTS.

Compiled to end of Season, 1922-1923.

CLUB.	Played	Won	Lost	Drawn	Goals.		Points.	
					For	Agst.	For	Agst.
CELTIC, - - -	66	18	24	24	99	107	60	72
HEART OF MIDLOTHIAN,	66	40	15	11	133	81	91	41
THIRD LANARK, - -	66	42	13	11	148	80	95	37
ST. MIRREN, - -	66	41	8	17	183	80	99	33
DUNDEE, - - -	56	34	13	9	134	68	77	35
HIBERNIAN, - - -	56	37	9	10	132	60	84	28
CLYDE, - - - -	50	39	4	7	142	42	85	15
PARTICK THISTLE, -	48	33	7	8	121	45	74	22
KILMARNOCK, - -	48	41	4	3	143	38	85	11
MORTON, - - -	46	31	9	6	105	41	68	24
QUEEN'S PARK, - -	44	36	3	5	130	38	77	11
MOTHERWELL, - -	40	28	6	6	91	41	62	18
AIRDRIEONIANS, - -	40	27	10	3	94	52	57	23
FALKIRK, - - -	36	20	10	6	71	41	46	26
HAMILTON ACAS., -	34	28	3	3	95	23	59	9
ABERDEEN, - - -	32	19	3	10	59	24	48	16
DUMBARTON, - -	30	20	6	4	73	40	44	16
RAITH ROVERS, - -	22	18	3	1	53	17	37	7
AYR UNITED, - -	20	13	3	4	45	21	30	10
PORT-GLASGOW ATH.,	16	13	1	2	62	11	28	4
ST. BERNARDS, - -	14	11	2	1	45	21	23	5
CLYDEBANK, - -	10	7	1	2	29	7	16	4
ABERCORN, - - -	8	7	0	1	33	9	15	1
LEITH ATHLETIC, -	8	6	1	1	21	14	13	3
RENTON, - - -	6	5	0	1	20	9	11	1
ALBION ROVERS, -	8	6	1	1	22	7	13	3
VALE OF LEVEN, -	4	4	0	0	20	2	8	0
CAMBUSLANG, - -	4	4	0	0	16	4	8	0
COWLAIRS, - - -	2	1	0	1	3	1	3	1
ALLOA, - - - -	2	2	0	0	4	0	4	0
Totals, - -	**948**	**631**	**159**	**158**	**2326**	**1024**	**1420**	**476**

SUMMARY OF LEAGUE RESULTS.

Season	Played	Won	Lost	Drawn	Goals		Points
					For	Agst.	
1890-91, ·	18	13	2	3	58	25	29†
1891-92, ·	22	11	9	2	59	46	24
1892-93, ·	18	12	2	4	41	27	28
1893-94, ·	18	8	6	4	44	30	20
1894-95, ·	18	10	6	2	41	26	22
1895-96, ·	18	11	3	4	57	39	26
1896-97, ·	18	11	4	3	64	30	25
1897-98, ·	18	13	2	3	71	15	29
1898-99, ·	18	18	0	0	79	18	36*
1899-1900, ·	18	15	1	2	69	27	32*
1900-01, ·	20	17	2	1	60	25	35*
1901-02, ·	18	13	3	2	43	29	28*
1902-03, ·	22	12	5	5	56	30	29
1903-04, ·	26	16	4	6	80	33	38
1904-05, ·	26	19	4	3	83	28	41‡
1905-06, ·	30	15	8	7	58	48	37
1906-07, ·	34	19	8	7	69	33	45
1907-08, ·	34	21	5	8	74	40	50
1908-09, ·	34	19	8	7	91	38	45
1909-10, ·	34	20	8	6	70	35	46
1910-11, ·	34	23	5	6	90	34	52*
1911-12, ·	34	24	7	3	86	34	51*
1912-13, ·	34	24	5	5	76	41	53*
1913-14, ·	38	27	6	5	79	31	59
1914-15, ·	38	23	11	4	74	47	50
1915-16, ·	38	25	7	6	87	39	56
1916-17, ·	38	24	9	5	68	32	53
1917-18, ·	34	25	3	6	66	24	56*
1918-19, ·	34	26	3	5	86	16	57
1919-20, ·	42	31	2	9	106	25	71*
1920-21, ·	42	35	1	6	91	24	76*
1921-22, ·	42	28	4	10	83	26	66
1922-23, ·	38	23	6	9	67	29	55*
Totals,	**948**	**631**	**159**	**158**	**2326**	**1024**	**1420**

* Champions.   † Joint Champions with Dumbarton.
‡ Tied for Championship with Celtic and lost the Deciding Match.

RANGERS' INTERNATIONAL HONOURS

Abbreviations.—E., England ; W., Wales ;
I., Ireland ; E.L., English League ; I.L., Irish
League ; S.L., Southern League ; C., Canada.

Archibald, Alec, forward.—E., 1922 ; W., 1921, 1922 ; I., 1923 ;
E.L., 1921, 1922 ; I.L., 1921, 1922.

Barker, John B., forward.—W., 1893, 1894 ; E.L., 1894 ;
I.L., 1895.

Bennett, Alec, forward.—E., 1909, 1910, 1911 ; W., 1904, 1908,
1909, 1910, 1911 ; I., 1907, 1909, 1913 ; E.L., 1905, 1908,
1909, 1910, 1911, 1912 ; I.L., 1912 ; S.L., 1911, 1912, 1913.

Bowie, James, forward.—E., 1920 ; I., 1920 ; E.L., 1915 ;
I.L., 1912, 1913 ; S.L., 1914.

Cairns, Thomas, forward.—E., 1922, 1923 ; W., 1920, 1923 ;
E.L., 1922, 1923 ; I.L., 1923.

Cameron, John, half-back.—I., 1886.

Campbell, John, forward.—E., 1899 ; W., 1899 ; I., 1899, 1901 ;
E.L., 1899.

Campbell, Peter, forward.—W., 1878, 1879.

Chalmers, William, goal.—I., 1885.

Crawford, David, back.—W., 1894, 1900 ; I., 1894 ; E.L., 1906.

Cunningham, Andrew, forward.—E., 1921, 1923 ; W., 1921,
1923 ; I., 1920, 1922 ; E.L., 1912, 1920, 1921, 1922 ; I.L.,
1914, 1920, 1922.

Dickie, Matthew, goal.—W., 1900 ; I., 1897, 1899 ; E.L., 1898.

Drummond, John, back.—E., 1895, 1896, 1898, 1900, 1901, 1902 ;
W., 1902 ; I., 1892, 1894, 1895, 1896, 1897, 1902, 1903 ;
E.L., 1895, 1896, 1901.

Duncan, J., back.—W., 1878, 1882.

Galt, James H., half-back.—W., 1908 ; I., 1908 ; E.L., 1912 ;
S.L., 1912.

Gibson, Neil, half-back.—E., 1895, 1896, 1897, 1898, 1899, 1900 ;
W., 1899, 1901 ; I., 1895, 1896, 1897, 1899, 1900, 1905 ;
E.L., 1896, 1897, 1898, 1899, 1900, 1901, 1902, 1903 ; I.L.,
1897, 1901.

Gibson, William, back.—I.L., 1895.

Gillespie, George, goal.—E., 1881, 1882 ; W., 1880, 1881, 1886,
1890 ; I., 1891.

Gordon, James E., half-back.—E., 1912, 1913, 1914, 1920 ,
W., 1913, 1920 ; I., 1912, 1913, 1914, 1920 ; E.L., 1913, 1914,
1915, 1920 ; I.L., 1910, 1913, 1914, 1920 ; S.L., 1912, 1913,
1914, 1915.

Gossland, James, forward.—I., 1884.

Gow, Donald, back.—E., 1888.

Gow, John Robertson, forward.—I., 1888.

Graham, John, forward.—I.L., 1902.

THE STORY OF THE RANGERS.

Haddow, David, goal.—E., 1894 ; E.L., 1894.

Hamilton, Robert C., forward.—E., 1899, 1901, 1903 ; W., 1899, 1900, 1902, 1911 ; I., 1899, 1901, 1902, 1904 ; E.L., 1898, 1899, 1901, 1903, 1904 ; I.L., 1898, 1904.

Heggie, Charles, forward.—I., 1886.

Henderson, George, half-back.—I., 1904.

Hendry, Joseph, half-back.—S.L., 1911.

Hill, David, forward.—E., 1881 ; W., 1881, 1882.

Hyslop, Thomas, forward.—E., 1896, 1897.

Inglis, John, forward.—E., 1883 ; W., 1883.

Kyle, Archibald, forward.—E.L., 1906, 1908.

Law, George, back.—E., 1910 ; W., 1910 ; I., 1910.

Livingstone, George, forward.—E., 1902, 1906 ; W., 1907 ; E.L., 1907.

Logan, James L., half-back.—E.L., 1913.

Low, Thomas P., forward.—I., 1897 ; E.L., 1897.

M'Creadie, Andrew, half-back.—E., 1894 ; W., 1893 ; C., 1891.

M'Creadie, Hugh, forward.—E.L., 1893.

M'Hardy, Hugh, back.—I., 1885.

M'Intyre, Hugh, half-back.—W., 1880.

M'Intyre, James, half-back.—W., 1884.

M'Neil, Moses, forward.—E., 1880 ; W., 1876.

M'Pherson, John, forward.—E., 1889, 1890, 1894, 1895 ; W., 1888, 1892 ; I., 1895, 1897 ; E.L., 1897, 1898, 1899 ; I.L., 1901, 1902.

Marshall, Robert, half-back.—I., 1892, 1894 ; E.L., 1895.

May, John, half-back.—E., 1908 ; W., 1906, 1909 ; I., 1906, 1908 ; E.L., 1906, 1907, 1908.

Meiklejohn, David, half-back.—W., 1922 ; E.L., 1923 ; I.L., 1922.

Miller, James, forward.—E., 1897, 1898 ; W., 1898 ; E.L., 1897, 1898 ; I.L., 1897.

Mitchell, David, half-back.—E., 1892, 1893, 1894 ; I., 1890, 1893 ; E.L., 1893, 1894.

Morton, Alan L., forward.—E., 1921, 1922, 1923 ; W., 1920, 1922, 1923 ; I., 1920, 1921, 1922, 1923 ; E.L., 1920, 1921, 1922, 1923 ; I.L., 1920.

Muirhead, Thomas, half-back.—E., 1923 ; I., 1922 ; E.L., 1922. 1923 : I.L., 1922, 1923.

Neil, Robert G., half-back.—W., 1896, 1900 ; E.L., 1901.

Oswald, James, forward.—E., 1889, 1895 ; W., 1897 ; E.L., 1894, 1895, 1896.

Reid, William, forward.—E., 1911, 1913, 1914 ; W., 1911, 1913 ; I., 1911, 1912, 1913, 1914 ; E.L., 1911, 1913, 1914, 1915 ; I.L., 1911, 1912 ; S.L., 1912, 1913.

Robb, William, goal.—I.L., 1921.

Robertson, John T., half-back.—E., 1898, 1899, 1900, 1901, 1902, 1903, 1904 ; W., 1900, 1901, 1902, 1903, 1904, 1905 ; I., 1901, 1902, 1904 ; E.L., 1900, 1901, 1903, 1904, 1905 ; I.L., 1904.

Smith, Alec, forward.—E., 1898, 1900, 1901, 1902, 1903, 1906, 1911 ; W., 1900, 1901, 1902, 1903, 1905, 1907 ; I., 1900, 1901, 1902, 1903, 1904. 1906, 1911 ; E.L., 1898, 1900, 1901, 1902, 1903, 1905, 1907, 1908, 1911, 1913 ; I.L., 1897, 1898, 1901; S.L., 1912.

Smith, Nicol, back.—E., 1897, 1899, 1900, 1902 ; W., 1898, 1899, 1900, 1901 ; I., 1899 , 1900, 1901, 1902 ; E.L., 1897, 1898, 1899, 1900, 1901, 1902 ; I.L., 1897, 1901, 1904.

Speedie, Finlay, forward. E., 1903 ; W., 1903 ; I., 1903 ; E.L., 1905.

Speirs, James H., forward.—W., 1908.

Stark, James, half-back.—E., 1909 ; I., 1909 ; E.L., 1907, 1909.

Vallance, Thomas, back.—E., 1877, 1878, 1879, 1881 ; W., 1877, 1879, 1881.

Walker, John, forward.—W., 1897, 1904 ; I., 1895, 1898, 1904 ; E.L., 1896, 1897, 1903, 1904 ; I.L., 1904.

Watson, James, forward.—W., 1878.

Wylie, Tom, forward.—I., 1890.

NOTES ON THE PLAYERS.

T. HYSLOP was a Stoke player in 1896 when capped against England.

JOHN M'PHERSON was a Cowlairs player when capped against England in 1889 and 1890, and against Wales in 1888.

JAS. OSWALD was a Third Lanark player when capped against England in 1889, and a St. Bernards player when capped against England in 1895.

J. T. ROBERTSON was an Everton player when capped against England in 1898, and a Southampton player when capped against England in 1899.

GEO. LIVINGSTONE was a Celtic player when capped against England in 1902, and a Manchester City player when capped against England in 1906.

A. BENNETT was a Celtic player when capped against Ireland in 1907, and against Wales in 1904 and 1908.

JOHN DRUMMOND was a Falkirk player when capped against Ireland in 1892.

N. GIBSON was a Partick Thistle player when capped against Ireland in 1905.

G. GILLESPIE was a Queen's Park player when capped against Ireland in 1891, and when capped against Wales in 1886 and 1890.

JOHN WALKER was a Hearts player when capped against Ireland in 1895 and 1898, against Wales in 1897, and against the English League in 1896 and 1897.

D. CRAWFORD was a St. Mirren player when capped against Ireland and Wales in 1894 and against the English League in 1906.

J. DUNCAN was an Alexandria Athletic player when capped against Wales in 1878.

R. C. HAMILTON was a Dundee player when capped against Wales in 1911.

A. L. MORTON was a Queen's Park player when capped against Wales in 1920.

R. G. NEIL was a Hibernian player when capped against Wales in 1896.

A. CUNNINGHAM was a Kilmarnock player when capped against the English League in 1912 and against the Irish League in 1914.

" VICTORY " INTERNATIONALS, 1919.

Victory International matches, two each against England, Ireland, and the English League, were played in the spring of 1919. They are not included in the official records and are consequently omitted from the foregoing list. Rangers players who took part in the Victory matches are :—

	E.	I.	E.L.
J. E. Gordon, -	2	2	2
Jas. Bowie, -	2	1	1
Jas. Blair, -	2	1	—
T. Cairns, - -	—	1	—
A. Archibald, -	—	—	2

In the following synopsis of the number of International honours awarded Rangers players up to the end of season 1922-23, the Victory Internationals of 1919 are not included. Scotland played Canada only once—in 1891. The Scottish League met the Southern League five times, the latter body being, from 1911 to 1915, independent of the Football League of England. The combined figures are unequalled among Scottish clubs :—

England, - - - - - -	85
Wales, - - - - - -	82
Ireland, - - - - - -	81
English League, - - - -	101
Irish League, - - - - -	38
Southern League, - - -	13
Canada, - - - - - -	1
Grand Total, - -	**401**

ATHLETIC RECORDS MADE ON IBROX PARK.

AMONG football clubs, the Rangers were pioneers in athletics and cycle-racing. The following existing Scottish records have been made on IBROX PARK :—

All Comers.

100 Yards, -	9⅘ sec. - -	W. R. Applegarth	1913
120 Yards -	11⅗ sec. - -	R. E. Walker -	1909
150 Yards -	14⅗ sec. - -	R. E. Walker -	1909
440 Yards -	48⅖ sec. - -	W. Halswell -	1908
600 Yards -	1 min. 11⅘ sec.	W. Halswell -	1906
Three-quarter Mile	3 min. 10⅖ sec.	A. G. Hill -	1921
1000 Yards -	2 min. 15 sec.	A. G. Hill -	1920
1½ Miles - -	6 min. 48⅖ sec.	A. J. Robertson	1909
2 Miles - -	9 min. 9⅗ sec. -	A Shrubb - -	1904
3 Miles - -	14 min. 27⅕ sec.	A. Shrubb -	1904
4 Miles - -	19 min. 23⅖ sec.	A. Shrubb -	1904
5 Miles - -	24 min. 55⅘ sec.	A. Shrubb -	1904
6 Miles - -	29 min. 59⅖ sec.	A. Shrubb -	1904
7 Miles - -	35 min. 4⅗ sec.	A. Shrubb -	1904
8 Miles - -	40 min. 16 sec.	A. Shrubb -	1904
9 Miles - -	45 min. 27⅗ sec.	A. Shrubb -	1904
10 Miles - -	50 min. 40⅗ sec.	A. Shrubb -	1904
11 Miles - -	56 min. 23⅖ sec.	A. Shrubb -	1904
One Hour -	11 mls. 1136 yds.	A. Shrubb -	1904
120 Yds. Hurdles	15⅘ sec. -	R. S. Stronach -	1905
High Jump -	6 ft. 2½ ins. -	B. H. Baker -	1921
Mile Walk -	6 min. 44⅘ sec.	E. J. Webb -	1919
1½ Miles Walk -	10 min. 21⅕ sec.	R. Quinn -	1910
2 Miles Walk -	13 min. 57⅕ sec.	E. J. Webb -	1909
3 Miles Walk -	21 min. 39⅕ sec.	A. E. M. Rowland	1909

Several of A. Shrubb's times are world's records.

CLUB OFFICIALS.

J. Campbell was Honorary Match Secretary in 1875-76, and Peter M'Neil from 1876-77 to 1882-83. Angus Campbell was Honorary Secretary from 1878-79 to 1880-81, both seasons inclusive. J. M. Watt was President in 1876-77 and Honorary Treasurer in 1878-79 and 1879-80. Moses M'Neil was Honorary Treasurer in 1876-77.

Season.	President.	Vice-President.	Hon. Secretary.	Hon. Match Secy.	Hon. Treasurer.
1882-83.	A. Harkness (died) George Goudie.	William S. Hays.	J. W. MacKay.	P. M'Neil.	A. Campbell. J. F. Ness.
1883-84.	Thomas Vallance.	George Goudie.	Walter Crichton. James Gossland.	J. W. MacKay.	Robert White.
1884-85.	Thomas Vallance.	George Goudie.	James Gossland.	J. W. MacKay.	Robert White.
1885-86.	Thomas Vallance.	Robert B. Kerr.	William S. Hays.	James Gossland.	Robert White.
1886-87.	Thomas Vallance.	Peter M'Neil.	Walter Crichton.	James Gossland.	T. C. B. Miller.

Year					
1887-88.	Thomas Vallance.	Peter M'Neil.	Samuel Ricketts.	James Gossland.	T. C. B. Miller.
1888-89.	Thomas Vallance.	George B. Caldwell.	Daniel B. M'Conechy	James Gossland.	T. C. B. Miller.
1889-90.	John Mellish.	James A. K. Watson.	John S. Marr.	William Wilton.	T. C. B. Miller.
1890-91.	James A. K. Watson.	Dugald MacKenzie.	John S. Marr.	William Wilton.	T. C. B. Miller.
1891-92.	Dugald MacKenzie.	John Cameron.	John C. Lawson.	William Wilton.	John S. Marr.
1892-93.	Dugald MacKenzie.	John Cameron.	William MacAndrew.	William Wilton.	John S. Marr.
1893-94.	Dugald MacKenzie.	John Cameron.	William MacAndrew.	William Wilton.	John S. Marr.
1894-95.	Dugald MacKenzie.	Robert Brown Kerr.	John Robertson Gow.	William Wilton.	John S. Marr.
1895-96.	Dugald MacKenzie.	John Robertson Gow.	George P. Hourston. John Robertson Gow.	William Wilton.	William MacAndrew.
1896-97.	John Robertson Gow	James Henderson.	James Walker.	William Wilton.	William MacAndrew.
1897-98.	John Robertson Gow	James Henderson.	James Walker.	William Wilton.	William MacAndrew.
1898-99.	James Henderson.	John Hutcheson.	James Walker.	William Wilton.	William MacAndrew.

DIRECTORS.

THE Club was incorporated on 27th May, 1899. William Wilton was appointed Manager and Secretary, and held that position till his death, on 2nd May, 1920.

1899-1900—James Henderson (*Chairman*), Walter Crichton, William R. Danskin, J. R. Gow, J. Hutcheson, A. B. Mackenzie, J. S. Marr, George Small, and J. Walker.

1900-1—James Henderson, J.P. (*Chairman*), W. Crichton, W. R. Danskin, J. Hutcheson, A. B. Mackenzie, D. MacKenzie, J. S. Marr, G. Small, and J. Walker.

1901-2—James Henderson, J.P. (*Chairman*), W. Crichton, W. R. Danskin, J. Hutcheson, A. B. Mackenzie, D. MacKenzie, J. S. Marr, G. Small, and J. Walker.

1902-3—James Henderson, J.P. (*Chairman*), W. Crichton, W. R. Danskin, J. Hutcheson, A. B. Mackenzie, D. MacKenzie, J. S. Marr, G. Small, and J. Walker.

1903-4—James Henderson, J.P. (*Chairman*), William Craig, W. Crichton, W. R. Danskin, J. Hutcheson, A. B. Mackenzie, D. MacKenzie, G. Small, and J. Walker.

1904-5—Councillor James Henderson, J.P. (*Chairman*), W. Craig, W. Crichton, W. R. Danskin, J. Hutcheson, A. B. Mackenzie, D. MacKenzie, G. Small, and J. Walker.

1905-6—Councillor James Henderson, J.P. (*Chairman*), W. Craig, W. Crichton, W. R. Danskin, J. Hutcheson, A. B. Mackenzie, D. MacKenzie, G. Small, and J. Walker.

1906-7—Councillor James Henderson, J.P. (*Chairman*), W. Craig, W. Crichton, W. R. Danskin, J. Hutcheson, David Lawson, A. B. Mackenzie, G. Small, and J. Walker.

1907-8—Councillor James Henderson, J.P. (*Chairman*), W. Craig, W. Crichton, W. R. Danskin, A. B. Mackenzie, David Lawson, John MacPherson, G. Small, and J. Walker.

1908-9—Bailie James Henderson, J.P. (*Chairman*), W. Craig, W. Crichton, W. R. Danskin, D. Lawson, A. B. Mackenzie, J. MacPherson, G. Small, and J. Walker.

1909-10—Bailie James Henderson, J.P. (*Chairman*), W. Craig, W. Crichton, W. R. Danskin, D. Lawson, A. B. Mackenzie, J. MacPherson, G. Small, and Colin Young, I.M.

1910-11—Bailie James Henderson, J.P. (*Chairman*), W. Craig, W. Crichton, W. R. Danskin, D. Lawson, A. B. Mackenzie, J. MacPherson, G. Small, and Colin Young, I.M.

1911-12—Bailie James Henderson, J.P. (*Chairman*), W. Craig, W. Crichton, W. R. Danskin, D. Lawson, J. MacPherson, G. Small, and Colin Young, I.M.
Bailie Henderson died in May, 1912.

1912-13—Sir John Ure Primrose, Bart. (*Chairman*), W. Craig, W. Crichton, W. R. Danskin, D. Lawson, J. MacPherson, and G. Small.

1913-14—Sir John Ure Primrose, Bart. (*Chairman*), W. Craig, W. R. Danskin, D. Lawson, J. MacPherson, G. Small, and Wallace B. Tod.

1914-15—Sir John Ure Primrose, Bart. (*Chairman*), W. Craig, W. R. Danskin, D. Lawson, J. MacPherson, G. Small, and W. B. Tod.

1915-16—Sir John Ure Primrose, Bart. (*Chairman*), ex-Bailie Joseph Buchanan, J.P.; W. Craig, W. R. Danskin, D. Lawson, J. MacPherson, and G. Small.

1916-17—Sir John Ure Primrose, Bart. (*Chairman*), ex-Bailie J. Buchanan, J.P.; W. Craig, W. R. Danskin, D. Lawson, J. MacPherson, and G. Small.

1917-18—Sir John Ure Primrose, Bart. (*Chairman*), Bailie Duncan Graham, ex-Bailie J. Buchanan, J.P.; W. Craig, W. R. Danskin, J. MacPherson, and G. Small.

1918-19—Sir John Ure Primrose, Bart. (*Chairman*), ex-Bailie J. Buchanan, J.P.; ex-Bailie D. Graham, J.P.; W. Craig, J.P.; W. R. Danskin, J. MacPherson, and G. Small.

1919-20—Sir John Ure Primrose, Bart. (*Chairman*), ex-Bailie J. Buchanan, J.P.; ex-Bailie D. Graham, J.P.; W. Craig, J.P.; W. R. Danskin, J. MacPherson, and G. Small.

1920-21—Sir John Ure Primrose, Bart. (*Chairman*), ex-Bailie J. Buchanan, J.P. ; ex-Bailie D. Graham, J.P. ; W. Craig, J.P. ; W. R. Danskin, J. MacPherson, and G. Small.

Manager—William Struth.

Secretary—W. Rogers Simpson, C.A.

1921-22—Sir John Ure Primrose, Bart., LL.D. (*Chairman*), ex-Bailie J. Buchanan, J.P. ; ex-Bailie D. Graham, J.P., O.B.E. ; W. Craig, J.P. ; W. R. Danskin, J. MacPherson, and G. Small.

Mr. Danskin died 20th March, 1922.

1922-23—Sir John Ure Primrose, Bart., LL.D. (*Chairman*), ex-Bailie J. Buchanan, J.P. ; ex-Bailie D. Graham, J.P., O.B.E. ; W. Craig, J.P. ; J. MacPherson, and G. Small.

1923-24—William Craig, J.P. (*Chairman*), Sir John Ure Primrose, Bart., LL.D. ; ex-Bailie J. Buchanan, J.P. ; ex-Bailie D. Graham, J.P., O.B.E. ; J. MacPherson, and G. Small.